Big Data *and* Business Analytics

Big Data *and* Business Analytics

Edited by
JAY LIEBOWITZ

Foreword by
Joe LaCugna, PhD, Starbucks Coffee Company

CRC Press
Taylor & Francis Group
Boca Raton   London   New York

CRC Press is an imprint of the
Taylor & Francis Group, an **informa** business
AN AUERBACH BOOK

CRC Press
Taylor & Francis Group
6000 Broken Sound Parkway NW, Suite 300
Boca Raton, FL 33487-2742

Printed on acid-free paper
Version Date: 20130220

International Standard Book Number-13: 978-1-4665-6578-4 (Hardback)

Library of Congress Cataloging-in-Publication Data

Big data and business analytics / editor, Jay Liebowitz.
  pages cm
  Includes bibliographical references and index.
  ISBN 978-1-4665-6578-4 (hardcover : alk. paper)
  1. Business intelligence. 2. Business planning. 3. Decision making--Statistical
methods. 4. Data mining. 5. Management--Statistical methods. I. Liebowitz, Jay, 1957-

  HD38.7.B54 2013
  658.4'72--dc23   2013004216

Visit the Taylor & Francis Web site at
http://www.taylorandfrancis.com

and the CRC Press Web site at
http://www.crcpress.com

Contents

Foreword

Joe LaCugna, PhD
Enterprise Analytics and Business Intelligence
Starbucks Coffee Company

The promise and potential of big data and smart analysis are realized in better decisions and stronger business results. But good ideas rarely implement themselves, and often the heavy hand of history means that bad practices and outdated processes tend to persist. Even in organizations that pride themselves on having a vibrant marketplace of ideas, converting data and insights into better business outcomes is a pressing and strategic challenge for senior executives.

How does an organization move from being data-rich to insight-rich—and capable of acting on the best of those insights? Big data is not enough, nor are clever analytics, to ensure that organizations make better decisions based on insights generated by analytic professionals. Some analysts' work directly influences business results, while other analysts' contributions matter much less. Rarely is the difference in impact due to superior analytic insights or larger data sets. Developing shrewd and scalable ways to identify and digest the best insights while avoiding the time traps of lazy data mining or "analysis paralysis" are new key executive competencies.

INFORMATION OVERLOAD AND A TRANSLATION TASK

How can data, decisions, and impact become more tightly integrated? A central irony, first identified in 1971 by Nobel Prize winner Herbert Simon, is that when data are abundant, the time and attention of senior decision makers become the scarcest, most valuable resource in organizations. We can never have enough time, but we can certainly have too much data. There is also a difficult translation task between the pervasive ambiguity of the executive suite and the apparent precision of analysts' predictions and techniques. Too often, analysts' insights and prescriptions fail to recognize the inherently inexact, unstructured, and time-bound nature of strategically important decisions. Executives sometimes fail to appreciate fully the opportunities or risks that may be expressed in abstract algorithms, and too often analysts fail to become trusted advisors to these same senior executives. Most executives recognize that models and analyses are reductive simplifications of highly complex patterns and that these models can sometimes produce overly simple caricatures rather than helpful precision. In short, while advanced analytic techniques are increasingly important inputs to decision making, savvy executives will insist that math and models are most valuable when tempered by firsthand experience, deep knowledge of an industry, and balanced judgments.

LIMITATIONS OF DATA-DRIVEN ANALYSIS

More data can make decision making harder, not easier, since it can sometimes refute long-cherished views and suggest changes to well-established practices. Smart analysis can also take away excuses and create accountability where there had been none. But sometimes, as Andrew Lang noted, statistics can be used as a drunken man uses a lamppost—for support rather than illumination. And sometimes, as the recent meltdowns in real estate, mortgage banking, and international finance confirm, analysts can become too confident in their models and algorithms, ignoring the chance of "black swan" events and so-called "non-normal" distributions of outcomes. It is tempting to forget that the future is certain to be different from the recent past but that we know little about how that future will become different. Mark Twain cautioned us, "History doesn't repeat itself; at best it sometimes rhymes." Statistics and analysts are rarely able to discern when the future will rhyme or be written in prose.

Some of the most important organizational decisions are simply not amenable to traditional analytic techniques and cannot be characterized helpfully by available data. Investments in innovation, for example, or decisions to partner with other organizations are difficult to evaluate *ex ante*, and limited data and immeasurable risks can be used to argue against such strategic choices. But of course the absence of data to support such unstructured strategic decisions does not mean these are not good choices—merely that judgment and discernment are better guides to decision making.

Many organizations will find it beneficial to distinguish more explicitly the various types of decisions, who is empowered to make them, and how. Many routine and tactical decisions, such as staffing, inventory planning, or back-office operations, can be improved by an increased reliance on data and by automating key parts of the decision-making process—by, for example, using optimization techniques. These rules and decisions often can be implemented by field managers or headquarters staff and need not involve senior executives. More consequential decisions, when ambiguity is high, precedent is lacking, and trade-offs cannot be quantified confidently, do require executive engagement. In these messy and high-consequence cases, when the future is quite different from the recent past, predictive models and optimization techniques are of limited value. Other more qualitative analytic techniques, such as field research or focus groups, and new analytic techniques, such as sentiment analysis and social network graphs, can provide actionable, near-real-time insights that are diagnostically powerful in ways that are simply not possible with simulations or large-scale data mining.

Even in high-uncertainty, high-risk situations, when judgment and experience are the best available guides, executives will often benefit from soliciting perspectives from outside the rarefied atmosphere of their corner offices. Substantial academic and applied research confirms that decisions made with input from different groups, pay grades, and disciplines are typically better than decisions that are not vetted beyond a few trusted advisors. Senior executives who find themselves inside "bubbles" of incomplete and biased information may be misled, as when business cases for new investments are grounded in unrealistically optimistic assumptions, or when a manager focuses on positive impacts for her business unit rather than the overall organization. To reduce this gaming and the risks of suboptimization, there is substantial value and insight gained by seeking out dissenting views from nontraditional sources. In strategically important and ambiguous situations, the qualitative "wisdom of crowds" is often a better guide to smart decision making than a slavish reliance on extensive data analysis—or a myopically limited range of perspectives favored by executives. Good analysts can play important roles too since they bring the rigor and discipline of the scientific method above and beyond any data they may have. The opportunity is to avoid the all-too-common refrain: we're doing it because the CEO said so.

Many executives may need to confront the problem of information distortion. Often this takes the form of hoarding or a reluctance to share information freely and broadly across the organization. Its unhelpful twin, "managing up," may also manifest itself: sharing selectively filtered, positively biased information to curry favor with more senior decision makers. These practices can impair decisions, create silos, truncate learning, accentuate discord, and delay the emergence of learning communities. In the past, hoarding and managing up have been rational and were sometimes sanctioned; now, leadership means insisting that sharing information up and down the hierarchy, transparently and with candor, is the new normal. This is true both when insights confirm existing views and practices and also when the data and analysis clash with these. Conflicting ideas and competing interests are best handled by exposing them, addressing them, and recognizing that they can improve decisions.

EVOLVING A DATA-DRIVEN LEARNING CULTURE

For organizations that have relied on hard-won experience, memorable events, and other comfortable heuristics, the discipline of data-driven decision making may be a wholly new approach to thinking about how to improve business performance. As several chapters in this volume indicate, it is simply not possible to impose an analytic approach atop a company's culture. Learning to improve business performance through analytics is typically piecemeal and fragile, achieved topic by topic, process by process, group by group, and often in fits and starts. But it rarely happens without strong executive engagement, advocacy, and mindshare—and a willingness to establish data-driven decision making as the preferred, even default approach to answering important business questions.

Executives intent on increasing the impact and mindshare of analytics should recognize the scale and scope of organizational changes that may be needed to capture the value of data-driven decision making. This may require sweeping cultural changes, such as elevating the visibility, seniority, and mindshare that analytic teams enjoy across the company. It may mean investing additional scarce resources in analytics at the expense of other projects and teams, much as Procter & Gamble has done in recent years, and for which it is being well rewarded. It may also require repeated attempts to determine the best way to organize analytic talent: whether they are part of information technology (IT), embedded in business units, centralized into a Center of Excellence at headquarters, or globally dispersed. Building these capabilities takes time and a flexible approach since there are no uniformly valid best practices to accelerate this maturation.

Likewise, analytic priorities and investments will vary across companies, so there are clear opportunities for executives to determine top-priority analytic targets, how data and analysts are resourced and organized, and how decision making evolves within their organizations.

NO SIMPLE RECIPES TO MASTER ORGANIZATIONAL COMPLEXITY

The chapters in this volume offer useful case studies, technical roadmaps, lessons learned, and a few prescriptions to "do this, avoid that." But there are many ways to make good decisions, and decision making is highly idiosyncratic and context dependent: what works well in one organization may not work in others, even for near-peers in the same businesses or markets. This is deeply ironic: we know that strong analytic capabilities can improve business results, but we do not yet have a rigorous understanding of the best ways for organizations to build these capabilities. There is little science in how to build those capabilities most efficiently and with maximum impact.

Smart decisions usually require much more than clever analysis, and organizational learning skills may matter more than vast troves of data. High-performing teams identify their biases, disagree constructively, synthesize opposing views, and learn better and faster than others. Relative rates of learning are important, since the ability to learn faster than competitors is sometimes considered to be the only source of sustainable competitive advantage. There is a corresponding, underappreciated organizational skill: a company's ability to forget. Forgetting does matter, because an overcommitment to the *status quo* limits the range of options considered, impairs innovation, and entrenches taken-for-granted routines. These "core rigidities" are the unwelcome downside to an organization's "core competencies" and are difficult to eradicate, particularly in successful firms. Time after time, in market after market, highly successful firms lose out to new products or technologies pioneered by emerging challengers. Blinded by past successes and prior investments, these incumbent companies may be overly confident that what worked in the past will continue to work well in the future. In short, while big data and sophisticated analyses are increasingly important inputs to better decisions, effective team-learning skills, an ability to learn faster than others, and a fierce willingness to challenge the *status quo* will increase the chance that data-based insights yield better business outcomes.

Executives confront at least one objective constraint as they consider their approach to data-driven decision making: there is a pervasive shortage of deep analytic talent, and we simply cannot import enough talent to fill this gap. Estimates of this talent gap vary, but there is little reason to think it can be filled in the near term given the time involved in formal education and the importance of firsthand business experience for analysts to become trusted advisors. With some irony, Google's Hal Varian believes that statisticians will enjoy "the sexiest job for the next decade." Analysts who combine strong technical skills with a solid grasp of business problems will have the best choices and will seek out the best organizations with the most interesting problems to solve.

There is also an emerging consensus that many managers and executives who think they are already "data driven" will need to become much more so and may need deeper analytic skills to develop a more nuanced understanding of their customers, competitors, and emerging risks and opportunities. Much as an MBA has become a necessary credential to enter the C-suite, executives will increasingly be expected to have deeper knowledge of research methods and analytic techniques. This newly necessary capability is not about developing elegant predictive models or talking confidently about confidence intervals, but about being able to critically assess insights generated by others. What are the central assumptions and what events could challenge their validity? What are the boundary conditions? Is A causing B or vice versa? Is a set of conclusions statistically valid? Are the findings actionable and repeatable at scale? Is a Cronbach's *alpha* of 5 percent good or bad?

There is nothing automatic or easy about capturing the potential value of big data and smarter analyses. Across several industries, markets, and technologies, some few firms have been able to create competitive advantages for themselves by building organizational capabilities to unearth valuable insights and to act on the best of them. Many of these companies are household names—Starbucks, Walmart, FedEx, Harrah's, Expedia—and there is strong evidence that these investments have been financially prudent, richly strategic, and competitively valuable. Rarely did this happen without strong and persistent executive sponsorship. These leading companies invested in building scalable analytic capabilities—and in the communities of analysts and managers who comb through data, make decisions, and influence executives. These companies are not satisfied with their early successes and are pioneering new analytic techniques and applying a more disciplined approach to ever more of their operations. Embracing and extending this data-driven approach have been called "the future of everything." The opportunity now is for executives in other firms to do likewise: to capture the value of their information assets through rigorous analysis and better decisions. In addition to more efficient operations, this is also a promising path to identify new market opportunities, address competitive vulnerabilities, earn more loyal customers, and improve bottom-line business results.

Big data *is* a big deal; executives' judgments and smart organizational learning habits make big data matter more.

Preface

So why *Big Data and Business Analytics*? Is it that the White House Office of Science and Technology Policy held a conference on March 29, 2012, citing that $200 million is being awarded for research and development on big data and associated analytics? Is it that, according to *KMWorld*, big data revenue will grow from $5 billion in 2011 to $50 billion in 2017? Or is it just that we are entrenched in the three Vs: volume of data, variety of data, and the velocity of data?

With the barrage of data from such domains as cybersecurity, emergency management, healthcare, finance, transportation, and other domains, it becomes vitally important for organizations to make sense of this data and information on a timely and effective basis to improve the decision-making process. That's where analytics come into play. Studies have shown that by 2018, there will be a shortage of 140,000 to 190,000 business data analysts in the United States alone. These analysts should know machine learning, advanced statistical techniques, and other predictive analytics to make sense of the various types of data—structured, unstructured, text, numbers, images, and others.

This book is geared for filling this niche in terms of better understanding the organizational case studies, trends, issues, challenges, and techniques associated with big data and business analytics. We are extremely pleased to have some of the leading individuals and organizations worldwide as contributors to this volume. Chapters from industry, government, not-for-profit, and academe provide interesting perspectives in this emerging field of big data and business analytics. We are also very pleased to have Joe LaCugna, PhD, who oversees Enterprise Analytics and Business Intelligence at Starbucks Coffee Company, write the Foreword based on his many years of working in this field, both in industry and academe.

This effort could not have happened without the foresight of John Wyzalek and his Taylor & Francis colleagues. I would also like to especially thank my family, students and colleagues at the University of Maryland

University College, and professional contacts for allowing me to further gain insight into this area.

Enjoy!

Jay Liebowitz, DSc
Orkand Endowed Chair in Management and Technology
The Graduate School
University of Maryland University College
Adelphi, Maryland
Jay.liebowitz@umuc.edu

About the Editor

Dr. Jay Liebowitz is the Orkand Endowed Chair of Management and Technology in the Graduate School at the University of Maryland University College (UMUC). He previously served as a professor in the Carey Business School at Johns Hopkins University. He was ranked one of the top 10 knowledge management (KM) researchers/practitioners out of 11,000 worldwide and was ranked number two in KM strategy worldwide according to the January 2010 *Journal of Knowledge Management*. At Johns Hopkins University, he was the founding program director for the graduate certificate in competitive intelligence and the Capstone director of the MS-Information and Telecommunications Systems for Business Program, where he engaged more than 30 organizations in industry, government, and not-for-profits in capstone projects.

Prior to joining Hopkins, Dr. Liebowitz was the first knowledge management officer at the National Aeronautics and Space Administration's (NASA's) Goddard Space Flight Center. Before this, Dr. Liebowitz was the Robert W. Deutsch Distinguished Professor of Information Systems at the University of Maryland–Baltimore County, professor of management science at George Washington University, and chair of artificial intelligence (AI) at the U.S. Army War College.

Dr. Liebowitz is the founder and editor-in-chief of *Expert Systems with Applications: An International Journal* (published by Elsevier), which is ranked third worldwide for intelligent systems/AI-related journals, according to the most recent Thomson impact factors. The journal had 1.8 million articles downloaded worldwide in 2011. He is a Fulbright Scholar, an Institute of Electrical and Electronics Engineers (IEEE)-USA Federal Communications Commission Executive Fellow, and a Computer Educator of the Year (International Association for Computer Information Systems, or IACIS). He has published more than 40 books and myriad journal articles on knowledge management, intelligent systems, and IT management. His most recent books are *Knowledge Retention: Strategies and Solutions* (Taylor & Francis, 2009), *Knowledge Management in Public Health* (Taylor & Francis, 2010), *Knowledge Management and E-Learning* (Taylor & Francis, 2011), *Beyond Knowledge Management: What Every Leader Should Know* (Taylor & Francis, 2012), and *Knowledge Management*

Handbook: Collaboration and Social Networking, second edition (Taylor & Francis, 2012). In October 2011, the International Association for Computer Information Systems named the Jay Liebowitz Outstanding Student Research Award for the best student research paper at the IACIS Annual Conference. He has lectured and consulted worldwide. He can be reached at jay.liebowitz@umuc.edu.

Contributors

David Belanger
Chief Scientist
AT&T Labs and Stevens Institute
    of Technology
Hoboken, New Jersey

Joseph Betser
Senior Project Leader—
    Technology, Strategy, and
    Knowledge
The Aerospace Corporation
El Segundo, California

Mike Bugembe
Head of Analytics
JustGiving.com
London, United Kingdom

Bill Burkart
Vice President
Agency Services
Acxiom Corporation
Foster City, California

Jie Cheng
Vice President of Consulting
Acxiom Corporation
Southfield, Michigan

Daniel Conway
Department of Industrial
    Engineering and Management
    Sciences
Northwestern University
Evanston, Illinois

Matt Dobra
Associate Professor
Economics
Methodist University
Fayetteville, North Carolina

Artur Dubrawski
Senior Systems Scientist
The Robotics Institute
Carnegie Mellon University
Pittsburgh, Pennsylvania

G. Scott Erickson
Professor
Marketing and Law
Ithaca College
Ithaca, New York

Jeni Fan
Lead Associate
Advanced Analytics
Booz Allen Hamilton Inc.
Chevy Chase, Maryland

Paul Kent
Vice President of Big Data
SAS Institute Inc.
Cary, North Carolina

Diego Klabjan
Associate Professor
Department of Industrial
    Engineering and Management
    Sciences
Northwestern University
Evanston, Illinois

Juergen Klenk
Principal
Advanced Analytics
Booz Allen Hamilton Inc.
McLean, Virginia

Radhika Kulkarni
Vice President
Advanced Analytics R&D
SAS Institute Inc.
Cary, North Carolina

Joe LaCugna
Enterprise Analytics and Business
    Intelligence
Starbucks Coffee Company
Seattle, Washington

Arun K. Majumdar
Co-Founder
VivoMind Research
Rockville, Maryland

Katherine Marconi
Professor and Program Director
Health Care Administration
    and Health Administration
    Informatics
University of Maryland University
    College
Adelphi, Maryland

Daniel Pitton
IT Compliance Director
U.S. Department of Transportation
National Highway Traffic Safety
    Administration
Washington, DC

Farzan Rohani
Senior Data Scientist
Google Inc.
Mountain View, California

Helen N. Rothberg
Professor
Strategy
Marist College
Poughkeepsie, New York

Udo Sglavo
Principal Analytical Consultant
SAS Institute Inc.
Cary, North Carolina

Yugal Sharma
Lead Associate
Advanced Analytics
Booz Allen Hamilton Inc.
Rockville, Maryland

John F. Sowa
Co-Founder
VivoMind Research
Rockville, Maryland

Murray Stokely
Manager and Software Engineer
Distributed Systems and Parallel
    Computing
Google Inc.
Mountain View, California

Tim Suther
Chief Marketing Officer
Acxiom Corporation
Chicago, Illinois

Eric Tassone
Senior Quantitative Analyst
Google Inc.
Mountain View, California

Ian Thomas
Senior Director
Microsoft Online Services Division
Sunnyvale, California

Charles Thompson
Senior Consultant
Research Triangle Institute (RTI)
    International
Washington, DC

Omer Trajman
Vice President
Field Operations
WibiData
San Francisco, California

Daqing Zhao
Director of SEM Analytics
Ask.com
Moraga, California

1

Architecting the Enterprise via Big Data Analytics[*]

Joseph Betser and David Belanger

CONTENTS

---

[*] All trademarks, trade names, and service marks are the property of their respective owners.

INTRODUCTION

The emergence of new technologies, applications, and social phenomena creates novel business models, communities, and system complexities. Some of these changes are nonlinear and create changes in kind, such as new driving business forces and new organizational structures, which in turn, drive new ways of interacting and conducting business. Facebook, LinkedIn, Google, and Twitter, combined with mobile devices, introduce such emerging technologies, which generate tools for easy community building, collaboration, and knowledge creation, based on social networks. Such emerging changes cause e-mail communication to be subsumed by social network communications, as well as by text messages and tweets. The communities that are created can be based on professional interest, business interest, and social factors. The introduction of cyberthreats to the emerging enterprise makes the challenge richer still, adding multiple layers of complexity to modern enterprises. We review these challenges and how big data analytics assists us in decomposing some of these challenges into more tractable components.

CHALLENGES

The challenges that are brought about by this structural sea change of paradigm shifts are immense. This chapter will not tackle all of them but merely address how big data analytics will assist with a number of these challenges. Challenges that will be discussed in less detail include the societal changes that are brought about by these technology drivers, cyberimpacts, and some new technologies and industries that will revolutionize our economy going forward. We will stress at the conclusion of the chapter that a critical enabling resource that we must cultivate is STEM (science, technology, engineering, and mathematics) education. The supply of the STEM talent pipeline does not meet the growing needs of our high-technology economy, and much of the promise of big data analytics is contingent on ample and a growing supply of STEM talent.

EMERGING PHENOMENA

As phenomenal growth took place in processing power, data storage, network speeds, mobility, and higher semantic capability of a myriad of online applications, the pace of innovation has increased dramatically. The ability to conduct quick searches on vast amounts of data that are available on the World Wide Web (WWW) and other enterprises resulted in multiple new capabilities. It allows national security applications to provide relevant data products to warfighters in record time, enables more targeted and effective advertisement, and allows faster and more effective communications within the enterprise, to name just a small number of innovations. However, an outcome that was not anticipated is the dramatic flattening [1] of enterprises and organizations created by this information revolution. Much like the steam engine and the light bulb created the industrial revolution, the WWW and all those emerging applications are drastically restructuring our enterprises, industries, and even societies.

SOCIAL NETWORKS

When social networking and online blogging began during the past decade or so, it appeared that these were not mainstream activities that would actually define the evolution of technologies, infrastructures, applications, users, communities, and societies. However, these activities soon resulted in knowledge creation and collaboration at a pace that was not previously seen. Some collaborators were physicists all over the world studying bubble chamber results of elementary particle experiments generated by a handful of expensive high-energy accelerator facilities. Other collaborators were teenagers sharing music downloads, individuals sharing recipes, or worldwide customer support organizations supporting a worldwide customer population. What was common in all cases is that collaboration was at a faster pace, and in many cases near real time, and it enabled the creation of virtual communities at a rate never seen before. This turn of events in fact created the concept of Communities of Practice (CoP) and Communities of Interest (CoI). These CoPs and CoIs kept growing in size, scope, and number to the point that they drive significant business model changes as well as societal changes. The relationship between the individuals and peers becomes intertwined with some enabling technologies, and the enterprise becomes a far more dominant structure that comprises the information world in which we live and work.

PERSON-CENTRIC SERVICES AND COMMUNITIES

It is well known that the same online search yields different results for different users. This is because the searches are customized for each user, according to previous searches, websites visited, geolocation, and personal preferences of that user. Sometimes social network relationships, such as Facebook friends and LinkedIn connections, Amazon choices, eBay searches, and previous shopping history also affect the results of searches and advertisements. The services afforded to users become increasingly more effective and targeted in a way that can exceed the capability of human sales and marketing individuals. National security applications can similarly provide users with information most relevant to their mission and current activity in a more effective and timely fashion.

TECHNOLOGY DRIVERS AND BUSINESS ANALYTICS

The computational power of handheld devices, along with the dramatic storage capability, graphic capability, networking capability, and overall versatility, creates an enormously complex and capable enterprise. The discussion that follows studies in more detail how big data business analytics helps make sense of this very challenging undertaking.

FROM NUMBERS TO BIG DATA

How Did We Get Here?

Since the beginning of applications of computers to business problems, in the 1950s, and certainly since the mid-1960s when the first successful database management systems started to appear, there has been a steady increase in the amount of data stored and in the recognition of the value of that data beyond the simple computerization of routine tasks. In big data parlance, the *volume* of data has increased steadily and substantially from the 1960s through the present time. The combination of the Internet and the WWW in the mid-1990s, however, signaled a sea change not only in the amount of data but also more significantly in the rate at which data arrived, *velocity;* the diversity of sources from which it arrived and the types of data available to nearly everyone, *variety.* More important than the quantitative changes, there has been a huge, qualitative change in the amount of *detail* that is carried and maintained by these databases. These changes, combined with dramatic changes in the technology available to analyze and derive information from these data, the cost and availability of processing and storage for the data, and source/delivery mechanisms such as smartphones and sensors have in turn driven changes in the opportunities that can be created by excellence in the use of data and information. More than that, they have driven changes in what we consider to be data available for analysis, what we view the possible results to be, how we view information itself, and most important, the ability that we have to use the results to impact real events.

For several decades, the primary focus of data management was on the ability to process the transactions that make up the core of many business processes, with perfect reliability and with ever-increasing numbers of transactions per second. This replaced manual processes, and over a fairly short amount of time enabled the rate of transactions and the total number of transactions to exceed what would have been economically possible without the machines. Examples of this are the airline reservation systems and the credit card systems. These systems are highly optimized for the large numbers of transactions that they can process, with near-perfect reliability, each second. The goal was to create systems that achieved the so-called ACID[†] properties as efficiently as possible. With each decade, the size of the databases increased by about a factor of 1000, so that what was a large database in the 1970s (perhaps many megabytes) was replaced by terabyte-scale bases in the 1990s, and petabytes in the 2000s. Given the current explosion in sources of data, both the number of individual sources and the volume from each source, there is every reason to

---

[*] For example, IBM's IMS Data Base System.
[†] ACID—atomicity, consistency, isolation, durability.

expect this pace to increase. The basic model of the databases also evolved from hierarchical and network* to relational. These models became very effective at storing data that had the structure of fields within records† (attributes in tuples). Of course, there were exceptions to the transaction processing models, for example, scientific databases made up of huge volumes of numbers,‡ databases made up of images (e.g., NASA databases), and databases made up of events (e.g., network data). With the dominance of the relational data model, structured query language (SQL) became the de facto standard for accessing data.

By the late 1980s and early 1990s, it had become clear that there must be more value in the data available than simply managing transactions or recording events. The existing data provided deep insight into behavior of customers, activities on inventories, trends in financial transactions, and a host of other useful functions. Alas, in transaction systems, changes are made *in situ;* therefore, historical data was often lost, and longitudinal studies were difficult. In many ways, the emergence of data warehouses addressed this problem, making data more available to a larger cross-section of people, and retaining data that no longer had direct operational use but was very useful for decision support and optimizing operations. The sources of the data were largely the same, driven by transactions and events, and the type of data was still typically numbers or characters in fields organized into records (i.e., the relational model), but the additional type of management opened up many new possibilities in terms of analysis and recognition of the value of the detail available. In general, a wider variety of people had access to these warehouses, and they often contained a broader cross-section of data.

All of this would have been fine, except that in the late 1990s the development of the WWW, on top of the Internet, was making huge amounts of information available to large percentages of the United States (and the world). With the advent of the WWW, many things changed. There has been no reduction in the need for reliable, high-volume transaction processing, but it has become only one of a number of different modes of data management. First, there are now many important applications that do not require strict ACID properties but may be able to relax either the

---

* Databases structurally based on the concept of parent/child records or owner/member records.
† A picture of a relational attribute and tuple.
‡ For example: astronomy, meteorology, high-energy physics, genomics.

requirements for availability or consistency in a networked environment.* For example, an application that monitors network traffic to detect security attacks is interested in very low latency and near perfect availability of the data, but may be willing to sacrifice some consistency to obtain it. This engineering tradeoff allows it to run at the speed of the network, an essential property, without sampling, which could lose important information, but with a generally small sacrifice in terms of consistency. Second, much, and then most, of the data available no longer looked like a relatively small set of numeric- or character-based fields collected in the form of a record. Semistructured and unstructured data have become, in volume and velocity, at least the equal of structured data. It is certainly not hard to observe this on the Internet and WWW. Browsers are based on the notion of semistructured data. There is structure in the form of the web hypertext, but the individual web pages are made up of text, image, and often video and audio. None of these has the convenient structure of a relational database, and none of it is reasonably accessed by an SQL-like language. These changes have not only led to many changes in what we can generate and access as data, but have driven fundamental changes in the structure of the way data itself is managed. Among many other things, the emergence of NoSQL[†] (not only SQL) data management systems have fundamentally changed the calculations on what we can do with data systems. The map/reduce systems, such as Hadoop, which these data management systems run, have vastly increased the scale of processing data.

But the WWW and the resultant consumer access to vast amounts of largely unstructured data was just the first wave of changes in data volume, velocity, and variety. While having the effect of making these data available at any time and to nearly anyone, and at least as important, making nearly everyone a potential (and often actual) source of data, they accessed only a small fraction of the potential generation and use of data.

Two existing trends, and one emerging trend, have filled this void and are dramatically increasing volume, velocity, variety, and especially timely detail of data both generated and consumed. These are mobility, machine-to-machine communication, and the trend toward "open" data.

---

[*] This concept is important because of a very well-known theorem, known as the CAP theorem, which states roughly that in a partitioned environment (e.g., separated by a network) one cannot have complete consistency and availability. [Ref: 2.]

[†] For example: Cassandra, HBase, BigTable, and working with systems like Hadoop.

Mobility creates more data and more demand for data. It reduces the time during which an item of information is perceived to have value* to seconds or minutes (how long are you now willing to wait, given that you have a smartphone, for an update of a news item or sports score?), and it reduces the effort you expect to expend to obtain information† to feet or inches (the distance between your hand and pocket). From the point of view of data, every activity on the mobile device generates data about the device and the networks that it is using, the applications that you are using and what you are using them for, your location, and a variety of other values. Some of this data is consumed and returned directly to you in the form of personalized, online advertisements or other applications, some is consumed to optimize the performance of the device and its networks and to detect network problems, and much of it is stored for later data analysis. Of course, you can perform all of the activities that you do on a smartphone with a fixed device in your home, but you can't do it wherever you are at any given time.

Mobility, in the form of devices like smartphones, has increased the amount of data by a few orders of magnitude. Much of this is the result of the "always on" nature of the medium, but even more of the pure data consumed, and therefore in flight, is a result of the convergence of entertainment with communications and computing. Simply put, today video is the primary driver of bandwidth use on networks, fixed and mobile. Much of this video is what we classically think of as entertainment, professionally developed movies and television. This results in a huge amount of data moving across networks, though a limited amount of new information (since the sources are quite limited). However, much more of it is the result of cameras (image and video) on every new smartphone. These devices are used to record a vast variety of things, mundane or exciting, which are in turn stored and made available to many (e.g., "friends") or everyone (e.g., YouTube). There are now venues where the amount of upstream content in the form of video exceeds downstream. Even this deluge of data, easily hundreds of petabytes per day, will be supplanted in terms of velocity, and perhaps volume, over the next decade.

What could possibly generate more data than seven billion folks multitasking with video applications all their waking hours? The answer is a few trillion machines communicating with each other 24 hours a day.

---

* Sometimes referred to as the half-life of the perceived value of information.
† Sometimes referred to as the inconvenience threshold.

The advent of wireless communication, both that which we associate with mobility (i.e., cellular) and more nomadic wireless (e.g., WiFi, Zigbee, UWB), has made it possible to place sensing devices nearly anywhere. Today, most of these devices are communicating numbers and characters among each other or to a central location for analysis. For example, your cell phone is communicating a large array of data about its status, signal strength, connectivity, and location with a frequency that is limited largely by the capacity of the network to transmit the data and the ability of the carrier to make use of the data. There is also an increasing array of devices that can be attached to your body and transmit medical and activity information (e.g., blood pressure, pulse rate, blood glucose level, pace of motion) to clinical systems. As the ability to mine unstructured data, especially image and video, matures (a matter of only a few years), the data supplied by these devices spreads to image and video and will see another quantum leap in the amount of data, but much more important, also in the value of data.

Finally, data because of its value, even if only for operations, has traditionally been considered a proprietary resource. Before the advent of the Internet, web, and broadband communications, this was purely a pragmatic choice. Only large corporations had the resources and expertise to purchase and operate the kind of machinery needed to move, store, and analyze the data. Now, a large percentage of the world has such capability. So we have seen first hardware, then software, move from the province of large corporations to consumers.

Will data be next? Of course it will! Hardware has become remarkably standardized over the last two decades, and while corporate computers are bigger and faster than most found in homes or pockets, they are increasingly large because they are clustered in large groups. Most people do not have an array of thousands of PCs in their homes, but Google and Amazon do, and through the "cloud" one can, in theory, have access to them. Software, through open source and cloud, is following in that direction, though proprietary software is still a significant force. Sites are beginning to appear* that make significant data available to anyone who can make use of it. This trend will certainly increase quickly, but data has some properties that hardware and software do not. Among the most obvious are privacy and integrity. One can be harmed by data about oneself falling into the wrong hands (e.g., identity theft) and equally by

---

* For example, COSM.com (formerly Pachube.com), data.gov.

data that is incorrect even in the right hands (e.g., credit score errors). The resolution of the tension between privacy on the one hand and openness on the other will take years to resolve, and the details are not yet clear. What is clear is that upcoming generations have a different expectation of privacy, since they were raised in the presence of pervasive mobile devices. It is fairly clear that openness is generally the friend of integrity. For example, Wikipedia seems to rival traditional encyclopedias in terms of overall quality of the data, for most articles. This is largely because of its open, self-correcting structure.

Why Does It Matter?

In this section we outline a potential application to illustrate the nature and some of the power of *big data*. The application is hypothetical but entirely possible given access to the right data. In this discussion, we will assume that all users have opted in. That is, they have indicated that they are willing to share their data to have access to the service.

Suppose that you are interested in an application on your mobile device that would notify you if someone with certain common interests was within a short walking distance from you at this moment. Perhaps they should be within half a mile. What data would be required to provide such a service? First, a way to indicate interests would be needed. This might be done by noting the searches that you and the person whose interests match yours have performed over the past few days. Using an appropriate algorithm to cluster people with similar interests based on their recent search patterns, a set of possible contacts could be determined. This is already a big data problem, because the search data is typically text (variety), and usually large (volume, velocity). Given a set of people with common interests, the next step is to see if any of them are within half a mile of you right now. The data required for this is provided by the GPS on most smart devices and available to the application if you have opted in to allow it to be seen. Though this data is numeric, it typically has significant volume and velocity and, more than that, is useful only in real time. That is, where you were a few minutes ago is of no interest. The above conditions being met, each of the people identified would be notified by an instant message with enough information to make the contact.

Regardless of whether you actually want such a service, it is likely that, given interesting enough topics, many consumers would sign up. It could even generate "flash" groups. Our interest here, however, is to understand what is different about the data processing required to provide such a service. As observed earlier, the differentiating property of big data is the amount of detail that can be provided. In this case, detail about the interests of tens or hundreds of millions of people, as reflected by data from search engines, social networks, specific interest (e.g., health-related) sites, tweets, or other sources, is well beyond anything available in the transactional world. It is possible, of course, that transactional data would also be used in such a service. Location data, also reflecting the position of tens or hundreds of millions of people, is also at a level of detail beyond what traditional databases could digest; but more than that, the half-life for this type of application is very short. Detail reflects not only the minuteness of the information but also the amount of time for which it has value.

How Has Technology Evolved to Support These Requirements?

Of course, most of the new capabilities are the result of a very dynamic technological base that has matured over the past decade and made them possible, but another way of looking at this is from the opposite direction. What is now required that has made these technologies necessary? For example, brute scale has made better compression essential even as the disk price, per megabyte, has come down dramatically. It has also made algorithms like map/reduce and NoSQL databases necessary.

Following are some technology directions that both make big data possible and will make many of the things in big data easier to accomplish:

- **Data Stream Management:** The velocity associated with big data often results in the influx of data from widely distributed sources that has more of the characteristics of a stream than of discrete transactions. In particular, the appropriate immediate processing is much like a filter. A set of algorithms is applied, usually in parallel, to quickly determine what to do with a particular piece of data, before it is passed on to a database or data warehouse for storage and further processing.
- **Cloud:** The technical and economic structure of cloud services (as a service) have made it possible for many organizations to use and publish large amounts of data and analysis.

- **NoSQL Databases:** Since much of the actual data in new databases is not in the form of a set of character-based fields in a collection of relations, a number of more flexible data access languages have evolved. There is now a fairly large set of such languages competing to become standards.
- **Bandwidth:** The ability to move large amounts of data, especially video data, is dependent on the huge increases in bandwidth available, not only in core networks but also in access to most endpoints, including mobile endpoints.
- **Mobility/Wireless:** Mobile access to all forms of data, with high bandwidth, anywhere, anytime, dramatically increases both the supply and demand for data and information. In addition, wireless communication makes many of the machine-to-machine communications possible. There are many effective types of mobile access, including cellular, nomadic, and ad hoc networks.
- **New forms of data** (e.g., text, speech, video, image): Not only the availability of these types of data (they have been both available and digitized for a long time) but also the availability of technology to manipulate and analyze them have allowed the explosion in a variety of data. For example, data mining on speech data, at the scale of millions of conversations per day, is now a reality and is used by many call service centers.

REDEFINING THE ORGANIZATION

Thinking about Redefining

Ready access to data, quickly and with rich analysis and visualization, has qualitatively, as well as quantitatively, changed the communication patterns and hence the decision processes in many companies. The first several generations of data processing were largely concentrated on record keeping and automation of existing processes. The expected, and common, result was a certain amount of disintermediation, so that the sources of data became connected to the consumers by machines, as opposed to armies of people with attendant hierarchies. While there was a considerable amount of data mining and analysis, it was largely based on direct analysis of single, sometimes large, data stores and was largely used for decision support and optimization within well-defined corporate silos. The current big data world has changed these communications patterns even more dramatically in terms of disintermediation, automation, and insight into the workings of processes. In this context, big data should be understood not primarily as being bigger or faster data sets than before, but as the ability to access, integrate, and process data that provides detail rich enough to impact business processes both qualitatively more deeply than before and as the process is running (i.e., in real time for that process). Size is often a characteristic of this data, but several industries such as credit card, telecom, and finance have been processing this size of data for many years and are still seeing dramatic changes due to big data. An obvious example is location data associated with cell phones, vehicles, or anything else that moves. That data, combined with other data, yields stunning insight into the patterns of behavior of communities, as well as the entities in them, not merely their transactions.

Let's talk about how this is happening and how it will happen.

Some Challenges

We start by articulating the challenge presented by big data in terms of how we think about its use and value. Some of the technical challenges have been discussed in previous sections.

The fundamental challenge is pretty straightforward. Your competitors, current and potential, might be getting more value out of their data than you are—first in terms of restructuring the enterprise, becoming faster, and reducing cost; second in terms of making better decisions based on real, up-to-date information; and finally, among the leading edge, in terms of new products and new approaches to markets. Loosely put, the player who knows more about its markets and customers, sooner, and acts on that knowledge will usually win!

Some Opportunities

Given the challenge articulated above, there are many opportunities presented by big data that are the result of reengineering the way we think about our business, and consequently the ways we can organize it. We will present two here.

1. Feedback Control: Restructure the key processes that run the company as tight feedback control processes. Don't just make a bunch of new silos; create views that cross, optimized silos.
2. Latency of Information Access: Restructure the communication paths in the company to reflect the ability to get information quickly and accurately across barriers.

Before going into detail about reengineering, it is useful to think about the characteristics of big data that create opportunities today that did not exist previously. Clearly, it is not simply volume or velocity. These represent as much barriers to be overcome as they do opportunities. What is new and extremely powerful about big data as we see it today is the level of detail that it contains and the timeliness of that detail. As an example, consider the combination of location and activity data in real-time marketing. Currently, a lot of companies can track exactly what a consumer is doing online, very close to the time when they are doing it. This can result in pushing advertisements targeted exactly at the particular consumer and what he or she may be interested in at the time. What makes this work is the combination of very detailed data about web activity combined with exact knowledge of what the target is doing at exactly that moment. In the mobile world, one can add location data to that equation, allowing the targeting to be informed not only by *what* but by *where*. This would enable offering a coupon to your smart device as you are passing the store with the offer. Examples like this abound in marketing, healthcare, finance, and many other areas. The central concept in all of these examples is the availability of data in extreme detail and in time to impact real-world events.

Restructuring Opportunities

Every business has a collection of long-running, essential processes on which its operation and revenues depend. These processes can be modeled as workflow or state machines and are often programmed as such. Perhaps the most public example is the ability of many online sales companies and most shipping companies to track the progress of every order between the order itself and delivery. At each point in the process there is a data trail indicating whether a particular package has reached that point. Often there is web access so that a recipient can track delivery progress. It is a short step from that capability to providing the data-mining capability to automatically alert if any package fails to reach a given point in the expected time. That is a control feedback loop to monitor, and control if possible, the execution of each thread through the process.

There are many other examples, including provisioning in communications services, providing intelligence products to the warfighter, and trials and manufacturing in pharmaceuticals. All are characterized by the fact that they look like very long-running (e.g., hours, days, months) transactions. They are also characterized by the fact that they typically cross a number of data and organizational silos, sometimes crossing databases in different companies. Provisioning in communication is a good example. It lies between sales/ordering and maintenance/billing, and its function is to make some service or network capability available to a customer. With modern electronics, many provisioning functions are fully automated and very quick—witness the provisioning of mobile service when you buy a cellular device. Others require physical activity, such as laying fiber in the ground, and can take months. Most are somewhere in between. All of them require the access and update of a number of databases, such as logical inventory (what IP addresses are available), physical inventory (what network facilities will be used, if any need to be updated), customer information (what does the customer already have, will there be conflicts), access to other companies (local number portability), and several others. As with any process, logical or physical, there is little reason to believe that the process is running perfectly as intended, for all transactions, without actually creating a feedback loop that ensures the correct completion of each transaction. Often this is simplified to "the same number of transactions leave as enter over some time period." At large scale, the input/output condition can be satisfied while many transactions are permanently hung up in the interior of the process. The goal is to be able to track each transaction's thread through the process, with alerts when any delays or errors occur, and feedback control at all points of data exchange. This raises a number of challenges, including the following:

- The amount of data typically gets very large, very quickly.
- Many, if not most, of the data systems in these threads are legacy and were not designed to be integrated with their peers except through the handoff of data downstream. Others may be ad hoc, not designed for use with other data systems. There is no reason to expect common keys throughout the process for tracking, nor that the systems are set up for convenient data retrieval.

- In high-velocity and complex processes, it is unlikely that the control part of the process can productively be handled by humans (too many) or that the root cause can be found in "real" (as defined by the customer) time. A *patch* control process will likely be needed. Sometimes this can be as simple as *power cycle* (i.e., restart the thread). Sometimes it will require default values to move forward.

How does this help in reengineering the company? First, it recognizes the fact that, though they are there for good reasons, silos are not the friend of complex, multi-silo processes. More than that, the solution is not to attempt to just make bigger silos. If the data systems are moderate in volume and velocity, and homogeneous in technology and variety, one can think of creating a level of indirection that makes them appear to be a single federated database for corporate purposes. If the databases, individually, represent big data, this will be very complex, and almost certainly suffer from poor, sometimes crippling, performance.

One approach to this problem uses what are essentially a combination of web and database technologies to create a "view" of the data that is as integrated as possible, but sometimes requires human intervention. The view is, for practical and performance reasons, virtual where possible, and materialized if necessary. In typical operation, this integration would attempt to create, as accurately as possible given lack of consistent join capability, a thread for every transaction through a process and would use a rule set of alerts if any thread fails to perform as expected. In the best of cases, it would also execute some control procedures when such a failure is detected.

A second opportunity is to restructure the communication paths in the company to reflect the ability to get information quickly and accurately across barriers. This approach is as much about web and social networking technologies as it is about big data, but it reflects two facts:

1. The purpose of web and social networking technologies is, as was phone technology before them, to move information and/or data (albeit some it used for entertainment) around the world, and to get it to the right place, at the right time, in the right form.
2. Though it doesn't start with the letter "V," *latency* is as important in the big data world as the three Vs. Latency is the delay in getting essential information to all people who can use it (and have a right to).

Most managers have experienced the desire to "spin" information that is going outside their control in an organization. The advent of web-oriented systems, service-oriented architectures, and interactive systems makes the justification for this very tenuous. Even under these conditions, if the presentation is sufficiently opaque, or the delivery sporadic or delayed, there is de facto information hiding. In a big data world, where the data is as liberated as possible and the analysis and visualization automated, there is little justification for hiding from those with a right to the information. A real example, with a service that was fairly new, had a few million customers but was adding in the tens of thousands per business day. An interactive, visual analysis of the lift due to regional or national ads within a few hours was down from the previous days or weeks. This meant that each morning the product manager could see exactly what the evening advertising campaign was doing. As expected, this person was accustomed to reporting these facts a few levels up at the beginning of each week, and the higher levels would then convey to their peers. Once it became known that the data was available each morning, in an easy-to-use and interactive format, the traditional communication patterns broke down. The product manager was exposed to questions from several levels above upon getting in each morning. Decision turnaround was cut by an order of magnitude. Most importantly, the data was able to quickly reach levels of management who had the ability to manipulate the product and advertising strategy, and this was able to change in days, as opposed to weeks and months.

What is the message? For people within a fast-moving information system, expectations of how information is delivered and used need to be adjusted. It will dramatically reduce the half-life of perceived value of information but will, at the same time, dramatically increase the potential value of the information. Finally, it is an example of a special kind of social network. These are called "communities of interest," networks formed not by explicit social relationships but by common interests. Each employee is a member of a number of such communities, and the communication along the paths in the graph of a community is much more intense than across nonaligned edges. Communications patterns within organizations have been studied a number of times—e-mail is, for example, well studied. Informal communications patterns are found to be much richer and more complex than the organizational hierarchy. This is interesting, but the concept above is a way of using and institutionalizing that fact in a way that is dynamic and flexible. One can speculate that analyzing these communities within an organization can lead to optimization and an intraorganizational set of communities, though it is not clear yet how or what value it will have. It is clear that with the proper use of big, real-time information, they can form and can make a huge difference.

PREPARING FOR A BIG DATA WORLD

Science, Technology, Engineering, and Mathematics

It is clear that the ubiquity of data, and particularly of the very detailed, timely data associated with big data, will create demand for professionals to manage and manipulate the data, and for a population able to understand the uses and implications of the new data world. The shortage of people with deep analytical skills is estimated [3] as ranging from 140,000 to 190,000 in the United States alone. The same source estimates the shortage of data-aware managers and analysts to be roughly 1.5 million. This is the tip of the iceberg. As the benefits of big data permeate nearly every industry, they will also impact every enterprise and every consumer. This is already true for fields like retail, online advertising, finance, defense, healthcare, aerospace, and telecom, among other industries. The implications to our economy, and the economy of every nation, are enormous.

At the same time, we are facing a decline in the production of graduates at all levels in the STEM fields, of which technologies associated with big data are an exploding part. As indicated in [4], both bachelor of science and associate degrees in STEM fields, as a percentage of all such degrees, have been declining for nearly a decade. The absolute numbers for each degree type have been essentially flat for that period of time, while the total number of degrees has increased. This source estimates that approximately one million more STEM professionals will be required over the next decade than will be produced with current trends. The unavoidable conclusion as it relates to big data is that not only will there be a substantial increase in demand for people with the skills required to allow our economy to take advantage of this technology, but also that supply, given the momentum view, isn't increasing and will face increased international competition for people with these skills across the STEM fields. Furthermore, evidence [4, 5, 6] suggests that the "pipeline" of mathematically trained people coming out of high school and interested in the STEM fields is well short of the upcoming demand.

The United States alone has far too many initiatives and approaches to the STEM education problem to enumerate here, many with impressive initial results, but too little evidence of which of these will have the critical properties of measurability, scalability, and sustainability. It is reasonable to discuss thought processes that may be of use. In the next section, we outline just a few.

RECOMMENDATIONS

1. Leverage expertise wherever possible. World-class use of the current volumes, velocities, and varieties of data is an inherently multidisciplinary activity. Only a relatively small number of very deep scientists and engineers will be creating new, fundamental technology, but orders of magnitude more data scientists, domain experts, and informed users will be required to maximize the value of data. At AT&T Labs, a multidisciplinary research lab called InfoLab was created about 15 years ago to address opportunities in what is now called big data. It has observed over the intervening time a large list of useful techniques, technologies, and high-value results.

2. Leverage technology aggressively. The difference between force-fitting a technology and using the best available technology, at scale, can be huge. Think in terms of small, multidisciplinary teams (where small is a single-digit number), armed with the best technology available. Right now it is not clear what the winning tools across the big data landscape will be five years from now. It is clear that a revolution in the basic set of tools is appearing to address a variety of issues in this area. In this world, worry less about standards than productivity at scale. Ignore tools that don't scale easily.

3. It's all about the data! Initiate a proactive effort to make data easy for the teams to access. Experience indicates that getting the required data is often more than 75 percent of a data analysis effort, especially when real-time data is involved.

4. Use crowds and networks where possible. Hide data from employees only where it is absolutely necessary, and encourage people to look at data critically. It may provide some surprising insights, and will certainly increase data integrity.

5. In your own interests, get involved in improving STEM education. There are many approaches to improving all levels of education. Some, such as use of virtual classrooms, inverting the learning model via online learning, seem very promising. Examples are mentoring programs to increase retention in STEM, outreach to help minority and female students understand what STEM employees do, interaction with education partners on industries' needs in the area, and investigation of online classes in big data. Most importantly, generate whatever data you can on techniques and outcomes. Much of the current data in this space is anecdotal, and that will not be sufficient to make the needed progress.

In summary, the trends in terms of value and spread of data use guarantee rapid and broad increases, while the trends of skilled workers in these fields are not likely to keep up, at least in the short term. Proactive work to address your skill needs will pay disproportionately large dividends.

REFERENCES

1. Friedman, T., *The World Is Flat—A Brief History of the 21st Century*, Farrar, Strauss & Giroux, 2005.
2. Shim, Simon S.Y., The CAP Theorem's Growing Impact, *Computer*, 45(2), February 2012.
3. McKinsey & Company, *Big Data: The Next Frontier for Innovation, Competition, and Productivity*, McKinsey Global Institute, Cambridge, May 2011.
4. Office of Science and Technology Policy, The White House, Report to the President: *Engage to Excel: Producing One Million Additional College Graduates with Degrees in Science, Technology, Engineering, and Mathematics*, http://www.whitehouse.gov/sites/default/files/microsites/ostp/pcast-engage-to-excel-final_feb.pdf, February 2012.
5. TechAmerica Foundation, *Recommendations for Education and the Advancement of Learning (REAL) Agenda Commission: Taking Steps to Invest in Promise of Their Future and Ours*, http://www.techamerica.org/Docs/fileManager.cfm?f=taf-real-report.pdf; April 2012.
6. Carnevale, A., N. Smith, and M. Melton, *STEM: Science, Technology, Engineering, Mathematics*, Georgetown University Center on Education and the Workforce Georgetown University; http://www9.georgetown.edu/grad/gppi/hpi/cew/pdfs/stem-complete.pdf; 2011.

2

Jack and the Big Data Beanstalk: Capitalizing on a Growing Marketing Opportunity

Tim Suther, Bill Burkart, and Jie Cheng

CONTENTS

DO YOU KNOW JACK?

Had he lived in the twenty-first century, Jack—he of the beanstalk fame—perhaps would have been a C-suite marketing executive with a LinkedIn profile maxed out with connections and a résumé filled with genuine success stories. Consider his circumstances:

Dismissing his mother's directive to sell the family's lone asset and instead acting off the vague promise of a funny-looking but convincing old man, he trades a cow-gone-dry for a handful of beans (textbook outside-the-box thinking—the hallmark of any forward-thinking executive). Jack's mother, a conservative nineteenth-century pragmatist entrusted with providing food for her family, scorns Jack, sending him to bed without supper while casting the beans out the window.

Had Jack's story ended there, his would have been the tale of an unremarkable corporate middling, one whose aspirations were tempered by immature overreach and miscalculation. But as we know, Jack's story continues …

He awakes the next morning to find a giant beanstalk outside his window. Seeking a reversal of fortune (and as any faithful Freudian would assume, his mother's approval) he sets out on a blind journey, desperate to extract value from the massive growth.

Jack succeeds but not without overcoming the most daunting of challenges: competition, this time in the form of a menacing giant. He accomplishes this not through brute force but through skill and daring, remarkably gaining the sympathies of his adversary's spouse (without any discernible quid pro quo, mind you) while returning time and time again to gather gold coins, a golden-egg-laying goose, and other valuables.

Jack and the Beanstalk is a classic read for most of us and a perfect opportunity for parents to hone a repertoire of "fee-fi-fo-fum" variations. But for our purposes, it presents an apt metaphor that sums up nicely the challenges for twenty-first century corporations that seek to find genuine long-term success.

THE CHALLENGE: MEGA AND GIGA, MEET ZETTA

Companies today are overgrown with information, including what many categorize as big data. The jungle includes information about customers, competition, media and channel performance, locations, products, and transactions, to name just a few—data that in isolation presents a multitude of intimidating and bewildering options that can lead to poor decision making, or worse, to inaction.

Just how big is big data? Nearly two *zetta*bytes (a football stadium piled with magic beans to the upper deck or, more scientifically, about 500 billion DVDs) of data were created in 2011, the fifth consecutive year the amount exceeded our ability to store it.

But, it's more complicated than simply *volume*; the nature of the data has dramatically changed. Two other V words—*variety* and *velocity*—are used to describe big data, and they are wreaking havoc as well. Some analysts believe that multistructured data, like images, videos, and social chatter, now represents 80–90 percent of the total data output.* The value of some data, like "intent to buy," can be fleeting, so the ability to process in real time is important. And, the quality of much digital data is suspect, caused by the inadequacies of cookies. The bottom line? Most of today's information systems are not designed for the three Vs of big data, leaving marketers to feel overwhelmed by the tsunami of data. Taming big data means redesigning these systems.

---

* http://clarabridge.com/default.aspx?tabid=137&ModuleID=635&ArticleID=551

1 million comments

2 million YouTube videos viewed

500 Billion online comments

10 million display ads

1.4 million Facebook status updates

2 Zettabytes (1 trillion Gigabytes)

Meanwhile, an interesting paradox has emerged for marketers: The number of ways to reach consumers has never been more; they can check in, "like," pin, and follow, in addition to a host of traditional marketing options. But amazingly, despite all these new tools, it has never been more difficult to *engage* consumers—to have a meaningful, trust-building conversation. Consumers truly are boss, choosing when, where, how, and *if* they engage with brands.

Consumers skip or even block ads and flit between mediums. Television viewing used to be the tribal campfire for families, but now television seems to be just another light source among many. Research indicates that consumers with tablets are usually doing something disconnected from what's in front of them on TV. As viewing evolves from one screen to many simultaneously, marketers are left to play a cat-and-mouse game, struggling to determine the impact of an individual marketing impression. It's enough to spin even Jack's head.

Changed consumer behavior has also eroded the efficacy of traditional advertising models. You know this intuitively if you've browsed your local four- or eight-page newspaper recently—if a company in your city or town still prints one. Fifteen years ago, a heavy national TV schedule could reach 80–90 percent of a target audience in three weeks. Now it's lucky to reach 60 percent. Fifteen years ago, 40 percent of impressions would be concentrated on the top 20 percent of heaviest TV viewers. Now it's 60–80 percent. Twenty years ago, there were 28 TV channels. Today, there are more than 165 channels. Today, it takes 405 spots to deliver the equivalent media weight of one spot from 15 to 20 years ago.*

And of course, while *consuming* information, consumers are busy *creating* their own, with photos, reviews, calls, texts, likes, follows, pins, check-ins, pings, and tweets, among many others. Indeed, last year, U.S. consumers were busier than Jack's new army of gold-counting accountants: Each minute on the Internet yielded 700,000 Google search queries and 48 hours of new video uploaded by YouTube users, and Facebook users shared 674,478 pieces of content.† That's each minute—every 60 seconds.

This vast and rapidly expanding pool of data has also created an ever-widening gap between those who view data as an asset and those who don't. In particular, while technology and some media companies have amassed enormous value, most brands have yet to tap into big data's value. As a result, margins are under assault and loyalty has fallen sharply.

Research reveals that just 25 percent of consumers are very loyal today, while another 25 percent exhibit no loyalty at all.‡ And nearly all brand measurements are down, including awareness (down 20 percent), trust (down 50 percent), and esteem (down 12 percent).§

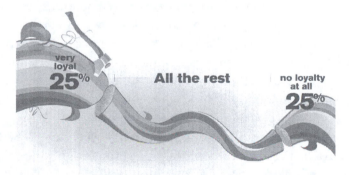

* http://www.simulmedia.com/2012/04/simulmedia-investors-fund-new-6-million-round/
† http://www.domo.com/blog/2012/06/how-much-data-is-created-every-minute/
‡ http://www.accenture.com/us-en/Pages/insight-acn-global-consumer-research-study.aspx
§ http://www.amazon.com/Brand-Bubble-Looming-Crisis-Value/dp/047018387X/ref=sr_1_1?ie= UTF8&s=books&qid=1253624008&sr=1-1

Some, however, are enjoying huge financial success by leveraging the value from big data. Among the top 10 most valuable companies worldwide,* at least five—Apple, Microsoft, IBM, China Mobile, and AT&T—have created major value through the strategic use of big data. Moreover, venture capitalists have invested another $2.5 billion into big data in the last year alone.[†] They clearly recognize, as do we, that data is on par with labor and capital in its ability to generate value.

Intriguingly, most of the value generated by data to date has been used by *selling* advertising better to brands—but very little has been used to help brands *buy* and execute advertising better. As a result, many of these data-fueled innovations are proving disruptive to traditional business models.

During the 2011 holiday season, Amazon made news with its Price Check app, which allows consumers to scan barcodes on products in local stores and instantly compare prices with those on Amazon's website. For a limited time, consumers who made a purchase through the app, thus abandoning their local retailer, received a $5 discount on purchases (up to $15.)

Even without a discount incentive, consumers were already honing their "showrooming" skills. According to Forrester Research, consumers who are in the store ready to buy abandon a purchase for two primary reasons: they found the item cheaper online or found a better deal down the street.[‡] Consumers were always sensitive to price; now smartphones and an app make it easy (and fun) to compare prices and locate merchandise elsewhere. (Did we already mention consumer loyalty is in rapid decline?)

The example underscores what's at stake for brands: the need to engage more intelligently with consumers in an always-on, connected way. Yes, brands need to *develop real-time insights*—to help them better anticipate and serve customers. But, developing insights alone won't be sustaining. Brands need also to *control* those insights.

It's curious; while every brand is actively exploring how to better use data, few are taking sufficient steps to *protect* the insights they generate. For sure, brands have elaborate information technology security to ward off cybercriminals. Instead, a brand's data rights (particularly the data generated in marketing and advertising) need more protection. In fact, in many cases, brands are actually inadvertently *giving* this data away.

---

* http://ycharts.com/rankings/market_cap

† http://www.itworld.com/big-datahadoop/287477/big-data-bringing-down-big-bucks-venture-capitalists

‡ Understanding Shopping Cart Abandonment, Forrester Research, May 2010.

For instance, using a media buying "trading desk" can appear to add inexpensive reach, but it could come at a steep price if the brand fails to receive data that customers generate from using the service. That data provides clues to future customer interests and value, and the response behavior helps determine whether or not marketing campaigns are actually working.

More ominously, many services (not limited to trading desks) use that data to create proprietary profiles of customer behavior, which in turn are used to provide service to others, potentially including the original brand's competitors. For some services, the data is actually auctioned to the highest bidder. No brand wants its proprietary insight to help its competition, yet inattentiveness allows that to happen.

OLD IS NEW

The challenge—managing data—is not new. It began when smart, usually large companies recognized the inefficiency in maintaining disparate customer databases for nearly every activity.

Developing and implementing sophisticated (at the time) algorithms, these companies began targeting their marketing more precisely, often to specific households. They began to connect transactions to customers to products to marketing activity to value generated, planting the "beans" for data-driven marketing.

We see today's challenge as similar, albeit more complex. Companies still need to manage across customer databases and build richer customer views, but cultivating meaningful insights is not as simple as merging newly aggregated data into existing databases. The sheer volume of big data overwhelms traditional systems. Additionally, privacy sensitivities require thinking more strategically about what data is captured and how it's used.

The challenges are great, but companies must take concrete, fundamental steps to survive and prosper against such formidable odds.

THE POWER OF FIVE

One: Get Multidimensional

As some companies have proven, data can unlock enormous value. But *what type* of data is most valuable? Is it what customers actually buy?

What they say they want? What they search for? Data from their social media activities? Or the digital breadcrumbs they leave as they travel the Internet? Is the data that brands observe about customers more important than that which customers volunteer directly? And, what about the role of the algorithm, the calculated insights marketers make? Surely there must be one source of data that is most valuable, a silver data bullet (or bean), right?

Unfortunately, no single signal consistently describes and predicts consumer behavior. As with the blind men and the elephant in the old parable, to see the whole, leaders must think multidimensionally, refining insights from all relevant perspectives about their customers.

Let's look at why. Past purchases are important, but even the most loyal customers spend most of their time engaged with other brands. Additionally, a brand's "best" customer may be, in fact, an even better customer for a competitor. Knowing what customers do when not engaged with your brand can provide clues in how to increase your share-of-wallet or help you create new products or services (creating new wallets in which to share).

Asking customers what they want is important but also incomplete. Unfortunately, customers don't always know what they want. (Did anyone really know they wanted an iPod until they saw it?) Moreover, consumers often have an unrealistic view of the world. Sixty-three percent of Americans think they are of above-average intelligence, a mathematical impossibility.* Connecting what consumers believe with what they actually do is vital.

What about search? Is a search explicitly for a product, in fact, the best indicator? Statistically, the results are mixed.† Moreover, while search is an awesome tool to *fulfill* demand, it does nothing to *generate* demand.

Of course, over the years, word of mouth has been a powerful marketing ally. Is its modern incarnation, the social graph, the answer? Once again, it's interesting but incomplete. While it has loads of potential, the linkage between social behavior and purchases is at best fragile.

And, what of digital breadcrumbs? They hold enormous potential to complement search as an expression of intent. But, like many emerging technologies, marketers are still learning how to use them effectively.

---

* http://www.amazon.com/The-Invisible-Gorilla-Intuitions-Deceive/dp/0307459659
† http://www.luthresearch.com/node/119

Technologists struggle with data quality challenges as well; for example, digital data gets gender wrong about half the time.*

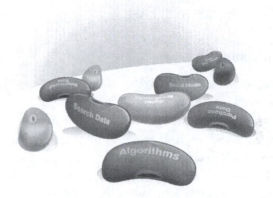

There is no one data point that accurately describes or predicts consumer behavior; no single color paints the portrait with so many different colors on the palette.

Recall our man Jack, who could have retired after his first trip with a bag of gold coins but returned several times and reaped a golden-egg-laying goose, a cool harp, and other valuables. To *tap the full potential of their marketing*, companies today must cultivate and control *multidimensional* insights about their customers.

The strategy requires that all relevant online, offline, and attitudinal data—data that is observed, inferred, volunteered, and predicted—be activated, evaluated, and applied. This means treating multidimensional data as an enterprise asset, unlocking it from the silos that trap customer data today.

It's not easy. Think about how difficult it is to set up a weekly interdepartmental conference call addressing your company's spring softball team and who should play center field or pitch. Multiply that challenge almost infinitely when you consider that employees will now be required to share customer data across channels and campaigns.

Creating multidimensional insights, then, requires a strategic commitment to judging marketing success at the enterprise level. Successful

---

* http://www.mediapost.com/publications/article/179772/google-shifts-data-focus-from-retargeting-to-remar.html?

campaigns or optimized channels are nice, but you achieve real success by growing the value of your customer portfolio. To do that requires technology to activate and evaluate data at scale—we call this enterprise data management, a system that creates continuous insights that drive better connections with the right customers.

Two: Work Inside Out

Multidimensional insight creates the foundation. Now, let's talk about how to get the most out of that investment.

Most companies have customers with significant differences in value. Some buy more or cost less to serve, or are highly influential on others. In banking, half the checking accounts are unprofitable.* Some wireless-service providers track the number and frequency of support calls made by high-maintenance, high-cost end users and waive their termination fees. Most are familiar with Vilfredo Pareto's principle, which says the top 20 percent of customers often account for about 80 percent of total profits. (In our experience, it's not unusual to see top customers worth 5 or 10 times more than average customers.)

Why then do so many continue to undervalue customer profitability measures in marketing? Companies will declare loudly, "Our customers are our most important asset," yet marketers regularly underinvest in nurturing their value. Sixty percent of companies spend 20 percent or *less* of their marketing dollars on customer retention.† Over half of brands cannot identify their best customers, and less than 10 percent use insight to personalize loyalty programs and offers.‡

Remember the funny-looking old man who traded the magic beans to Jack? He never checked back with Jack; in a highly profitable (beans for a cow) customer relationship, he never asked, "How else can I help?" Maybe later the old man traded the cow for some catchy TV spots; but while entertaining TV ads abound (we're partial to those with talking babies), they fall short of efficiently maximizing the value of the customer portfolio.

Instead, companies should think *inside out*. The *inside* is the customer portfolio you have—calculate the value of your current customer

---

* http://www.celent.com/node/26864
† http://loyalty360.org/resources/article/acxiom-loyalty-360-announce-results-of-joint-study-making-every-interaction
‡ http://loyalty360.org/resources/article/acxiom-loyalty-360-announce-results-of-joint-study-making-every-interaction

relationships and use it to drive investment decisions. The key concept is *proportional*—a customer worth five times more than another gets five times the investment. Unprofitable customers get special treatment by focusing on service cost-to-profit ratios and strategic attrition. The *out* of *inside out* then uses that insight to find others who act, look, or think like your best customers. Over time, the value of the customer portfolio increases dramatically.

> *"It's a higher standard; success happens when you acquire new customers who match the profile of your best customers."*

Working inside out requires a system and process that assess customer lifetime value (incorporating purchase, influence, and service costs) and facilitate proportional investment. The process continually adjusts based on what customers do and don't do. This process and system are also crucial for acquisition efforts. Many unprofitable relationships are a direct result of poor acquisition discipline and criteria. Acquisition success is not just about newly booked customers. It requires a higher standard: success happens when you acquire new customers who *match the profile of your best customers*. Part of the secret of increasing the value of your customer portfolio is to stop destroying it.

This inside out, customer-*centric* approach is distinct from merely offering great customer service. Of course, all customers deserve great service, but some deserve greater … those who create more value.

For Jack, this means continuing to wave to the cow buyer in the market square (you never know when you might have a cow to sell and the funny-looking old man hasn't been around) while sending the giant's wife an annual holiday card and the occasional tray of chocolate-dipped fruit.

Three: Work Outside In

The Internet is an amazing source of insight. Consumers search for your product, "like" or talk about it, and if you're lucky, they bookmark it, pin it, or give it good reviews. They navigate the web and, where permissibility and privacy allow, reveal clues to interest and intent. All in, there is an enormous Petri dish of consumer behavior to be found on the Internet.

To date, most organizations use this *outside* data narrowly, just for digital advertising. What a missed opportunity. The consequences of a display ad gone wrong are inconsequential—it was cheap to buy and will be cheap to correct. But using this *outside* data *in* your organization is another matter. For example, if digital data reveals that intent is geographically concentrated, wouldn't you also adjust your circular or local advertising? If digital data reveals that a particular classification of customers' behavior is changing, wouldn't you adjust your customer relationship management (CRM) programs? And, if digital data reveals a virally popular theme, wouldn't you adjust your TV messaging and capitalize on it?

Of course, the answers to these questions are obvious, but actually answering them requires a strategic commitment to view customer data as an enterprise asset. That, in turn, requires a system and process to activate, evaluate, and apply this outside intelligence across all media, not just digital media.

Four: Link Intersecting Insights

Over the years, marketers have relied on many tools to understand customers: primary research, purchase and response data, loyalty systems, customer data warehouses, customer personas, and optimal messaging for the right product at the right time. A major brand might invest several hundred million dollars in customer insight.

Media buying, on the other hand, traditionally has relied on a very different set of data, unfortunately based on a small number of households, around 25,000.* Moreover, media strategy traditionally sought to woo buyers as if they all were the same. David Pottrack of CBS famously dispelled that notion when he said, "Reliance on the 18–49 demographic is hazardous to all media and marketers."†

Meanwhile a parallel universe has emerged, where publishers analyze and classify digital behavior in audience segments. A rallying cry has emerged, "I can reach *your* audience!" Sadly, while that intent is noble, publishers really know just a fraction of a brand's audience. Much of this audience data is collected via cookies and is often wrong. However, it does bring an important value: context, what a potential customer is doing right now.

So while publisher "audiences" are a poor substitute for a brand's customer insight—how could data collected over a few days possibly compare

---

* http://io9.com/5636210/how-the-nielsen-tv-ratings-work--and-what-could-replace-them
† http://adage.com/article/media/cbs-viewers-age-sex-matter-marketers/149534/

with the $500 million invested by a brand?—publisher data does provide fantastic insight into what customers are doing right now, the *context* of a given interaction.

The intersection of insights responsibly leverages what a brand knows about *customers* with what its partners know about *context*. Increasingly, marketers will insist on a blind match of their customer data with partner contextual data to better target and measure advertising of all kinds. In digital advertising, it means matching a destination site's registration list against a brand's customer file. For television, it means matching set-top box data (from tens of millions of households, not 25,000) against the customer file.

This won't happen without advertiser leadership. Many publishers and agency incentive systems are predicated on *volume*. But most marketers don't need *more* advertising; they need advertising *better placed*. Using brand customer data to drive targeting accomplishes that, but advertisers need to insist on this practice and enforce it with incentives. In the world of big data, better data is required—and that's the intersection of insights.

> *"Many publishers and agency incentive systems are predicated on volume. But most marketers don't need more advertising; they need advertising better placed."*

The intersection of insights has important privacy and data rights considerations.

Performing a blind match across customer and contextual insight requires a "safe haven," an intermediary that both advertiser and publisher trust to

1. Process the match securely and accurately
2. Ensure data is protected (keeping advertiser from seeing proprietary publisher data and vice versa)
3. Ensure both parties comply with industry best practices for privacy
4. Operate with no stake in the sale of any particular media (to avoid temptation)

Data rights are also an important consideration. Determining who can access and use the data generated in the match process is important. For example:

- Can performance data across publishers be provided back to the advertiser?
- At what level of detail will performance data be returned at all?
- What rights does the publisher have to use generated data—to commingle it? To sell it? To use it indirectly to sell more media to others?

All of these are important considerations. A useful exercise is to carefully review and update agreements with partners to ensure they accurately reflect their data rights objectives.

While clearly the intersection of insights requires attention to agreements and the involvement of a safe haven, it's worth it. For example, one of our major clients examined a full year's worth of TV ad spend, which totaled $31 million, and found it could have achieved the same results for $9 million by using its customer file to place media. A major financial institution used a similar approach for digital advertising to increase approved applications fourfold.

Five: Build Trust

The first four imperatives (multidimensional insight, inside out, outside in, and the intersection of insights) create a powerful economic engine; we'll see just how powerful in a moment.

But first, a note of caution: Creating these insights is so valuable that it may be tempting to use data inappropriately. Here, vision and fortitude are critical.

The data these imperatives unlock should be used *for* customers, not to do something *to* them. This means optimizing for long-term value by building trust-based relationships, not quick scores. And while providing relevance to customers based on individual tastes and needs is paramount, leaders will be transparent in providing choice in the use of the data.

There is a huge opportunity for data, when used in a responsible fashion, to drive commerce and to make lives easier, safer, and healthier. But, what are the business principles that should guide the use of personal information? We believe there are several:

- *Security*—make data security a priority. Implement and maintain robust processes and programs to ensure appropriate monitoring, detection, and resolution of potential issues.
- *Choice*—provide choices for the use of personal data; either opt out or opt in depending on the type of data, intended use, and regulations.
- *Don't be creepy*—here's a litmus test: are your actions *for* the individual (not creepy) or *to* the individual (creepy). A creepy movie, story, or experience is usually about the unknown, the hidden motivation, the ulterior motive. Be as open as possible about your interactions with individuals; use data responsibly to help the individual; provide descriptions of your processes; and describe how you ensure personal data is kept safe.
- *Transparency*—(related to not being creepy) be clear about what data you capture, how it's used, and with whom you share it.
- *Compliance*—comply with regulations and industry guidelines. Avoid marketing to inappropriate segments of the population, and do not market inappropriately to vulnerable segments.
- *Relevance*—serve individuals with highly relevant and engaging content based on individual tastes and needs. Understand and act on explicit individual preferences.

THE PAYOFF

Let's review: the bags of gold, the goose that lays golden eggs, the magic harp—these things are available, as in Jack's case, to those who are willing to change a few paradigms. And, five imperatives are vital:

- *Get Multidimensional*—refine across all relevant data points, viewing customer information as an enterprise asset.
- *Work Inside Out*—invest proportionally to customer value.
- *Work Outside In*—use digital data to optimize all media.
- *Link Intersecting Insights*—connect customer and contextual insights to create high-performing marketing.
- *Build Trust*—solve for customer value, not just short-term results.

By embracing these imperatives, companies can expect three significant payoffs: measurable improvements in marketing performance, increased value of their customer portfolio, and more intelligent and defendable pricing.

15–30 Percent Lift in Marketing ROI

The overall report card of the advertising industry is not great: 37 percent of all advertising in the United States is wasted[*]; 80 percent of online advertising fails to reach its intended target.[†] The culprit for both sad states is the same: insufficient use of the right data. Unfortunately, between 80 and 90 percent of today's advertising is still based on age and gender.[‡]

As a result, advertising fails to produce because it's mistimed, misplaced, and mis-messaged, failing to capitalize on nuances in individual interests and intent. And when advertising doesn't fully work, marketers simply

---

[*] http://www.amazon.com/What-Sticks-Advertising-Guarantee-Succeeds/dp/1419584332/ref=sr_1_1?s=books&ie=UTF8&qid=1345165729&sr=1-1&keywords=what+sticks

[†] ComScore, March 2009: Research from eight U.S. brand campaigns with budgets between $400,000 and $2 million.

[‡] http://exelate.wordpress.com/2012/08/07/audience-data-quality-control-4-tips-to-help-marketers-navigate-third-party-data-providers/

spend more, adding further to the clutter. Somehow, we've ended up in a state of *more* advertising when *better* advertising is what we need. Thus, a key to improving marketing ROI is to get smarter about the place, time, and message of advertising.

> *"Somehow, we've ended up in a state of 'more advertising' when it's 'better advertising' we need. Thus, a key to improving marketing ROI is to get smarter about the place, time and message of advertising."*

On average by embracing these imperatives, our research indicates that marketers usually see a 15–30 percent increase in return on marketing investment. So, it's reasonable to redirect $15 million to $30 million of a $100 million ad budget to better alternatives, including dropping the savings directly to the bottom line.

Brands achieve better ROI through two important principles: smarter targeting and better measurement. Smarter targeting leverages a brand's multidimensional customer insight with the contextual insight of its media partners and laser focus on the needs of its most valuable customers. Outside data, like estimates of potential spend or the likelihood to engage with a specific media type, are fundamental to media decision making. Insight is connected to the moment of truth, when a consumer engages your brand, creating a personalized and resonating experience in real time. Finally, leaders employ effective media substitution strategies, looking for opportunities to drive results more cost-effectively.

The second principle is better measurement, a relentless focus on connecting what customers do (or don't do) because of specific marketing programs. What's inspected improves. Consequently, leaders seek a cycle of continuous insight, supported by a dramatic increase in the number of tests—how specific media, message, offer, and creative interrelate and how they actually contribute to objectives. The ultimate result? Improved ability to sense and ultimately influence consumer behavior and to bring those insights to market more quickly.

These benefits are often self-funding (brands can redirect current ad spend or rationalize redundant information systems), but these decisions require strategy and fortitude. Recall Jack, the faithful son, who sacrificed dinner and suffered the wrath of his mother to find greater fortune than a dry cow would fetch in the market square. (The cable pundits would have had a field day with that one.) It's easy to see with hindsight that Jack's decision produced the more valuable outcome, but he deserves credit for making the courageous choice.

10–15 Percent Increase in Customer Gross Margins

While enormously valuable, making marketing more efficient is just the start. The second opportunity is to make marketing more *effective*, by focusing on improving the value of the customer portfolio. While some companies can be successful competing on price or distribution or innovation, most companies will need to compete on their ability to attract and serve the right customers.

Our research indicates a huge opportunity for firms adopting this strategy: a 10–15 percent improvement in customer profitability. Therefore, for a company with $1 billion in annual revenue, that's potentially another $100 million to $150 million in gross profit a year.

Driving customer portfolio value is highly dependent on information systems and strategy—the goal is to invest proportionally to customers' projected lifetime value. The best projections of lifetime value are multidimensional, refined from purchases, stated intentions, and external measures like share of wallet and influence. Ultimately, you should use customer lifetime value (CLV)-oriented key performance indicators (KPIs) to guide decision making.

Tactically, leaders start by optimizing their current customer portfolio, increasing focus on relationships with the most potential, while redirecting from those offering less potential. Effective marketers will seek to optimize customer value at every interaction. It's crucial here to recognize return customers and connect vital information about them to engage appropriately.

The second big driver of customer portfolio value is better acquisition discipline. Often, customer·portfolio value is compromised by acquiring relationships with consumers who never have a chance to become great customers. Leaders should focus on acquiring those who look, act and think like their best customers. The intersection of insights is critical in accomplishing this by connecting what brands know about great customers with what its partners know contextually about potential customers, in particular what they're doing right now.

5–7 Percent Improved Pricing

The first two payoffs, improved efficiency and effectiveness of marketing, are complemented by a third, the ability to raise and defend pricing. And why is this important? Because the long-term health of your company and your employee's jobs are at risk if you can't.

Many firms lazily use a low price as the primary incentive to attract customers. Price is easy to comprehend and it does drive traffic, but it can have devastating and resonating impacts on the brand. As an alternative, marketers should create value-add opportunities for which consumers are willing to pay more; but that requires better understanding of consumer interests. Multidimensional insight is the foundational key to that understanding.

Our research indicates that for most companies, there is a 5 to 7 percent gross margin improvement opportunity (in addition to the 10 to 15 percent achievable through customer portfolio optimization). So, a company with $500 million in annual revenue has an opportunity for $25 million to $35 million in additional gross profit per year.

Consumers' sensitivity to pricing varies greatly—by category, by versioning, and by positioning. Many love to talk a mean game in describing their latest bargain-basement deal on a new car, flat-panel TV, or angora sweater, but no one brags about using the lowest-priced heart surgeon. Yes, this is an extreme example, but the point is, how long will your business last if you are competing in your industry only on price? Do you want your customers to choose your brand only because it's the lowest priced? Is that sustainable for your business?

As marketers, we often fall into the trap of looking for that one silver bullet. It doesn't exist, but magic beans are a different story. You see, there are alternatives to the paths marketers have been following. Even the hippest most up-to-date, digital-savvy, socially hot companies are often guilty of missing these big payoffs.

WHICH BEANSTALK IS YOURS: CREEPER, TRAILER, OR UPSHOOT?

There we have it. Jack of beanstalk fame, our young C-suite marketing executive, has created genuine long-term success—not by shouting louder or slugging it out in discount la-la-land, but by harnessing the power of big data to create better connections with the right customers.

Jack didn't just *find* the reversal of fortune he was after; he *made it happen.*

There is no escaping big data and the new landscape where consumers have unlimited choice and information about those choices. Embrace the opportunity to ride the wave of data rather than be swamped by it.

Yes, with blogs, tweets, likes, clicks, pins, and even the passé phone call, consumers are everywhere, sharing and learning like never before. Yes, this necessitates a better method of gathering and refining data. Yes, the challenge may seem daunting—thousands of beanstalks, thousands of opportunities, thousands of hungry giants—and it requires strategy, technology, and process to activate and evaluate disparate threads of information. But it is not only possible, it's vital to driving value.

Fortunately, the hurdles are not impossibly high or numbingly numerous. We have described five imperatives and three payoffs.

Imperatives:

1. *Get Multidimensional*—refine across all relevant data points, viewing customer information as an enterprise asset.
2. *Work Inside Out*—invest proportionally to customer value.
3. *Work Outside In*—use digital data to optimize all media.
4. *Link Intersecting Insights*—connect customer and contextual insight to create high-performing marketing.
5. *Build Trust*—solve for customer value, not just short-term results.

The payoffs, once again, are (1) measurable improvements in marketing performance, (2) increased value of your customer portfolio, and (3) more intelligent and defendable pricing.

Much like they were for a resourceful Jack and his widowed mother, the stakes are high in today's marketplace, and you need to market *smarter, more efficiently,* and *more effectively* as you reach for the gold and drive value. Climb the beanstalk!

No doubt, a hungry giant will be chasing you.

3

Frontiers of Big Data Business Analytics: Patterns and Cases in Online Marketing

Daqing Zhao

CONTENTS

INTRODUCTION

Computer technologies have changed our lives dramatically. The changes are still happening at an accelerating speed. Without a doubt, the digital information revolution will continue to change our society and culture.

As technologies advance, we have more and more ways to collect data. Using sensors, anything from our medical information to our Web surfing history, energy usage of our homes, and things that can be seen or heard or in some way measured now can be digitally recorded and stored. Digital data can be analyzed much better using computers and statistical tools than analog data. Computer technologies have the characteristic of increasing capability while lowering cost over time. Moore's law says that the number of transistors in an integrated circuit doubles every 18 months. Thanks to Moore's law, which has been true for decades, we get new computers with more processing power, larger storage, and wider network bandwidths at lower costs. As a result, we can collect more and more data, store and access them, as well as analyze them in more detail. Information which used to be too expensive to gather is now readily available. Data are being accumulated at an accelerating speed. With the abundance of data, more and more technical solutions for handling and utilizing the data are developed.

From the dawn of civilization to 2003, a total of five exabytes (one exabyte is one million terabytes) of information were collected; in 2010, collecting that amount took only two days (Siegler, 2010). New data sources include not only structured text and numerical data but also unstructured, free-format data, such as images, audio, and videos. Most data now are behavioral or sensor data in digital form, rather than insights and knowledge we are accustomed to seeing in print media. Data alone, without analysis, are not actionable. From sciences to government to companies, because of the limited number of people with data analytics expertise, more data are collected than can be analyzed. Most new data are stored and stay dormant. In time, this situation will only get worse. This is the big data era (Dumbill, 2012).

With the Internet and mobile technologies, people and devices are increasingly connected. A visitor can come from anywhere on earth to get information or do business, in the process leaving a trail of evidence of preferences and interests. Using a network, a large number of sensors can be connected and data aggregated into a single data set. Via the Internet, data can be shared and analyzed, and information can be consumed by a large number of people.

There are many examples of big data (Cukier, 2010). Now, collecting information about each and every visitor to a website is not only possible but necessary to optimize to achieve reasonable user experience and effectiveness. In astronomy, right now far more data about the universe are being collected than could be analyzed. In medicine, real-time information about a patient is available through small devices including smartphones. Together with lifestyle, behavioral data, and genomic information, doctors can use new information to improve patient's health significantly. Not only smartphones but smart TVs and smart homes all will collect more and more data about consumers. Every field has been or will be changed by the large amount of data available.

Before the advent of commodity storage and computing solutions, only the most important data were recorded in detail, such as financial data. Other data were collected only as samples and surveys. Web server log data were quickly purged without any detailed analysis. In the big data era, companies are collecting every page view, every click, every blog, and every tweet, as well as pictures and videos customers generate, in addition to transaction data, customer services data, and third-party data, to provide information about customers. A company may know more about its customers than not only families and friends know but also the customers themselves, which may be a scary thought. We may not remember all the websites and pages we visited during the last month, but web server logs never forget. We may not know many things about our friends, but information about them indirectly tells who we are.

Organizations and society are not yet ready to digest and to use information from the increasingly abundant data. Companies don't have enough data-savvy business managers to work with the data and turn them into business advantages. The bottleneck is not computing power but people, analysts and managers, operational processes, and culture.

BIG DATA ANALYTICS

Computers will not be able to outsmart humans in the foreseeable future. One reason is that the computing power of a single human brain is about the same as all the world's computers combined (Hilbert and López, 2011).

After millions of years of evolution and optimization, our brains have many features that are hardwired, but they are not yet adapted to handle a large amount of digital data. In processing data, computers have advantages in many ways, while humans have advantages in others. Computers are powerful tools to help people, and humans also need to learn to work with the technologies.

Things Computers Are Good At

Computers (including storage) have perfect memory, since they can record everything, every event of everyone. In the big data era, this is especially the case. Do you remember what you ordered for lunch for the last year? Or how much on average you spent on lunch? How about this kind of data for everyone in the country? Such information is readily available in the data customers left with their credit card processing companies. What did we say at some time in the past? Spoken words in a person's lifetime can now be easily stored in a thumb drive.

Computers are also very good at searching through a large amount of data to find a needle in the haystack, to identify fraud, to find evidence of criminal activities, to make the one-in-a-million perfect match, or to retrieve and send you the piece of information you are searching for. As the volume of data increases, the marginal value of additional data is lower. Using computers to handle more and more repeating tasks is the only scalable way to utilize big data efficiently.

Computers are very good at calculating tradeoffs among a large number of factors to come up with a conclusion. For example, let's say there is a potential customer, female, age 25–34, has a child less than 5 years old, Asian, earns $30K, rents a home, divorced, lives in zip code 90001, some college education, visited sites of Walmart, Coupons.com, Monster.com, drives a Toyota Camry, etc. Is she a buyer of product X? Computers can do much better than the best analyst, in milliseconds, remotely over the Internet. Credit scoring is another example. Even if our analysts are given all the information about customers, without the computer to do the calculations, we still won't be able to say how good their credit is. For a few customers, the analyst may have the advantage of meeting them to read more based on intuition, but in scale, the computer clearly wins. A model cannot tell whether an individual will have the behavior, but predicts how likely the behavior happens in a large number of people with similar profiles.

Given data, computers can help us build models to find repeatable patterns. Computers are very good at optimizing model parameters to predict how likely is it that some behavior will happen, using data of many similar people and their known behaviors. Using statistics and machine learning methodologies, computers are very good at finding out what insights or predictions we can get from the data, as well as what we cannot, and to what level of accuracy.

Events just don't happen in isolation. We may think of ourselves as individuals with our own freedom and judgment, but how we make decisions largely depends on who we are and what environment we are in. Our behaviors strongly correlate with those of our friends and neighbors. Before making a purchase, we inevitably have a sequence of activities, and we leave signals in our demographic profile, socioeconomic status, background, values, lifestyles, and preferences. When events happen, there is often some evidence left behind. If we collect a lot of data, we often find direct or circumstantial evidence of the event or behavior.

Once we have built models from the data to describe quantitatively how relevant a given set of variables and our concerned events are related, we can use the models to see what happens under some given scenario. This is computer simulation. Computers make extensive simulations possible. By selecting possible future scenarios, we can use computers to see how the concerned metrics change. This is just like flight simulators.

Computers can help us optimize using the models. Through generation of a large number of scenarios, including factors we can influence, we can evaluate which scenarios are most favorable or desirable. This is the most sophisticated use of computer modeling. We can try to get more of the good ones and fewer of the bad ones and to design strategies to best handle the situations. This is how we realize the value of data. The more data we have, the better model we have, and the better we can optimize. Most companies have managers look at the data at some level of aggregation and digestion and try to find value and opportunities to optimize using their heads. But as we discussed earlier, people are not good at estimating complicated tradeoffs among a larger number of factors.

Computers make scalable personalization solutions possible, offering the right information or product to the right people at the right time. Large-scale personalization is a great application of big data analytics. There is this narrative that the owner of a mom-and-pop store knows all of her good customers and builds personal relations, providing services tailored to their needs and preferences. As superstores come along, prices are lower because of scale, but at the expense of customer experience of personalized services. With computers and the Internet, companies now can know enough about the customers through the collection and analysis of a large amount of customer-level data. Large vendors now can provide personalized services at lower prices in scalable ways. The value of such personalization of services becomes more compelling as the cost of computers and storage continues to drop. Personalization solutions require not only customer data but also the computer power to do deep analysis on the data, as well as detailed data on products and services.

In addition to help improve services to customers, big data will allow companies to have better competitive intelligence (CI) as well. Companies can collect more detailed data about their own customers, products, and processes. Considering data as a valuable asset, they are very reluctant to share with competitors. It is usually more difficult to collect data about competitors. In order to gain insights of CI, companies often use syndicated data vendors, such as Nielsen and comScore, for services ranging from standard reports to custom data collections and analyses. In the big data era, individuals, organizations, and their relations are all more visible. Having easy access of customer sentiment and behaviors on the web, with a large amount of data from public sources as well as data vendors, inexpensive sensor data collections, and computer resources, companies will be able to have more comprehensive and accurate information about their competitors at lower costs. Data on the competitive environment should be part of the drivers for business decisions and optimization. At the same time, it is also more and more difficult to do business in scale and remain under the radar.

Computers Can't Do Everything

Even though computers can help a lot, they are only as good as the analyst who uses them. They follow the analyst's instructions.

Data, especially big data, are often disorganized and overwhelming like runoffs. Data may not have a taxonomy and context, and often there is no sufficient documentation. Some key data for some specific interest may not be collected at all. And then for sure no one, with whatever computer resources, would be able to make good predictions. Data are unreliable before they are thoroughly analyzed. Data collection is usually an engineering function. After building the data acquisition system, some data are collected and put into storage. Some quality assurance tests may be done on the software so that some numbers are there and some aggregate measures look reasonable. But this is no guarantee that the data are clean or even correct. Some subtle data issues may still be present. The more we analyze the data, from exploratory data analysis all the way to predictive modeling, the better we know the data and the better we identify issues. *Data are only as clean as the amount of effort used to analyze them.* This is similar to debugging a software product, which we all know is a long, laborious process. If we have not completely analyzed the data, they may not be correct. Without continued detailed analysis, additional issues may be introduced by new releases, and new usage exceptions may not be handled properly by an existing release.

Traditional Business Intelligence and Big Data

The traditional business intelligence (BI) is shaped like a pyramid (Dyche, 2007): from the standard report at the bottom to the multidimensional report, the segmentation/predictive modeling, and finally to knowledge discovery, which is at the top of the pyramid. Going from collecting a standard report to knowledge discovery, data maturity of the organization increases and there are fewer assumptions needed. This is similar to the capability maturity model in software development (Paulk, Curtis, et al. 1993).

The BI pyramid defines a sequence of efforts from simple to increasingly complex, as in crawl, walk, and run. Most organizations are somewhere in the middle in "maturity" level; they never go beyond the stage of multidimensional reporting or simple analysis. These companies may just have built a data collection infrastructure, or may not have the required analytic talents, or may not be ready due to organizational and cultural reasons to achieve a higher level on the pyramid. They never had a detailed analysis of the data; no predictive modeling was ever done. Again and again in our years of experience, we found data issues that are subtle enough to look normal without a detailed analysis. For example, a data warehouse may take many data feeds from different departments or regions, and only one of them has problems. The numbers are not missing, but they are not accurate or not correct.

If a company adopts a stepwise approach according to the traditional BI pyramid, business rules used to produce standard reporting will need to be decided beforehand. Before big data technology is available, because of the high cost of storage and computing power to process, most data are not collected or discarded. Only data deemed to be the most important are kept. Since analytic tools are built on databases, there is usually no easy way to analyze data in raw format. Therefore, assumptions have to be made about the data before we can look at them. We have to make decisions on data structure before loading raw data into a database. This can be a source of problems. Once the designs are implemented, they are difficult to change. Without the benefit of a thorough analysis, an initial design may hinder the optimal extraction of information and knowledge. This may not be optimal.

In big data, data volume is so large so that raw data are stored as the persistent data, on a cluster of distributed computers with local storage. Also because of the size of the data, data access and analysis will need to be done on the same cluster of computers. A characteristic of big data analytics tools is that we can process data in raw format in a distributed way by using a large number of servers to manipulate data on their local storage. With big data analytic tools, we can and should do a more thorough analysis before generating standard reports. After analysis, the data are more reliable and we know better the basic patterns in the data, so we can better identify which variables are important and should be put in reports.

Some big data can be in a free format. Then relevant information has to be extracted before analysis can be conducted. Depending on the nature of raw data, there is usually no unique way or surely successful methodology to extract information from such data. Various strategies have their own perspectives and may yield different amounts of information with different levels of utility.

Therefore, *we need to conduct a detailed analysis before building standard reports.* This approach does imply that people who know how to analyze the data should be a part of the decision-making process on the data structure. We often say that knowledge is power. With big data, now we need to add that knowing how to discover knowledge is power.

Models Have to Be Designed by People

It is up to the analyst working with the stakeholder to define the question to be answered, to decide the model to be built, to select the dependent variable, which is the one we try to predict, and to choose all the independent predictors as well. For example, to improve services to our customers, we have to first decide how we measure quality of services. Our metric can be the number of clicks or conversions, transaction dollar amount, lifetime value, time spent, or visit frequency, and so forth. These measures are related but not identical, each with pros and cons and different emphasis or perspective. After we decide to choose, say, conversion, the metric is called the *target*, in the modeler's language. We then gather a set of variables to predict conversions, for example, day of week, time of day, geo, age, or gender, and these are the predictors. Again, we have to decide whether to include a particular variable. Computer algorithms may determine that a variable we include in the modeling is not predictive, but they cannot tell if a critical predictor is missing. It is up to the analyst to make these decisions.

Computers have no way of knowing whether there is a problem in a model. This can be very subtle. For example, during the model-building process, if a predictor data contains information about the event it is supposed to predict, the model produced will appear to be more accurate than it really is. In such a case, when we apply the model, its performance will be poor. This is called a leakage in predictive modeling. Only analysts know if these mistakes are present. Inexperienced analysts may solve correctly the wrong problems, and even experienced analysts may have a lapse of judgment.

Finally computers have no goals to achieve. It is not computers but people who decide on the purpose of the analysis and how knowledge will be used to take action. Computer models have to be designed and managed by people. Even after having built and deployed automated solutions to achieve scalability, we still need some analysts to assess and ensure their quality of performance, and to find new ways to improve and optimize.

Perfect data are all alike; every wrong data is wrong in its own way. In addition to some relevant data not being collected, it is also possible that some data feeds, but not all feeds to the warehouse, are incomplete. So when we query the table, data are there, but some rows or some values are missing. Without detailed knowledge, it may not be easy to realize that there is a problem. There can be multiple definitions of the same field, and each of them may be used for some period of time. There can be multiple business rules based on reasonable but different assumptions. For example, at an online university, if a new student took a single course and paid for it but dropped out after the first couple of classes, is he considered a student? One analyst may say that the person paid tuition and was a student for the classes. Another may say that he is just someone who took a single class and could hardly be considered a student. Both are reasonable, but they would result in not only different student enrollment counts but also metrics like average revenue per student.

Some data are incomplete due to business nature. For example, we have data that a customer has interest in some products, but we have no data on her interest in other products. The data are sparse, so it is difficult to tell whether there is a lack of behavior or it is an incomplete collection of data. One example is the separate log-in and log-out data for Internet portals. Due to privacy policies, the two sets of data cannot be analyzed together. Since people do not always log in, either data set is incomplete. Credit card purchase data reflect only a customer's partial behavior because of possible cash purchases. Data are never ideal. It is up to the analyst to decide if models should be built and if they are useful. This underscores the insight that detailed data issues need a thorough analysis to uncover.

Modeling Needs to Scale as Well

In traditional practice, predictive models take a long time to build. For example, it may take several months or even more than a year to build a model in property insurance. The training data sets for model building are quite small, and sample data are often relatively expensive to collect. Models can be built only for repeatable patterns over a long period of time.

Nowadays in the time of big data, data are cheap and abundant. We build more and more models; some of them may degrade in performance in weeks. With big data, the number of predictors or dimension of predictors can be very large. In addition, some variables may be categorical with a large number of values. In this new situation, human interactive model building is not scalable. We no longer have enough resources to build all the models with a lot of human interaction.

Reasons for interested events can be complex. Without some detailed analysis, it is often unclear which of a large number of variables drive the event. In traditional modeling, the number of predictors often is not more than a few dozen. Now, it is not uncommon to have thousands of variables. Increasingly, we need to rely on modeling methodologies which help build models somewhat automatically, using techniques like out-of-sample testing and off-the-shelf modeling.

Bigger Data and Better Models

Any model has two parts, the data and the analytic framework. For many complex questions, the ultimate determining factor to improve the quality of models is data. Not only will better data lead to higher-quality models, a larger data set will also generate more accurate results. Statistical analysis of really large data sets can often help us better answer difficult questions. One such example is "wisdom of the crowd," which says that for many questions aggregating responses from a large number of people will give better answers than asking an expert.

Thus, if we want to know the price of an item, we should look it up in eBay auctions; if we are looking for the value of a keyword on Google paid search, we should place bids on the auction engine to find out; if we wonder how good a book is, let's look at its reviews on Amazon.com; if we want to compare which of the two web page layouts has better conversion rates, let's do an A/B test for a large number of site visitors to decide, and so forth.

Other examples are Google's spell checking in search and the Translation product, which are based on big data–driven models. Research shows that model results continue to improve as the amount of data becomes larger and larger (Norvig, 2011).

Big Data and Hadoop

There are some characteristics in big data analytics. In big data, often raw data are stored and appended but not updated. There are no aggregations for the purpose of saving storage. This is mainly because the volume of raw data is too large for normal database technologies to handle. When data sizes are larger than several hundred gigabytes, a single server will not be able to process the data in a reasonable amount of time. For example, it may take a day for a server just to scan one terabyte of data from a storage disk.

To get results in a reasonable amount of time at a reasonable cost, a technique now often used is MapReduce, a distributed computing paradigm developed at Google (Dean and Ghemawat, 2004). The basic idea is the following: We use a cluster of commodity servers with local storage to work as a single computer. We read and process intermediate results in parallel using many servers on local data, which is called the Map step. And then we aggregate at the end, which is the Reduce step. We may need to repeatedly execute Map and Reduce steps to complete a task. In order to address the issue of slow speed of disk read and write, we bring computing closer to the data. A cloud of servers using MapReduce often scales linearly as the number of servers increases, but not always. As data get larger and larger, a cloud of commodity servers is the only way to scale.

MapReduce is a data processing strategy that can be implemented on different platforms. Google has its own implementation. Ask.com built an

SAS cloud using the MapReduce paradigm for an online educational institution, which was discussed in an invited talk at SAS Global Forum (Zhao, 2009). The setup can process billions of ad impressions and clicks at the individual customer level in a scalable way. One advantage of using SAS to implement MapReduce is the availability of a large portfolio of statistics procedures already in SAS to process and analyze data. This is an especially good solution for organizations with SAS site licenses. Hadoop is an open-source implementation of MapReduce used widely on commodity servers and storage. Many major companies, such as Yahoo!, Facebook, and Ask.com, have large Hadoop clouds consisting of thousands of servers. Using these clouds, we can search the data to find a needle in a haystack in milliseconds; model computations usually would take years to compute, but now can be completed in minutes. Using cloud computing, we can build models in scale. In 2010, Google was using 260 million watts of electricity, enough to power 200,000 homes (Glanz, 2011). This implies that the total number of servers is on the order of several hundred thousand or more. At one location near the Columbia River at The Dalles, Oregon, where electricity is less expensive, Google has two football-field-sized data centers. Facebook, Yahoo!, and other Internet companies have similar large data centers.

ONLINE MARKETING CASE STUDIES

Wine.com One-to-One e-Mails

During the dot-com era, Digital Impact was an e-mail marketing company committed to the vision of "the right message to the right customer at the right time." It was one of the main intermediary players between customers and vendors. Now e-mail marketing is still a widely used and effective channel to engage customers.

In 1999, I led the analytics project to help the e-commerce site wine.com develop a one-to-one e-mail program. Armed with wine.com's house opt-in e-mail list, and permissions to send marketing e-mails, wine.com sent weekly newsletters, with each customer having a different set of six or eight recommended wines. Before using the one-to-one e-mail solution, weekly e-mails contained static wine offers, with every customer getting the same recommendation, selected by wine.com's merchandiser, along with some news articles on wine and related information. Wine.com had an inventory of more than 20,000 wines. Due to state-level alcohol regulations, there are distribution constraints for various states.

As one of the early pure e-commerce sites, wine.com had relatively clean data. We were able to get purchase and product data, as well as e-mail behavioral data. For each purchase, we obtained time of purchase, products, spend, and associated campaign. Wine product profiles were also quite complete, with product-level data on price, color, variety, vintage, country of production, the producer, and a description of the wine. Wine.com also gave us a set of taste profiles of the wine, including oak, sweetness, acidity, body, complexity, intensity, and tannin in a scale of 1 to 7. We also had e-mail response click streams linked to each wine, and we collected self-reported preferences and demographic data, such as age, gender, zip code, and others, as well as preference for types of wines, and optionally, drinking frequency, purpose of purchase, level of knowledge about wine, and so forth. There were no explicit customer ratings of products. Most customers had only one or two data points, while a small percentage of customers had a lot of purchases and e-mail clicks.

The goal of the one-to-one e-mail program was to lift purchase revenue. We achieved this by optimizing the selection of a subset of wines that a customer is more likely to buy. The efficacy of the program was measured by A/B testing against weekly static selections by merchandisers. Our challenge was to produce consistent lift over a long period of time and many e-mail campaigns.

We designed an algorithm called *preference matching*. Instead of building elaborate logistic regression or decision tree models to predict interest category, we put our focus on the most important predictor—customer behavior profile—which was built using the detailed wine product profiles. We built both implicit profiles from purchases and e-mail clicks data and explicit preference profiles. More active customers had more behavioral data points, so that they have more refined profiles. We also considered the overall popularity and seasonality factors included, for example, champagne wines are more popular near the new year.

We then decomposed purchases into values in product attributes. Even if a customer had only a single click, we still could generate a profile. We augmented the profiles by adding association rules such as "Customer who bought these also bought ..." An advantage of such an approach is that when the specific wine goes out of stock, its profile information is still very much usable. New releases have no purchase history, but as long as we know the product attributes, they can be immediately mapped to existing profiles. For new customers, we augmented their profile with nearest neighbors who had more purchases as "mentors."

The algorithm used cosine distances to measure similarity in taste profile by color, and we also used price range, as well as text attributes on producer name, region, and country of production, to recommend similar wines. In successive campaigns, we shuffled among higher-scored wines. This way, repeated campaigns took care of prediction errors. We also deduped recent recommendations and purchases so that we didn't repeat what customers obviously were familiar with. We used decaying memory functions to put more weight on recent profiles and factored in seasonality. We always use simulations to ensure recommendation quality and user experience. Through reinforced learning, which is repeated test and optimization, we find algorithms and weights that give the highest lifts.

The one-to-one e-mails using these algorithms increased revenue up to 300 percent relative to the control cell. The program performed by 40 percent over more than a two-year period. We found that lifts in revenue were more significant than those in click-through rates. This finding underscores the importance of selecting the right metric of customer service. We found that purchasing data were the most important in recommending wines that customers are more likely to buy again. E-mail response data were also predictive. This says that the customer puts money where his mouth is. Self-reported preferences tend to be broader in range than the purchased sets. It is "talk the talk" versus "walk the walk." Aggregated web behavioral segments were least useful, and it is likely that this had to do with the way in which the early dot-com web analytics vendor processed and aggregated the data.

We built similar programs for other vendors, for example, Intel Channel Marketing to recommend, in biweekly newsletters, time-sensitive news on product releases, price drops, white papers, marketing collaterals, and training, based on purchases and e-mail response behavior, achieving the goal of sending the right information to the right customer at the right time. The general strategy of these programs is to improve relevance, to help customers search information, and to engage the customers.

Yahoo! Network Segmentation Analysis

In 2003, Yahoo! was the web portal on the Internet with 200 million users. Yahoo had more than 100 properties or websites, such as Mail, Search,

Messenger, Personals, Sports, News, Finance, Music (Launch), Shopping, Health, and others, with many properties being ranked as top sites at the time in their respective categories. Yahoo!'s privacy policies forbade explicit user-level analysis using combined login data and logout data. So we did the analysis using only login data. We separately did a sample analysis on combined login and logout data, which was encrypted to comply with privacy policies, and found similar results.

We asked, Who are Yahoo!'s users and how do they use Yahoo!'s properties? The intention was to use monthly page views in different properties to build a monthly profile for each user, and use clustering algorithms to group users into a finite number of segments. Each user belongs to one and only one segment. The benefit of this approach is that we can target individual customers based on the segments.

Potentially every customer can be different, which would result in 200 million segments. For 100 properties, if we use 1 for users and 0 for nonusers, we would get 2^{100} possibilities, which is an astronomical number. In reality, people's behaviors had a limited number of usage patterns. We expected the number of segments to be a much smaller number, say only around 100.

Each property has its own typical usage levels. For example, Mail had an average of several hundreds of page views per user per month, while News had an average of a few dozen page views, and Shopping may only have a few page views. Some of the differences were due to the various stages of adoption of the products and others to just the nature of the product. We would expect that a user generates fewer Shopping page views than e-mail page views or Sports ones. We did some normalization so that even though Mail was the most heavily used property, there weren't too many people in the Mail segments. Shopping page views are low, but user values are high. We don't want to see Shopping page views getting swamped by those from Mail or Sports.

After some optimization on the cluster analysis, we got 100 segments. Not surprisingly, Mail was still the largest segment, with a third of all users. The Search segment was the second largest. Shopping was around a few percent. Eighty-five percent of customers were in the top 15 segments.

After the clustering, we did some analysis profiling the segments. Since we used only login data, we were able to append gender, age, and other information. We found that some properties were gender neutral, such as Mail and Search, but interestingly some segments were highly selective for gender and age groups. For example, News and Finance were used mainly by male and older users, Music by young females, and Sports predominantly by young males and healthy older females. Not surprisingly, Search users had high user values, while Music and Sports had very low user values.

One of the obvious strategies to increase customer value is to integrate the more engaging properties such as Mail or Sports, with better monetized ones, such as Search and Shopping. Implementing features of Mail Search together with Web Search is an obvious integration tactic, so that we can have more Mail customers use Search more often.

Yahoo! e-Mail Retention

Mail was the stickiest service of Yahoo! If customers become Y!Mail users, the likelihood of their coming back is much higher. Users of other web properties, such as Search and Shopping, are more fickle. Therefore, increasing Mail customers is good for Yahoo!'s overall retention.

At the time, 40 percent of new Y!Mail users never came back after their initial signup. An analysis indicated that for customers who had e-mail activity immediately after signup, the retention rate would become normal. A more detailed analysis found that frequent page views in certain sections, such as Help and Junk folders in Mail, were predictive for mail retention. We tried to find actionable retention drivers and strategies, such as sending welcome e-mails, to improve customer service, user experience, to reduce Mail churn, and so forth.

There are many ways to analyze the retention problem. One approach is to look at profiles and activities of a cohort of Mail users in one quarter and see if they come back the next quarter. Some analysts are more comfortable with this formulation due to its simplicity. One of the problems of this approach is that retention depends strongly on tenure. For newborns, when we plot infant mortality rates versus time, we find that the rates were high immediately after birth but they decrease and stabilize after a couple of weeks. Similarly, new e-mail customers tend to have high attrition rates initially, and the rates stabilize after some period of time. If we choose a time interval that is too large, we would lose information about this feature.

A more appropriate method to analyze customer retention is the survival analysis, a statistical method for analysis of patient survival data under medical treatments. If some treatment yields a higher survival rate than the placebo, it is said to have a certain efficacy. In consumer behavioral analysis, customer "survival" means customer retention as indicated by continued visits.

Customer Lead Scoring

In 2009, an online university was one of the largest online marketers, and it worked with a large number of lead-generation vendors. A lead is a customer name, contact information, and some basic profile of the area of study, high school degree, possible association with the military, and other fields, as well as the permission to contact.

For those of us familiar with online marking, customer life cycle is usually from an impression to a conversion. But for a lead, the experience from an impression to signup is just one third of the life cycle. After the university receives the lead, its call center and enrollment counselors will discuss with the candidate the topic of enrolling at the university. After months of effort, only a few percent of leads will enroll as students. Students can stop taking classes anytime, and those who are easy to enroll in the university may also be quick to drop out, with only a small percentage of them ever graduating many years later.

Lead vendors have their own media strategies, reaching various segments within the population to collect candidates with different levels of interest in college education. Being at different locations in the conversion funnel, some leads are ready to enroll immediately while others may be just looking around. Therefore, leads from the vendors often have very different enrollment rates. Because of the long enrollment process, it may take many months before we know the quality of a cohort of leads from a vendor. The university paid the vendors every month and had to agree with each vendor on price per lead and volume without the benefit of any direct information about the leads.

To assess the quality of leads, we need student data over a long period of time including not only enrollment information but also class completions. Ideally we should use lifetime values and brand values tied to the leads to determine media allocation and to buy a number of the best leads at the lowest cost while enhancing the brand.

One way to estimate quality is lead scoring. Analogous to credit scoring, the model uses given information at time of lead submission to score leads on the propensity for enrollment. This is similar to a car dealer running a credit report before deciding if we qualify for financing when buying a car. Using this approach, we can also build models on, say, completion of first one or three courses.

A lead may have been marketed multiple times from various channels. To build a good lead-scoring model, we need to track lead-level data in search, display, landing page, home site, call center, enrollment, courses completion data, and other factors. Ideally, we need to have a 360-degree view of a lead's signup and conversion process, as well as student life cycle. Lead quality may also depend on major, credits finished, demo, socio-economic status, first-generation students, lead source, lead form entries, and so forth. Some degrees and majors have different desirable student profiles and may require different scoring models.

Vendors also have different levels of fluctuation in enrollment rates from month to month. When we buy leads, we take risk in the value of leads relative to the cost of leads, just as when we buy stocks we take risk in the company's prospects. Using financial theory of efficient frontiers, we can calculate a larger price discount if the vendor has a higher variability in enrollment rates, and we can construct a portfolio of lead vendors with a lower risk than that of an individual vendor.

Customer Lifetime Value

Let's consider the case at online universities, although similar arguments can be made for customers of other vendors. Online universities often face the question of student retention, sometimes called *persistence*. If a student drops out, it is a loss to both the student, who has to pay tuition, and the university, which has to spend resources on recruiting and educational services. What are the overall costs and returns of a student during time at the university?

Student attrition is not just absence for a period of time. A student who takes off for a period of time before assuming study is still retained. Some assumptions have to be made about the point in time of a student's attrition, for example, by defining a churn as someone who has taken a break longer than a certain period of time. We then analyze events up to that time and find their correlation with risk factors, such as if the student had a baby, failed some courses, had a family member who became sick, etc., to estimate the probability of attrition. By definition, the retention curve is nonincreasing in time, while cumulative attrition is nondecreasing. Starting at 100 percent initially, a retention curve eventually goes to zero. This is because in time, a cohort of students will decrease in number as more and more students either drop out or graduate.

With retention curves, we can consider lifetime revenue generated by a student. Like financial assets, we pay acquisition and service costs and receive revenue when the student takes a sequence of classes, considering the duration of the degree program. Since a student may or may not take the next course, the lifetime value is the average of revenue minus cost, weighted by the probability of retention.

To calculate lifetime values, we assume that student acquisition costs, marketing costs, and enrollment costs are shared by all new students, but not by returning students. Course instructional costs and salaries of faculty and academic counselors are proportional to the number of courses the student has taken. Campus and online students have different service costs, fixed or variable.

Longer programs have higher student lifetime values. In traditional four-year universities, student attrition rates may be very low. In community colleges and online universities, attrition rates are quite high initially and then stabilize after a few courses. This is because these universities serve primarily adult and part-time students, who have more retention risk factors. Many students receive credit for their past college courses or work experience. Because of the varying number of transfer credits, each student needs to take a different number of courses to reach graduation. This also affects the lifetime value in a degree program.

We built retention curves by degree and program and other variables and calculate lifetime values for each segment. Retention rates may depend on some other variables, such as age and gender, lead source, geographic location, modality and socioeconomic factors, and others.

We can attribute expected value of a student to a lead source, a search keyword, or a display ad impression, and we then can use the information to optimize media spend.

Ad Performance Optimization

Tribal Fusion (part of Exponential Interactive) was one of the pioneers of the display ad network. Aggregating a large number of reasonably large high-quality web publishers, Tribal Fusion serves display ads for premium advertisers, using a revenue-sharing model. By 2005 it became one of the top three display ad markets, reaching around 70 percent of the U.S. unique users, with billions of impressions per month. One of the efforts at Tribal Fusion was ad performance optimization. We used information about the publishers, channels, customer geo information, past behavior, demographic data, data append, session depth, and other factors to score each impression.

Because various advertisers had different conversion patterns, we used an array of predictive models, one for each advertiser, on conversion rate (or click-through rate) to work together with the auction engine in the ad server. We modeled using individual event-level information to predict a conversion rate for each impression.

We wanted to build a separate model for each of the hundreds of advertisers, but too many models were needed and there was too little time for them to be built by humans. Instead, the models were generated using an automated script that ran overnight.

Revenue Prediction

One of the tasks we were given for an online university client was to predict enrollment and revenue in the future within errors of a couple of percent, for the next month and in three months.

We were given all student transactional-level data for the online university from the finance department for three years as well as all data from the data warehouse, which had all the lead and student enrollment data and others. So in principle, we knew all the enrollment and all the associated revenue. Predicting future enrollment and revenue should be quite possible.

In reality the situation was far more complicated. The main problem was that there was more than one definition of revenue recognition and enrollment numbers by modality, campus or online, made by past business analysts, using reasonable business rules. Some rules were built into the BI reporting product, which the Financial Planning and Analysis team watched every month as only truth they know. We underestimated the difficulty of finding out explicitly the rules. It turned out that with IT/BI turnovers and rules changing over time, few people knew or knew how to articulate the rules. Without the rules, the enrollment and revenue numbers we calculated from the data were off by random errors of around 7 percent, larger than the prediction accuracy we wanted to achieve. After several meetings, we still had no correct rules that could reproduce the numbers from the reporting product. We also saw one-time data anomalies here and there. For some data problems, the finance team provided corrections, but for others, information was limited or absent.

Within the short time constraint, we found a way to get around these limitations. We modeled time series of reported data. This assumes that the relation between enrollment and revenue for campus and online modalities would be stable over time. In this way, one-time data errors were diluted, and rule changes long ago were also less weighted.

In the end, we were able to predict customer and revenue numbers for three to six months within a couple of percent. Time series models do have the assumption that some level, trend, and periodicity continue over the time window of prediction. Without the link between student-level information and revenue, it would be more difficult to use this approach to calculate the impact of student demographics and lead source information.

As we later found out, one of the issues was that some revenue from online enrollments was credited to campus, as an incentive to increase the use of online classes. These were campus students who also took some classes online.

Search Engine Marketing at Ask.com

Ask.com (formerly Ask Jeeves) was founded 16 years ago, and now it is part of InterActiveCorp, the IAC. Ask.com attracts 100 million global users and is one of the largest questions and answers (Q&A) sites on the web. Over the last two years, Ask.com has revamped its approach to Q&A with a product that combines search technology with answers from real people. Instead of 10 blue links, Ask.com delivers real answers to people's questions—both from already published data sources and from our growing community of users—on the web and across mobile.

Similar to other websites with original content, Ask.com uses multiple strategies of customer acquisition, with search engine marketing (SEM) being one of them. Using SEM, Ask.com places ads on major search engines to acquire customer traffic using the pay per click model.

One of the efforts is to identify keywords where Ask.com has an advantage. This is achieved by determining bids for each keyword using external data from the search engines, as well as internal data sources. If there were only a small number of keywords, it would be easy to let one or more analysts manage them; but Ask.com's keyword portfolio is very large, covering a wide range of topics and categories. To set bids for an extremely large number of keywords, data mining applications are developed. These applications run every day with new bids being automatically generated and pushed to major search engines. Through the use of reinforced learning, the algorithms are used to determine and optimize bids based on past performance data and to make further adjustment using new data.

We also propose and test hypotheses and optimize algorithms and their parameters via A/B tests.

In the bidding algorithms, we build models for revenue estimation at keyword and keyword group (cluster) level. This information, along with other information and business logic, is used to generate bids. Some of the variables we use are ad depth, which is the number of ads on the landing page; search engine click-through rates (CTRs); landing page click-through rates; quality score and minimum cost per click (CPC); effective CPC; keyword categories; natural language clusters; and search behavioral clusters.

One of the main assumptions is that similar keywords have similar performance, which tends to be the case, but not always. We found that contextual similarity to be more useful than similarity in performance metrics.

To group similar keywords together, we performed keyword clustering using text mining algorithms. We also clustered the keywords using behavioral associations, as well as metrics of keyword historic performance. We mapped out similarity metrics among keywords so that we can use information from similar keywords to help keyword management and expansion, and to leverage learning from keywords with more data.

One of the biggest challenges is to select profitable keywords at big data scale. Hadoop and Hive as well as machine learning suite Mahout are used to process and analyze the data, predicting keyword performance and bidding for the right keywords at the right price at the right time.

Although improving return on investment is important, our goal is to maximize profitable traffic volume. The algorithms generally increase click traffic for keywords of higher quality scores and higher click-through rates and reduce it for keywords of lower quality scores and lower click-through rates. We also optimize user experience through adjustment of the number of ads shown as well as the layout of the search result pages, not only to achieve profit goals but also to improve customer experience.

LESSONS FOR MODEL BUILDING

In predictive modeling, often there is leakage, which is the unintended mixing of information about the target in its predictors. For example, in building a lead scoring model, *lead source* was used to predict conversion. But some values of the field were populated only for converters that came from a different data source than nonconverters came from. Then the lead source becomes more predictive than it really is, contaminating the model. When being deployed, the model will have a lower predictive power.

Another example for display ads is the conversion model. We may construct the data set by taking all converters and a random sample of nonconverters. We then predict conversion using user page view profiles. The problem, if we are not careful, is that in the sample of nonconverters there are customers who had no impressions of the display ad. Of course, one gets the trivial and useless prediction that those who never see the ads are less likely to convert. These errors can be subtle and can be overlooked even by expert modelers.

We worked with SBC Communications (now AT&T) to market digital subscriber line (DSL) services to consumers. DSL subscribers have one-year contracts. In a retention analysis, if churn events are measured for all customers in a month-to-month retention, we would find very high retention rates. This is because of the contracts with penalties if customers leave early. The analyst could declare that nothing needs to be done, but this approach would have omitted the renewal at the end of the contract. A better way is to model retention rates at the contract expiry, on only one-twelfth of the customers.

For a retention analysis, if we define retention rate as the fraction of customers who are acquired in one quarter and retained in the following quarter, we will find that those acquired early in the first quarter have a lower retention rate. This is because those customers have more time to churn. A correct way is to use survival analysis.

CONCLUSIONS

Big data analytics provide the most exciting opportunity in every field from science, government, and industry, affecting daily lives of everyone. Big data is a dream come true for data scientists, since we finally can have it all, to get exciting insights we could never have before.

Big data does not become big information and big knowledge without detailed analyses. Big data requires big and scalable storage solutions, as well as scalable analysis capabilities and applications. Analysis does not mean we can throw data at some machine-learning and statistics algorithms, such as neural networks, decision trees, support vector machines, and so forth and expect to have good results automatically.

The analyst should focus on the domain knowledge. Good modeling requires not only algorithms and procedures but also, more importantly, understanding of the business context, insights about the data, and how one may take actions based on results of the analysis. In modeling, it is most important to identify the key data. The analyst needs to understand how data are collected and know the context of data collection, as well as what data can and cannot be collected, and be able to balance the cost of collecting additional data and optimization of modeling. Identifying the smoking gun may make all the difference. Understanding of the business context and the data helps the modeler identify good data transformations. Using the link data in web pages, Google's search algorithm PageRank (Brin and Page, 1998) was a game-changing data transformation. In our wine.com case study, the wine similarity metric was also a key data transformation. Social graph is a key data transformation for fraud detection (Hardy, 2012). Using big data, it is especially important to identify the most import predictors and to come up with creative and useful ways to transform the data. Data are not reliable until after being seriously analyzed. Only detailed analysis can reveal subtle data issues. We have to do our due diligence on the data before we can be sure of their cleanliness and accuracy, as well as relevance.

Using the feedback loop to test hypotheses is a very effective way to gain better understanding of data insights as well as optimize models. To the extent possible, we should conduct simulations to see if changes are reasonable. Testing and optimizing in the real market can be crucial. We should always focus on customer experience, not model complexity or predictive accuracy.

Bigger data will support better models. The analyst's knowledge in natural sciences can be helpful in finding insights and building models in a given data set. Scientists are better at connecting the dots. We know Einstein's relativity was based on little data other than his "thought experiment," and now big data from space telescopes are providing support to his theory. Darwin wrote in *On the Origin of Species*, "Therefore I should infer from analogy that probably all the organic beings which have ever lived on this earth have descended from some one primordial form, into which life was first breathed." His conclusion was based on his limited data from the Galapagos Islands. Now 150 years later, scientists use genomic big data to confirm the existence of a common universal ancestor (Steel and Penny, 2010).

In the case studies, we sampled some applications of customer segmentation, lead conversion, retention, lifetime values, targeted e-mails, predictions of trends, and seasonality of revenue, as well as keyword segmentation based on text and search behavior, based on our experience. One of the key features of these models and analyses is that they are built on individual customer and event level. The only way to scale these types of efforts, in the amount of data and in the number of customers, is through the use of big data.

To conclude, we use good advice from one of the greatest scientists ever:

The best way to get good ideas is to have a lot of them.

—**Linus Pauling**

REFERENCES

Brin, S., and L. Page (1998). "The Anatomy of a Large-Scale Hypertextual Web Search Engine." *Computer Networks and ISDN Systems* 30: 107–117.

Cukier, K. (2010). "Data, Data Everywhere." *The Economist.* Feb 25, 2010. Retrieved from http://www.economist.com.

Dean, J., and S. Ghemawat (2004). "MapReduce: Simplified Data Processing on Large Clusters." OSDI'04: Sixth Symposium on Operating System Design and Implementation, San Francisco, CA, December.

Dumbill, E. (2012). "What Is Big Data? An Introduction to the Big Data Landscape." January 11, 2012. Retrieved from http://radar.oreilly.com.

Dyche, J. (2007). "BI Adoption Evolves." Retrieved from http://www.baseline-consulting.com.

Glanz, J. (2011). "Google Details, and Defends, Its Use of Electricity." *New York Times.* September 8, 2011. Retrieved from http://www.nytimes.com.

Hardy, Q. (2012). "Data Analytics Company Finds Fraud Is a Friend." *New York Times.* January 19, 2012. Retrieved from http://www.nytimes.com.

Hilbert, M., and P. López (2011). "The World's Technological Capacity to Store, Communicate, and Compute Information." *Science* 332: 60–65.

Norvig, P. (2011). "The Unreasonable Effectiveness of Data." October 11, 2011. Retrieved from http://www.youtube.com.

Paulk, M.C., B. Curtis, et al. (1993). "Capability Maturity Model for Software, Version 1.1." Retrieved from http://www.sei.cmu.edu.

Siegler, M.G. (2010). "Eric Schmidt: Every 2 Days We Create as Much Information as We Did Up to 2003." August 4, 2010. Retrieved from http://techcrunch.com. For more discussions on the topic, see Hilbert and López (2011).

Steel, M., and D. Penny (2010). "Origins of Life: Common Ancestry Put to the Test." *Nature* 465: 168–169.

Zhao, D. (2009). "The University of Phoenix Wins Big with SAS Grid Computing." SAS Global Forum 2009, Washington, DC. Retrieved from http://support.sas.com.

4

The Intrinsic Value of Data

Omer Trajman

CONTENTS

INTRODUCTION

Over the past few years, the business world has become increasingly focused on data. The collection, storage, processing, analysis, and deployment of data are taking over larger fractions of IT budgets. Businesses in every industry are launching big data initiatives. This trend is a result of the success of numerous organizations that over the past 10 years have used the data they collect to drive their business. The result is organizations that operate more efficiently and that have gained a defensible advantage over their competitors. The success of these organizations' use of data leads us to ask how we can measure the intrinsic value of data.

Data is an intangible asset in the same vein as patents or intellectual property. Indeed for intellectual property to have value, it must be recorded and embodied as data. Though organizations incur real costs to create, acquire, store, secure, process, and access data, most only track the cost of data storage and loss prevention [http://www.csoonline.com/article/206200/the-value-of-data]. This simplistic approach to accounting for only the cost of data storage suggests that most organizations consider data a commodity, the value of which is entwined in the cost of storage. In effect, organizations are valuing data the same as the underlying storage instead of considering the true potential value of data as an asset, distinct from where it is housed. This line of thinking belies the true value of data. While storage has fixed cost regardless of whether it contains any data, the data it contains has real value, and storage that contains data has additional cost. Evidence of the cost and value of data has been seen in some of the fastest-growing companies of the past decade [http://www.nytimes.com/2011/04/24/business/24unboxed.html] and the growing market for data security [http://www.prweb.com/releases/cyber_security/application_content_data/prweb8262390.htm].

To better understand the intrinsic value of data, we explore two types of data through the life cycle of data creation, data acquisition, storage, processing, and access. The first is data that is used to record some exchange of value such as a purchase. This is called *transactional data* after the transaction it records. Other data is also often generated around the event of a transaction. We call this peripheral data set *incidental data*.

Much of the analyst, press, and vendor literature, incidental and other nontransactional data (such as images and video) that companies generate is grouped together and identified as *unstructured data*. However, this data all clearly has structure. If it had no structure, it would be very difficult to find any value in the data. The term *unstructured* is intended to differentiate it from data that is transactional or has relational structure. This distinction helps organizations that have been actively managing transactional data for decades to understand that there are other types of data that they create and store.

Incidental data may be stored for varying periods of time but is rarely curated and analyzed the way transactional data is. The one exception to this is profile data. This is the set of relatively static data that includes personal attributes and demographics and has been used for decades. For every transaction that takes place, there is some amount of associated profile data (name, address, credit card). There is also a second type of incidental data that is more dynamic. This behavioral data results from *data exhaust* [http://www.economist.com/node/15557431], the by-product of how digital services work. When browsing the web, whether or not a consumer completes a transaction, the server their web browser connects to records every page and every item on each page that is requested by the consumer's browser. This stream of click records is one example of behavioral incidental data.

As we walk through the life cycle of data, we consider how to determine the real value of this data. We can plot the value of data over its life cycle as a framework to consider how an organization might determine the value of data. Finally, to get a macroscopic picture of what data is worth, we consider the differential value of those companies that have gained a competitive advantage by using data in ways that the rest of their industry peers have not.

A BRIEF HISTORY OF DATA

As a logical construct, data has existed for millennia [http://cs-exhibitions. uni-klu.ac.at/index.php?id=187]. Initially data was created as records to communicate facts and assist in long-term memory. When we talk about the dawn of history, we are referring to the first instances of data captured in tangible form. This data included pictures describing facts, parables, and transactions between entities. Later, as alphabets came into use, the types of recorded data remained the same. We still use data in similar ways today in the form of biographies, history books, journals, blogs, tweets, and of course to capture transaction records when we purchase goods.

For millennia, data was used to maintain a short-term context for complex calculations such as in mathematics and scientific experiments. We learn in school to do long-form division and multiplication, to derive formulas, and to maintain a journal of work in science classes. Much of the short-term context for data today is stored digitally, in computer memories. We ask Google to find directions and it generates turn-by-turn navigation. We ask Wolfram Alpha to compute a formula, which it calculates in its internal memory and then provides the results.

Just a few centuries ago, recorded data started being used in earnest as the input to trend analysis and reporting. Real data analysis became available to scientists with the emergence of power series, analytical geometry, and the application of arithmetic to sets of data. This emergence of data analysis coincided with the Renaissance as scientists applied statistics to their recorded observations of the world.

Estimates are that in 2011 the total amount of data created amounted to 1.8 zettabytes (1.8 billion terabytes). In addition to the industries involved in creating, capturing, and storing data, there is an entire industry devoted to the protection of data and a complementary underworld that attempts to undermine, devalue, or destroy data [http://securitywatch.eweek.com/virus_and_spyware/data_theft_attacks_still_driving_underground.html]. These data-related businesses exist because data today has value. It is even argued that we are in the early stages of a data-driven economy [http://bigthink.com/ideas/the-data-driven-economy?page=all].

TRANSACTIONAL DATA

At first blush, the value of data that records a simple transaction seems relatively easy to calculate. Writing down that a customer paid for an item and that the item was delivered has been the backbone of commerce for centuries. Today, recording a transaction is critical to fulfilling the transaction, accounting for the goods and services rendered, and paying taxes. This suggests that data may be valued as some fraction of the economic value of the transaction or event it describes. As we will soon discover, the intrinsic value of data is not so simple to derive, nor is it static.

To make our analysis more concrete, we'll use as an example Ellen, a consumer who buys a piece of music from James, a vendor, for $1. When Ellen hands James $1 and James gives her a recording and a writes a receipt, it is difficult to see how that receipt holds any value. James has his dollar, Ellen has a dollar's worth of music, and they both have a record of the transaction. Is value created simply by recording this transaction? The receipt may have value as an intermediary if the transaction was long lived. For example, if the music is on backorder but Ellen prepays for it, then her copy of the receipt allows her to claim her music upon delivery. For that time, the receipt (data record) is arguably worth as much as the purchased item.

Consider that in addition to serving as a placeholder while a transaction is in progress, the creation of data as part of the transaction holds significant potential value. Using a record of the exchange, James is able to demonstrate to tax authorities that he sold a piece of music and neither stole $1 nor received a gift from Ellen. He can invoke various business-related tax laws to calculate his profit, net the cost of sales. If Ellen were to be sued for copyright infringement, her only defense may be the record of the transaction demonstrating that she legally acquired the music. Each of these actions uses the data record to save James and Ellen time and money.

There are a few interesting concepts worth pointing out in our examples so far. A subtle yet critical detail is that as we first claimed, the data recorded in the transaction between James and Ellen does not, in and of itself, have any value. Writing down a record of the transaction after the fact does not mean that the data record is worth $1 or indeed anything at all. There is no way, without additional context, to identify the particular worth of the data record. Yet when the data is used—to justify a tax break or redeem a purchase—it potentially becomes as valuable as the transaction itself or more if used to avoid fines and litigation.

This second detail is something we will consider further later on in this chapter. The value of this particular data varies depending on the context. Clearly, as a receipt that Ellen must use to redeem her piece of music, it may be considered as valuable as the music itself. For James, in order to justify a lower tax on his income, the dollar value of the receipt is smaller. In this context, the value is the difference in tax payments between $1 in profit and the profit margin (the price difference between the cost of a piece of music and the $1 sales price).

Finally, the astute reader will have noticed that the value of data changes. At the time of transaction, simply as a record that Ellen has paid James $1 for a piece of music, it has little value. If Ellen does not receive the music immediately, the data record, in the form of a receipt, is worth $1. The moment Ellen receives her purchase, the receipt record has little or no value. At tax time, it is worth the delta in taxes to James. Once James pays his taxes, or perhaps once the statue of limitations on audits has passed, the record may lose all further value.

It may seem trivial to consider the value of a record of a transaction valued at most at $1 or the cost of storing one record's worth of bits. The reader should understand that these are contrived examples. When Ellen decides to purchase a car for $10,000, the purchase and sale or the record of transaction is much more valuable. The transaction record is necessary to pick up the car when it is delivered, to register the car with the state, and to pay taxes.

PROFILE DATA

We have discussed the value of a piece of data that records a simple trans-action. Rather than spend the remainder of this chapter on increasingly complex (e.g., multiparty) transactions, we will simply note that at a minimum, every party to a transaction may derive some value from the transaction record. This includes Ellen and James (the principal parties), James's supplier, the tax authorities, the marketing firm that advertised this piece of music, the firm that advertises James's shop, and any other advertiser that might want to convince Ellen to buy something related.

Advertisers in particular are interested in both transactional and inci-dental data. Incidental data is never necessary to complete a transaction. Historically incidental data was mostly comprised of profile data. Curated collections of profile data containing information on demographics, rela-tionships, preferences, and credit scores organized and sold by compa-nies such as Acxiom [http://www.crunchbase.com/company/acxiom] have been in use for decades. Acxiom licenses data about consumers from various vendors and sources, validates the data, and uses it to help compa-nies enrich their own consumer profile data sets. Firms such as Experian [http://www.crunchbase.com/company/experian] and Epsilon [http://www.crunchbase.com/company/epsilon] provide services to help target marketing campaigns based on purchase data and demographic data, while companies such as Unica [http://www.crunchbase.com/company/unica] and now various divisions of Experian build software that per-forms the matching and targeting.

Advertisers in particular have discovered that data regarding transac-tions as well as other incidental data can be used to increase the return on investment in advertising by better targeting consumers. The payment industry, experiencing competitive pressures on its primary fee-driven business model, is starting to realize the potential value of the data it collects and stores [http://techcrunch.com/2012/08/18/payment-data-is-more-valuable-than-payment-fees/]. Large collections of transaction records are captured and stored by payment processors as well as mer-chants and banks (and of course customers). Advertisers are able to realize value in the data because of collection of transaction records from a wide variety of merchants combined with profile data.

As a basic example, assume that Ellen is an accountant between the ages of 25 and 30, making $75,000 a year. She lives in a town with a population of 25,000 about 15 miles from the closest city. Combining this transaction data with Ellen's demographic data offers some value to an advertiser. With sufficient data points, an advertiser can draw some probabilistic correlation between any particular demographic attribute or combination of attributes and Ellen's predisposition to purchase a particular piece of music.

This profile data has some value and yet is still not as valuable as when combined with incidental data about Ellen's occupation or the products that she buys. If Ellen was a concert violinist and the music she purchased was a Bach sonata for strings, it would be likely that advertising various pieces of music featuring string instruments would be money well spent. Assuming for simplicity that all forms of advertising incur the same cost, the delta in spending between what Ellen would have bought without advertising or with irrelevant advertising and what she spends with higher targeted advertising is one way an organization could derive the value of profile data.

Generic demographic data is also useful when combined with many transaction records. If we look at all transactions records of James's sales and the accompanying demographic data, we may, for example, find that 20 percent of all sales of classical violin music were purchased by women ages 25–30 who live in small suburbs and work in finance. Combine this with local knowledge that this same demographic listens to classical radio and we have the data necessary to launch a highly targeted marketing campaign.

The value of additional data—in this case demographic data—and collated transactional data from several sources can be ascertained based on the potential net uplift in sales or conversely the cost savings in a targeted marketing campaign relative to the cost of a broad marketing campaign that returns the same sales. It is estimated that the uplift in sales due to Amazon's targeted production recommendation systems, which suggests to potentials customers what they might want to buy, is on the order of 20–30 percent [http://blog.kiwitobes.com/?p=58]. Amazon is a good example of the increased revenue that can be achieved when transactional and profile data are combined with behavioral data collected from user interactions on its website.

BEHAVIORAL DATA

The above example of using incidental profile data is based on marketing methodologies that have been used for decades. Companies such as Acxiom and Experian own data centers the size of football fields just to store and process ever more detailed demographic data for advertisers. However, over the past 10 years, a new type of incidental data has become available.

As consumers turned to the Internet in the late 1990s, various pioneers such as Amazon, Google, and Facebook figured out that there was information to be gleaned by recording and analyzing how people browse online. Since nearly every action on a website requires asking a web server for information, the web server has an opportunity to record that request.

These web request records, known as *web logs*, are used to ensure operational integrity and respond to user inquiries or complaints. They serve a purpose as the secondary system for validating a transaction. As it turns outs, these logs are also instrumental in reconstructing the path that a consumer followed on any given website. The so-called session for a user is derived from a stream of records denoting the user's individual clicks. Thus a click stream is sessionized, resulting in a vector that can be recorded, analyzed, and compared.

An Internet marketing firm no longer needs to rely solely on the correlation between transaction data and demographic data [http://mashable.com/2012/07/06/big-data-playbook/]. By utilizing user sessions, a savvy marketer can effectively observe as Ellen browses through various selections of music. Ellen may use the search function and specify *string music* as a keyword or she may choose *classical* as a category. The clicks recorded during this session provide a much more accurate representation of Ellen's intent to purchase string music over any other kind of music or any other item for sale on James's website.

Compared with transactional data records, which have immediate value upon creation that decreases as the data ages, incidental data has little value when it is created. It takes some quantifiable business need such as diagnosing an error in the system or processing such as sessionization to derive value from incidental data.

THE COST OF DATA

We have discussed the life cycle of a piece of data, written as a record of the transaction where Ellen purchases a piece of music from James for $1, as profile information about Ellen or captured information about how Ellen browses James's website. Throughout the life cycle, data may have different values and indeed the value may always be potential if it is never used. Yet when it is created, at the time it is written and until it is destroyed, the data has real cost. Whether the cost of printing on a piece of paper or storing in a computer's memory, each bit takes energy to create and consumes space. To understand the importance of identifying the intrinsic value of data, we need only to consider the cost of capturing and storing.

There is also a cost to protect data against accidental or malicious theft and destruction. As of 2012 the estimated cost of data loss is over $200 per customer record lost or stolen [http://www.ponemon.org/news-2/23]. The risk of data leakage, in particular sensitive data that includes personal information, puts millions of people at risk of identity theft each year and costs companies and the government billions of dollars [http://www.treasury.gov/tigta/auditreports/2012reports/201242080fr.pdf].

For James, a single transaction incurs a small cost to record and slightly more to secure. If James is a large music publisher, he may be recording millions of transactions per day, perhaps billions each year. The cost of storing and securing records of these transactions adds up, depending on how long he must keep the data and if he needs to maintain backup copies.

Today, organizations record the cost of storage medium on their balance sheets and they pay for data protection. These are standard assets that depreciate per a set schedule. This methodology fails to capture the value inherent in these assets when they hold different types of data. The value of a disk, the cost of protecting it, and the potential loss necessarily changes when there is data stored on it. We understand this fact intuitively. An empty USB stick has some market value that decreases over time. A USB stick with your financial information is much more valuable and has greater cost. It is at least as valuable as the total of your assets and with the risk of identity theft, perhaps as valuable as your available credit.

Consider a simple scenario. As of May 2012, Acxiom generates $1.13 billion per year in revenue, all based on the data it has that no one else has [http://investor.shareholder.com/acxiom/secfiling.cfm?filingID=733269-12-15]. What would an organization pay to have all of Acxiom's data? What would an organization that has all of that data (and the rights to use it) be worth? In 2012, after expenses, Acxiom generated $85 million in net revenue, created entirely by the use of data that it collects. We will plant a seed to discuss later: if two companies now have access and rights to all of Acxiom's data, does that reduce the value of that data?

VALUE OF DATA

Part of the reason that incidental data has gotten so much attention is that it is growing at a faster rate than transactional data is. Consider the amount of profile information posted on Facebook or the number of actions Ellen may take on a website before she generates a single transaction record. It is estimated that incidental data is being generated at a rate 10 times that of transactional data [http://cdn.idc.com/research/Predictions12/Main/downloads/IDCTOP10Predictions2012.pdf].

Earlier in the chapter we argued that transactional data must be stored because of the business-critical nature of the record. In this case, transactional data initially has the value of the transaction itself and that value then varies over time depending on the context and age of the transaction record. For an organization to be net positive on transactional data, the total storage cost must be less than the total value of data over time.

This calculation can be simplified. Ignoring the residual value of data, the cost of creating, storing, and protecting data must be less than the net value of the transaction. Put another way, if the net profit from the sale of a piece of music is $0.10 and it costs $0.10 to record and store the transaction, James has no immediate profit. To create net profit in the business he must either lower the cost of recording data or invest additional capital to use the data he recorded, deriving new value. Today, most organizations have done this math, and indeed storing records of transactions costs less than their net profit driver from those transactions. Additional uses of transactional data that increase profits for a company are then icing on the cake.

It is harder to put a monetary value on incidental data, although the Internet giants have calculated that storing incidental data is net positive to their returns. These web-based companies have been growing highly competitive businesses, often surpassing nonweb brick-and-mortar business in growth [http://www.internetretailer.com/2012/02/27/e-retail-spending-increase-45-2016]. The techniques pursued by companies such as Amazon, Google, and Facebook have validated that incidental data has some net value when put to use. Much in the way that transactional data has value when used (to redeem a purchase or in filing taxes), incidental data can be used to attract or retain customers, to increase the operational efficiency of a business, and to gain a competitive advantage.

DIFFERENTIAL VALUE

So long as Ellen continues to buy music from James, he may not have a particular interest in incidental data. That is the status quo among organizations today. There are two driving factors that would prompt James to start collecting and using incidental data. The first, as we discussed is to entice Ellen to buy more. The science behind retargeting has demonstrated that using behavior as an indicator of intent increases the return on investment of advertising by anywhere from 2 to 35 times [http://www.technewsworld.com/story/71236.html].

The other business driver is competition. Consider when James's competitor, Greg, begins a concerted effort to win Ellen's business. Whether Greg uses broad-spectrum advertising or buys a mailing list (from a data vendor such as Acxiom), Ellen now has the option of comparison-shopping. Where James opportunistically invested in collecting, storing, and analyzing incidental data because of the potential to get Ellen to spend more, he must now rely on incidental data to prevent churn and retain customer loyalty.

In the case of competition, storing and using incidental data starts to become necessary, thus changing the value dynamics of the data. If James can figure out that Ellen visits his website directly (rather than through a search engine), he may resist offering discounts, believing that Greg's search engine advertising will not affect his customer's loyalty. James may have a social media relationship with Ellen, and when she talks about her music listening habits online, he can correlate this with purchases she made to identify whether she has started shopping elsewhere. James can also record her browsing habits on his website to identify whether she has reduced the time she spends "window shopping."

Recall the question posed earlier regarding the value of Acxiom's profile data should another entity have access to all of it and the ability to use or resell all of it. Conceivably, Acxiom would lose some competitive advantage since a marketer would now have two companies from which he could purchase his marketing database. The same may hold true with behavioral data. The information that Amazon collects regarding browsing habits helps Amazon better target advertisements to its customers. A competitor could mount an effective campaign to lure away an Amazon customer given the behavioral data that Amazon has collected.

Conceivably, when an organization has exclusive access to incidental data, that data has higher value than if the data is available to competitors. We saw that organizations can generate higher returns using more effectively targeted marketing strategies. When an organization has exclusive insight into consumer behavior, its strategies can be better targeted than its competitors.

For example, if a consumer browses Amazon looking for string music, Amazon will have a higher chance of inducing a purchase when it continues to advertise string music to that consumer compared with any other type of generic advertisement that its competitors may offer. If the consumer browses both Amazon and Best Buy looking for string music, both companies have the same incidental data and the consumer is likely to receive targeted advertisements from both competitors. Statistically, the chance that they will buy from Amazon then decreases [http://www.businessnewsdaily.com/841-online-targeted-advertising.html].

This data differential leads to a financial differential when data is put to use. Simply collecting and storing the data does not, on its own, add any value [http://blogs.forrester.com/rob_karel/11-03-29-stop_trying_to_put_a_monetary_value_on_data_its_the_wrong_path]. The financial differential can be observed in the market capitalization of companies like Amazon relative to their competitors such as Target and Walmart over the past few years. Similarly, Google was able to dominate the Internet search market (once considered mature) by creating AdSense for targeting online advertisements to the consumers most likely to click on them. Facebook has famously used incidental data collected from extensive sitewide instrumentation to fine tune their website for maximum user engagement. Facebook also employs a similar mechanism to target ads to users [http://www.technologyreview.com/featured-story/428150/what-facebook-knows/].

COMBINING DATA

Data also changes value when it is combined with other sets of data. Transactional data has value when it is combined with other transactions. Consider an individual credit card statement. All the transactions listed in a statement are a useful reference and perhaps can be used to assist in creating a personal spending budget. Retailers that have access to all the transactions from all customers can use the data to help optimize their supply chain [http://insiderprofiles.wispubs.com/article.aspx ?iArticleId=6628], perform market basket analysis [http://factpoint.com/ pdf2/1.pdf], and improve their ability to cross-sell and upsell [http:// tynerblain.com/blog/2009/12/16/why-cross-selling-works/].

Incidental data may never have value at the granularity of individual records. A single piece of profile data with no additional context does not add any immediate value. Profile data is useful when multiple pieces of data are filled in. An individual click or page load on a website is all but useless (except perhaps in the rare case of an error). Behavior data becomes useful when combined to help find patterns. A cross-section of user clicks can be used to understand what draws users' attention, and a series of clicks from one user can show how that individual is navigating the site. A collection of series is even more valuable since it shows how users browse a website.

For example, if one particular grouping of similar clicks leads to sales (identified by combining session data with transactional data), the site owner now has a prototypical *sales click pattern*. If the users have profile data, the click pattern can be classified based on the various profile attributes of each user. Instead of guessing wildly as to what will drive more sales, a reasonable hypothesis is that getting more people to follow the sales click pattern that users with similar profiles have followed will lead to more sales. Thus collections of incidental data have value relative to some proportion of the quantity of data.

DEPRECIATING VALUE

It is less clear whether and how the value of data degrades over time or as it is used. We saw that value of individual transactional records is effectively "used up" once a purchase is fulfilled and taxes paid. Some types of data must be retained for seven years due to regulatory requirements. Even beyond that time, collections of transactions may be valuable many more years into the future in the context of analyzing long-term buying trends.

It is clear that incidental data has little value as isolated records. At the time that individual records are generated, the value of a record depends on the context of other data with which it is combined. For example, data generated from a consumer clicking on an offer has potential value if the consumer's prior browsing history is available or as an event in the consumer's browsing session. When the click has context, the advertiser can try to understand what prompted the user to be interested in that offer. The value of incidental data exists so long as the data provides useful context for new data. Even when incidental data is related to a specific event in the past or an individual who has passed away, the attributes associated with that day may be useful in the future.

Collections of data may prove valuable so long as there are useful unanswered questions. Any anthropologist will testify that the more detail we know about any given historical event, the more questions we have. Since the future context is unknown, it is always possible that incidental data may reveal some hidden behavior that has recently changed. This is the secret and the challenge that companies like Google and Facebook now struggle with. All the data is potentially valuable in perpetuity when you keep everything.

DOLLAR VALUE OF DATA

An interesting research project outside the scope of this chapter is to explore the detailed value of data through collection, combination, usage, and depreciation. Translating detailed usage of data (in and of itself an act of collecting incidental data about data) could be compared with concrete alternatives where data is not collected or collected but not combined or simply not used. Although we do not have a detailed analysis, we can do a macroanalysis. By looking at the previously mentioned organizations that have established a data-driven methodology, we can compare business metrics that already have value assigned and compare the difference.

To understand the scale at which data-driven organizations collect data, consider that most organizations have less than one terabyte of data per $1 million in revenue [http://www.wallstreetandtech.com/data-management/231500503]. These are based on installed storage, not raw data; thus the comparison is not perfect. It does suggest that most organizations are storing only the data that has obvious immediate value, which is primarily transactional data.

In comparison consider that Facebook has estimated revenues of $3.7 billion and a reported 100 petabytes of incidental data, resulting in a ratio of 27 terabytes of data per $1 million in revenue [http://techcrunch.com/2012/08/22/how-big-is-facebooks-data-2-5-billion-pieces-of-content-and-500-terabytes-ingested-every-day/]. This is 135 times the average for Internet services companies. That Facebook does not produce content, contrasting with media and entertainment companies, which produce significant content, further highlights the relative amount of incidental data that they collect. Facebook stores 35 times the number of terabytes per $1 million revenue as the average media and entertainment company.

Companies such as Facebook and LinkedIn store extensive profile data to help drive advertising revenue. Most of their behavioral data is a by-product of profile data (such as browsing what other people post). Google collects primarily behavioral data about what people are searching for. We can therefore compare the potential value of these two types of incidental data that companies collect based on advertising revenue per user [http://en.wikipedia.org/wiki/Average_revenue_per_user]. As of August 2012, Facebook's value per user per quarter is $1.21, LinkedIn's is $1.76 and Google's is $7.14 [http://money.cnn.com/2012/05/16/technology/facebook-arpu/index.htm]. Thus behavioral data seems to be four to six times as valuable as profile data.

We can also assess the value that capital markets assign to companies that collect, store, and make use of all their data, both transactional and incidental. Looking at price-to-earnings ratios as an indication of market value, by rough measures the difference in value between companies that use incidental and transactional data is conservatively 2 times and at extremes up to 20 times. Among retailers, looking at price-to-earnings ratios over the past 10 years, Amazon's ratio has varied between 35 to nearly 300 [http://ycharts.com/companies/AMZN/pe_ratio#zoom=10] while Walmart's has been steady at around 15 [http://ycharts.com/companies/WMT/pe_ratio#zoom=10] and Target's has been in the range of 11 to 18 [http://ycharts.com/companies/TGT/pe_ratio#zoom=10]. Some of this can be attributed to Amazon's optimized distribution costs since they do not need to ship goods that someone may never buy to a remote store. Walmart and Target also have well-optimized supply and deliver chains. Some of the change in the ratio is most likely due to Amazon's use of incidental data in product recommendations, which as previously discussed led directly to an increase in sales.

CONCLUSION

Data, particularly incidental data, has potential value (and actual cost) when it is collected and stored. In most organizations the bulk of this potential value is never realized while the cost of storage is captured in the form of capital and operational expenditures. Indeed most organizations look at data as a commodity where every byte has the same cost and value as every other byte on the same tier of storage on which it resides. In other organizations such as Acxiom, data has concrete value because it is sold. The market demand for a given byte of data dictates its potential value over time. For a few organizations, some of which we highlighted, data is the fuel of growth. The incidental data they collect is used to drive new business on a day-to-day basis. The lack of data would halt or significantly slow their growth engine.

Though we don't have a bulletproof formula for deriving the intrinsic value of data, it is clear that the use of transactional and incidental data creates net value. Incidental data does not immediately possess value like transactional data does. Incidental data must be collated and processed before realizing value. When organizations seek a deeper understanding of how consumers interact with their companies, incidental data gains potential value. For organizations that develop a cadence of analyzing incidental data and pursuing growth strategies such as attracting new customers or increasing customer spend, this same incidental data becomes as critical to the business as transactional data.

For these organizations, data has real value because it is used to drive the business forward. Each piece of data that is collected adds some incremental value to the business when translated into higher user engagement (which becomes more advertising dollars) or directly by driving increased sales. In these organizations, there is a calculable return on the investment of adding instrumentation to collect and store new data sets. Without the incidental data to fuel business's growth, organizations are subject to the whims of the market and broad-based marketing strategies.

Indeed, we have observed over the past decade that organizations with leading growth in their industries are those that use all of their data. This leads us to believe that any organization that does not use its data will decline due to competitive pressures. The data collected by each of these successful organizations has value only because the data is put to use. Thus an entity that has nothing but the data that Facebook has amassed also gains nothing but the associated liabilities. The brand and product that Facebook creates using data is how the data that Facebook collects gains value. For an organization to make use of the data that Facebook has collected, that organization would need a channel through which to exploit the data. In many ways this is similar to an organization that has a stock of physical goods and no distribution channel.

To a close approximation we now have a means to assess the intrinsic value of data in an organization that is data driven. The relative volumes of data for data-driven organizations are measured in orders of magnitude relative to all other organizations. The value of all of that data is also highly dependent on the type and use of that data with behavioral data valued more than profile data. The result is a market value of between 2 and 20 times that of organizations that do not fully utilize their data.

As the cost of storage and processing continues to drop, our ability to store and analyze more data will increase steadily. It will be interesting to see how the data value curve evolves. There may be a time where we reach an apex and can identify the precise quantity of data that maximizes value.

5

Finding Big Value in Big Data: Unlocking the Power of High-Performance Analytics

Paul Kent, Radhika Kulkarni, and Udo Sglavo

CONTENTS

Here's a scenario that might be painfully familiar to many of you. You're the vice president of marketing for a major financial services company—a leading provider of consumer credit cards—and critical decisions must be made. It's late on a Monday afternoon and you've been locked in a conference room all day with your marketing managers, who have been hashing out plans for the upcoming quarter's demand-generation campaigns.

The stale sandwiches linger—along with strategic questions about your upcoming investments.

You have 20 million customers, eight separate marketing programs, and 210 different communications—which translates into slightly more than one *billion* eligible customer-offer assignments. Sounds complicated, doesn't it? What if you consider the realities of budget and policy constraints?

- Your marketing budget is capped at $10 million.
- For each of your eight marketing programs, you can't make more than 2.5 million offers from any single program.
- Each customer can receive no more than two offers.
- No customer should receive more than one offer from any marketing program.

How will you maximize your profit? Which customers get which offers, such as cash advances, balance transfers, or airline discounts? The marketing analyst in your department has painstakingly run several scenarios and crunched the numbers and has presented his proposed optimum outcome. The only problem? Bob, one of the campaign managers, claims that increasing the number of offers for his program and decreasing Elizabeth's number by the same amount will increase overall profit. In years past, that kind of last-minute objection might derail the team's entire proceedings and send them spinning off into pointless abstract debates or introduce significant delay. And you would have had no quick, factual basis upon which to resolve what might just be a turf war. After all, with all of that data and accompanying constraints, you're looking at a massive computational problem, and it could take many hours to recalculate a new scenario, right?

Not necessarily—not today. That's because our marketing analyst can simply access his computational grid from his laptop and—using sophisticated new high-performance analytics (HPA) routines and algorithms— run the new scenario to verify if Bob's claim is indeed true. And he can do it in less than two minutes.

HPA is transforming how companies—like our fictitious financial services firm—process their vast amounts of data, extract insights, and sift through millions of scenarios. It is literally changing the nature and speed of the challenges that companies are able to address.

HIGH-PERFORMANCE ANALYTICS: THE OPPORTUNITY AND THE CHALLENGE

We've all heard the "scare stats" countless times, but the latest figures on data volumes show an unbelievable, ever more inconceivable scale: In 2012, computers will create 2.5 exabytes of data every day (each exabyte is 1 quintillion bytes). In fact, 90 percent of the data in the world today has been created in just the last two years.* Just 12 years ago, the largest data warehouse in the world was "only" 100 terabytes. Today, that size seems almost quaint in a world where billion is the new million.

We're in the era of big data—but what do we mean by that? In our view, big data is a relative, not absolute, term. It means that the organization's need to handle, store, and analyze data (its volume, variety, velocity, variability, and complexity) exceeds its current capacity and has moved beyond the IT comfort zone.† Big Data is the classic dual-edged sword—both potential asset and possible curse. Most agree that there is significant, meaningful, proprietary value in that data. But few organizations relish the costs and challenges of simply collecting, storing, and transferring that massive amount of data. And even fewer know how to tap into that value, to turn the data into information.

Is the enterprise IT department merely an episode of TV's *Hoarders* waiting to happen—or will we actually find ways to locate the information of strategic value that is getting buried deeper and deeper in our mountains of data? Quite simply: *What are we going to do with all of this data?*

At its essence, high-performance analytics offers a simple, but powerful, promise: Regardless of how you store your data or how much of it there is, complex analytical procedures can still access that data, build powerful analytical models using that data, and provide answers quickly and accurately by using the full potential of the resources in your computing environment.

With high-performance analytics, we are no longer primarily concerned with *where* the data resides. Today, our ability to compute has far outstripped our ability to move massive amounts of data from disk to disk. Instead, we use a divide-and-conquer approach to cleverly send the processing out to where the data lives.

---

* http://www-01.ibm.com/software/data/bigdata/
† For more information, visit http://www.sas.com/big-data/

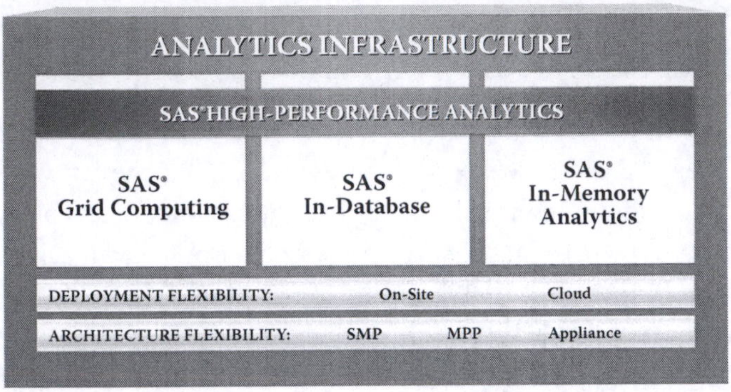

FIGURE 5.1
Several distributed processing options—in-memory, in-database, and grid computing—let enterprises take advantage of HPA advancements while providing scalability and flexibility. These options enable you to make the best use of IT resources while achieving unprecedented performance gains.

As our scenario at the beginning of this chapter illustrated, ultimately, HPA is about the value of speed and its effect on business behavior. If the analytic infrastructure requires a day to deliver a single computational result, you're likely to simply accept the answer it provides. But if you can use HPA to get an answer in one minute, your behavior changes. You ask more questions. You explore more alternatives. You run more scenarios. And you pursue better outcomes.

But how do we bring the power of high-performance analytics to data volumes of this scale? We believe there are three basic pillars—three innovative approaches—to bring HPA to big data (Figure 5.1):

- *Grid Computing: Distribute the Workload among Several Computing Engines*—Grid computing enables analysts to automatically use a centrally managed grid infrastructure that provides workload balancing, high availability, and parallel processing for business analytics jobs and processes. With grid computing, it is easier and more cost-effective to accommodate compute-intensive applications and growing numbers of users appropriately across available hardware resources and ensure continuous high availability for business analytics applications. You can create a managed, shared environment to process large volumes of programs in an efficient manner (Figure 5.2).
- *In-Database Analytics: Move the Analytics Process Closer to the Data*—With in-database processing, analytic functions are executed

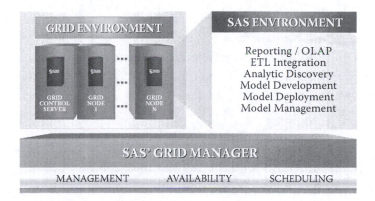

FIGURE 5.2

Grid implementations provide a managed, shared environment for processing large volumes of data and analytic programs quickly and are ideal for a broad variety of analytical tasks. Grid computing splits individual jobs and runs each piece in parallel across multiple symmetric multiprocessing (SMP) machines using shared physical storage.

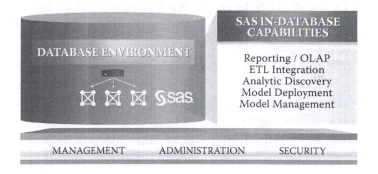

FIGURE 5.3

In-database technologies use a massively parallel processing (MPP) database architecture for faster execution of key data management and analytic development and deployment tasks. Computations run inside the database to avoid time-consuming data movement and conversion.

within database engines using native database code. Traditional programming may include copying data to a secondary location, and the data is processed using the programming language outside the database. Benefits of in-database processing include reduced data movement, faster run times, and the ability to leverage existing data warehousing investments (Figure 5.3).

- *In-Memory Analytics: Distribute the Workload and Data Alongside the Database*—In this approach, big data and intricate analytical computations are processed in-memory and distributed across a dedicated set of nodes to produce highly accurate insights to solve complex problems in near-real time. This is about applying high-end analytical techniques to solve these problems within the in-memory environment. For optimal performance, data is pulled and placed within the memory of a dedicated database appliance for analytic processing (Figure 5.4).

We will describe each of these pillars in greater details using specific customer examples. Each pillar is appropriate for a specific class of analytical challenges. All are an improvement over traditional single-machine computation.

PILLAR 1: GRID COMPUTING—HARNESSING THE FULL CAPACITY OF YOUR HARDWARE ENVIRONMENT

Flexibility and Cost Advantages

Grid computing lets you create a managed, shared environment for quickly processing large volumes of data and analytic programs using dynamic, resource-based load balancing. (You can split individual analytical jobs and run each piece in parallel across multiple symmetric multiprocessing machines using centralized, shared physical storage.) In this manner, IT can create and manage a lower-cost, flexible infrastructure that scales to meet changing computing requirements. HPA based on grid computing lets the enterprise:

- *Manage jobs and users more efficiently*—Central administration lets you monitor and manage multiple users, groups, and applications under a given set of constraints. IT can meet service-level demands by easily reassigning computing resources to manage peak workloads and changing business needs.
- *Avoid user or source disruptions*—Multiple servers in a grid environment enable jobs to run on the best available resource. If a server fails, you can transition its jobs seamlessly to other servers—providing a highly available business analytics environment.
- *Enhance IT performance*—Multiprocessing capabilities let you divide individual analytics jobs into subtasks that run in parallel on

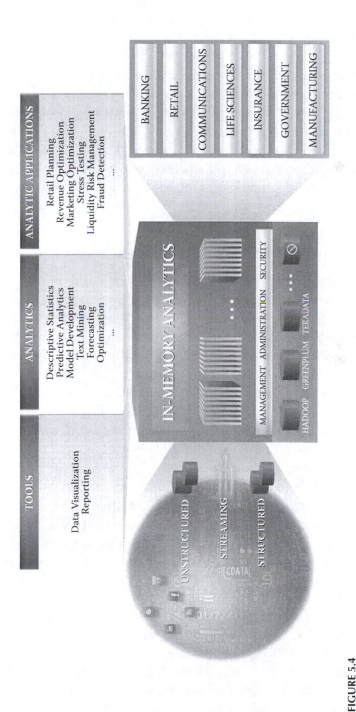

FIGURE 5.4

In-memory analytics divides analytic processes into easily manageable pieces with computations distributed in parallel across a dedicated set of compute nodes or blades. In-memory approaches let you tap big data with sophisticated analytics to address complex, industry-specific problems much faster.

the best available hardware resource in a grid environment. Faster processing of data integration, reporting, and analytical jobs speeds decision making across the enterprise.

Grid computing architectures create some of the efficiencies that big data and HPA require. Grid computing enables you to automatically submit jobs to a centrally managed grid of shared computing resources so complex analytics run faster and continuously. Grid computing also lets you leverage the favorable economics associated with low-cost commodity hardware resources. You can add incrementally without disruption, which eliminates the guesswork of sizing your environment for your future needs.

Breakthrough Analysis: From Days to Minutes

In retail, time is the enemy. That's the word from Scott Zucker, vice president of business services for Family Dollar Stores, Inc., operator of 7,100 general merchandise variety stores in 45 states. The company is fighting that enemy by turning to HPA to shrink data-processing speeds from days to less than an hour. That's enabling the company to examine product, time, and location—the critical levers—at a much higher level of granularity than ever before. Where previously Family Dollar looked at class or subclass by week or month, today it's looking at individual stock-keeping units (SKUs) by store and day. And that means the company manages 10 times more data today than it did just five years ago.

"Profit is made—in other words, you win or you lose—at the store/SKU level," he told us. "We used to plan our pricing at the store and SKU level for three- or six-month seasons and hope the financials worked as anticipated. With high-performance analytics, we're crunching through huge levels of data on a daily basis and making changes in a much shorter window. For instance, one process used to take 36 hours to calculate—now, it's less than 45 minutes."

That's the kind of speed that kills—competition. The company can implement a promotion and, within a day, have a solid read on its performance instead of waiting a month to take action. "Look, all analytical exercises are iterative," said Zucker, "and the more complex problems take 6 or 10 iterations. That sort of back-and-forth could take weeks. Now we can show the data the next day. That really has a significant bearing on your ability to improve operations, to move quickly, and shorten the time to results. If you don't have these kinds of tools to deal with big data, you're at a major competitive disadvantage."

PILLAR 2: IN-DATABASE PROCESSING—RAPID INSIGHTS

Scoring 1.2 Trillion Rows of Data

When you buy an item at a retail grocer, chances are you've seen the point-of-sale coupons that emerge from the register, enticing you to return and save on items you're likely to buy or may be interested in. As the largest consumer-behavior marketing company in the world, Catalina Marketing predicts shoppers' buying behaviors to generate customized point-of-sale coupons, ads, and informational messages at 23,000 retailer stores and 14,000 pharmacies across the United States, as well as another 7,000 stores worldwide by analyzing more than 250 million transactions every week.

But Catalina aspired to an even greater level of sophistication and precision. Its recent initiative stores transaction histories over a three-year period on 140 million consumers and uses high-performance analytics to generate more-targeted messages and offers based on that historical knowledge. Eric Williams, Catalina's former executive vice president and chief information officer, explained the rationale to us.

"A hundred years ago, a merchant knew all about you—your purchases, preferences, and tastes," he said. "Today, it's very challenging for a retailer to make the right recommendation for additional products or services to a specific individual based on historical purchases—the volumes have just grown too large. Instead, we've settled for segments of demographically similar customers. But cheap data storage and high-performance analytics are changing that. Now we can arm sales associates with timely and prescient information about what you've purchased previously and what's coming in the next inventory refresh. Now you can have your floor staff equipped with mobile devices displaying that information to give every shopper a personalized experience."

Today, Catalina can build new models in a day, not a month, that enable it to acquire new clients. Those models can more accurately gauge customer preferences—especially for the hundreds of new products that come out every week. Using in-database scoring, the company processes databases with as many as 1.2 trillion rows of information. "We've been helping clients reach the right people with the right messages for 25 years," Williams said. "But with the predictive capabilities of high-performance analytics tapping into the historical purchasing data of almost every grocery shopper in the country, we're able to achieve a greater level of precision than ever before—a level no competitor can touch."

Knowing Which Relationships to Court

With millions of dollars on the line—as well as crucial customer relationships—mobile-phone service providers need to make the right call on past-due accounts. On one hand, late-paying customers will generate profit as long as they are happy. On the other, some delinquent accounts will never pay, so why bother trying to hold onto them?

The trick is separating one from the other—in real time—while they're engaged with the call center. Applying in-database analytics to a model that predicts a customer's propensity to pay, a major U.S. telecommunications service provider brings in millions of dollars each month by knowing which relationships to cultivate—and which ones to hang up on.

Before adding in-database analytics to its IT mix, the provider was already generating $7–$10 million a month from an older version of its propensity model that identified customers more likely to churn. After refining the model and applying in-database analytics, the company added $1 million in revenue.

With in-database analytics, the model comes to the data—stored in a single enterprise data warehouse—instead of moving the data to the model. By eliminating hundreds of steps involved in the process of moving the data and doing the required transformations for analysis, the provider has results in minutes, not hours.

With high-performance analytics, the provider can predict payment, nonpayment, or delinquency for each of its 40 million accounts—not just for a segmented subset, allowing it to make the right decisions.

Call-center representatives access real-time payment predictions about each customer they're talking to, whether by phone or online chat. Based on those insights, the reps can immediately identify the best offer to give each customer. Bringing its refined model to 40 million records— versus extracting, transforming, and loading 350,000 records from different sources and applying the former model—the provider reports an incremental lift of 13 percent, an additional $900,000 to $1.4 million in recouped bad debt each month.

Faster Execution, Greater Efficiency

These kinds of results and financial advantages are happening thanks to *in-database* technologies. This technique uses a massively parallel processing database architecture for faster execution of key data management and analytic development and deployment tasks. The analytical algorithms move closer to the data by running *inside* the database as native routines to avoid time-consuming data movement and conversion. This HPA architecture provides several advantages by helping to

- *Ensure data governance*—In-database analytical processing can reduce or even eliminate the need to replicate or move large amounts of data between data warehouses and the analytical environment or data marts.
- *Increase IT efficiency and decrease costs*—You can use the existing infrastructure and resources, which protects investments and increases operational efficiency, yielding a faster time to value and reducing total cost of ownership.
- *Improve model-scoring performance*—By eliminating the need to move data between modeling environments and the database for analytic scoring, you can more efficiently deploy processing-intensive predictive models and achieve results faster.

Ideally, in-database analytics should support a wide range of third-party data warehouses and databases, including EMC Greenplum, IBM DB2, IBM Netezza, Oracle Exadata, Teradata, and Teradata Aster.

PILLAR 3: IN-MEMORY ANALYTICS

Quickly Responding to Market Preferences and Trends

Macy's, one of the world's largest and best-known retailers, has amassed a huge and loyal base of customers who shop at its stores, by mail order, and online at Macys.com. Like Family Dollar, Macys.com thrives on its ability to analyze its data at the SKU level. "We were aggregating away from products and trying to extrapolate and understand what product assortments are more readily available," said Kerem Tomak, Macy.com's vice president of analytics. "But with high-performance analytics, you can run hundreds or thousands of models at the product level—the SKU level—because you have the big data and the analytics to support those models.

"That's a huge breakthrough for us. Now we can see and understand how the business is performing in the marketplace. We can see how products are selling on Macys.com, for instance, versus how they're selling in stores. Or we can see the impact of our marketing efforts on sales results in both channels. The challenge boils down to the ability to gather big data and turn it into daily insights so that we can respond to any consumer-preference or marketplace changes. High-performance analytics is the way we make that happen."

From 167 Hours to 84 Seconds

Imagine it's your job to manage billions of dollars in consumer mortgages. You'd better know your current risk position pretty much all the time. But what if you had to wait a whole week just to find out where you stand right now? That's how it was for many lenders during the period leading up to the financial crash of 2008. As their portfolios continued to grow, so did their data volumes, meaning they were capturing much more information than they could process. And risk teams simply could not work fast enough to keep pace with demands for new and refined models.

At one industry giant, the risk-management team operated a separate hardware environment to run a performance-intensive routine that identifies characteristics and candidates for modeling. Unfortunately, the average processing time was 6.5 hours, leading most analysts to limit their data explorations due to simple pragmatics. They "settled" because they didn't have time to do their best. Worse, when the modeling team executed the same routines in its production environment, it required 167 hours of processing time—essentially, a full week.

High-performance analytics has turned all that around. Risk assessments that used to take a week are now ready in *just 84 seconds—more than 7,000 times faster!* Analysts now actually have the time—and motivation—to iterate models many more times than previously possible, and they no longer have to make modeling shortcuts to meet computational limitations. And that increased capacity to iterate and experiment is saving the company tens of millions of dollars because better models are being produced.

The company faced similar big data challenges in its marketing operations. To minimize churn, maximize customer lifetime value, and execute more profitable cross-sell and upsell campaigns, the marketing team needs to target as many as 15 million recipients. But it couldn't process all that data without high-performance analytics.

Now, using HPA, the lender has achieved tremendous gains in its database marketing—as much as 215 times faster—dramatically compressing the model-development life cycle and allowing teams to test and validate additional variables for greater reliability in their models. The result: Team productivity has improved dramatically, and the models are more reliable. With 15 million prospects, even a minor improvement to the typical 1 percent response rate quickly translates into tens of millions of dollars in revenue.

Tackling Complex Challenges

In-memory analytics is the pinnacle of HPA. The key is its ability to divide analytic processes into easily manageable pieces with computations distributed in parallel across a dedicated set of processing blades. With in-memory analytics, you can use sophisticated analytics on the biggest data sets ever to tackle complex problems quickly and solve dedicated, industry-specific business challenges faster than ever. Sometimes, the computational breakthroughs come not from the volume of the data involved but also from the CPU-intensive techniques that are required.

In-memory analytics give you concurrent, in-memory, and multiuser access to data, no matter how big or small. This type of HPA software is optimized for distributed, multithreaded architectures and scalable processing, so you can run new scenarios or complex analytical computations extremely fast. You can instantly explore and visualize data and tackle problems you could never feasibly approach due to computing constraints. In-memory analytics lets you

- *Make decisions faster*—You get quick access to more targeted information so you can seize opportunities and mitigate threats in near-real time.
- *Gain more precise answers from complete data*—You can run more sophisticated queries and models using *all* your data to generate more precise models that can improve business performance.
- *Establish a reliable, scalable analytics infrastructure*—Overcome traditional IT constraints, and get answers to difficult business questions quickly, with speed and flexibility.

In-memory analytics was designed expressly to address the complex queries and analyses that leverage big data or need large amounts of computational horsepower such as data exploration, visualization, descriptive statistics, model building with advanced algorithms, and scoring of new data—all at breakthrough speeds. This is the preferred framework for risk management, revenue optimization, text analytics, marketing campaign optimization, analysis of social networks, and other compute-intensive, data-intensive problems.

WHAT DOES IT TAKE TO SUCCEED WITH HIGH-PERFORMANCE ANALYTICS?

HPA isn't simply an incremental discipline. It involves innovative shifts in how we approach analytic problems. We view them differently and continue to find new ways to solve them. It's more than simply taking a serial algorithm and breaking it into chunks. Success requires deeper, broader algorithms in multiple disciplines and the ability to rethink our business processes.

In our experience, HPA solutions to complex business problems require innovation along two different dimensions. First, algorithms and modeling techniques must be invented and built to exploit the power of massively parallel computational environments in three major areas:

- *Descriptive* analytics—You can report and generate descriptive statistics of historical performance that help you see what has transpired far more clearly than ever before.
- *Predictive* analytics—You can use data relationships to model, predict, and forecast business results in impressive ways and predict future events and outcomes.
- *Prescriptive* analytics—You can identify the relationships among variables to develop optimized recommendations that take advantage of your predictions and forecasts and foresee the likely implications of each decision option.*

---

* For more information: http://www.informs.org/Community/Analytics

Second, HPA tools and products must be built, incorporating these high-performance analytics techniques, to enable the following three purposes:

- Visualization and exploration of massive volumes of data
- Creation of analytical models that use multidisciplinary approaches such as statistics, data mining, forecasting, text analytics, and optimization
- Application of domain-specific solutions to complex problems that incorporate both specific analytical techniques as well as the business processes to support decision making

What makes HPA so compelling to businesses across the spectrum—and makes them willing to undertake this fundamental rethinking of analytics—is the ability to address and resolve transformational business problems that have the potential to fundamentally change the nature of the business itself. By processing billions of observations and thousands of variables in near-real time, HPA is unleashing power and capabilities that are without precedent. Your business could witness the same results, for example, by taking the following steps:

- Implementing a data-mining tool that creates predictive and descriptive models on enormous data volumes
- Using those variables to predict which customers might abandon an online application and offer them incentives to continue their session
- Comparing these incentives against one another and the budget, in real time, to identify the best offer for each customer

That's the kind of emphatic value that HPA can provide and why it's continuing to garner the attention of many enterprises today.

CONCLUSION

The HPA journey can take many paths. Since every organization is unique and business needs can vary considerably over time, there isn't any single correct answer when it comes to HPA implementations. In this chapter, we've outlined three HPA approaches that can deliver breakthrough value for enterprises. Each approach has intrinsic value, depending on the nature of the problem at hand. Of course, it is important to note that HPA and big data needn't be inextricably linked. There are some classes of analytic problems that involve only modest amounts of data but are nonetheless compute intensive. These, too, can benefit from HPA techniques and principles.

Amazingly, the discipline of high-performance analytics continues to move forward at a rapid pace. As storage gets even more affordable and greater amounts of processing power become ever-cheaper, it's easy for us to envision "analytical streaming" in real time where insights are not discrete events but are part of the minute-by-minute operation of the enterprise, woven into the fabric of every meaningful business process. Moving further down the cost curve will enable us to further democratize analytics and move it beyond the specialized analyst and into the hands of virtually every employee, increasing the breadth and depth of the value. By pushing out the power of this style of HPA, we have the opportunity to achieve exponentially outsized gains driven by new levels of rapid analysis.

6

Competitors, Intelligence, and Big Data

G. Scott Erickson and Helen N. Rothberg

CONTENTS

INTRODUCTION

The advent of the big data era has brought a lot of different definitions and perspectives. Big data, cloud computing, business intelligence, and other concepts seeping into regular usage can mean different things to different people. This is especially true to those of us who have been working in related areas such as knowledge management and competitive intelligence for a number of years. And then there is the challenge of determining what the changes mean to practices related to knowledge development and knowledge protection.

Our milieu is the intersection of knowledge management (KM) and the development of intellectual capital (IC) juxtaposed with the vulnerability such work creates in relation to competitive intelligence (CI). Essentially, the more organizations codify, digitize, leverage through distribution, and share their whole bundle of knowledge assets throughout their external networks, the more access points they provide for competitor incursions. Thus, there is a strategic balance to be struck between developing knowledge assets and protecting them. Smart organizations will assess costs and benefits of knowledge programs, finding the sweet spot where the competitive gains from better KM are optimized without unduly opening up the firm to competitive efforts.

Big data brings a whole new set of issues to this discussion. Initially, we are now talking about a lot more than "knowledge" assets. The field typically defines data as measures without meaning attached, information is data with organization and meaning, and knowledge is information subjected to reflection (Zack 1999). We've long believed that there was potential value in information and data (*preknowledge*) as well as in the knowledge assets, usually the sole subject of study in our field. Just as IC recognized value in intangible assets beyond formal intellectual property, so big data and its concentration on this preknowledge finds more value beyond standard intellectual capital assets. Data and information are of increasing value and should be managed as an asset just as knowledge and intellectual property are.

Big data also brings cloud computing and remote hosting into the picture. As we'll discuss shortly, this step can place data security in a second party's hands, again raising the stakes on asset vulnerability. Finally, an effective knowledge or preknowledge asset strategy implies recognition of and sensitivity to environmental conditions. The new types of information assets, new sharing and processing conditions, and the nature of the firms involved have the potential to bring new complications to the operating environment of organizations. Essentially, the benefits and risks of pursuing big data solutions are likely to vary dramatically, depending on the circumstances facing individual firms.

Put it all together, and the move toward big data presents an interesting scenario related to how optimize the development and protection of all sorts of intangible assets. In this chapter, we'll look at what we already know about the circumstances that may confront firms in this regard, and raise further questions that decision makers might ask as they strategize their approach to big data and cloud computing.

KNOWLEDGE MANAGEMENT, INTELLECTUAL CAPITAL, AND COMPETITIVE INTELLIGENCE

While space precludes a full background review of key concepts like KM, IC, and CI, a short reminder is in order before we move on to the main discussion. KM refers to activities designed to better manage the knowledge assets or intellectual capital of the organization. This intellectual capital is the collection of intangible assets containing know-how related to job performance (human capital), organizational processes or culture (structural capital), and external relationships (relational capital) (Bontis 1999, Davenport & Prusak 1997, Edvinsson & Malone 1997). So IC refers to the stock of knowledge assets, then KM refers to the strategies and processes for using them to best effect. KM helps to identify the type of knowledge (e.g., tacit/explicit) and then employ the best tools and techniques to exploit it (IT systems, communities of practice, etc.) (Choi & Lee 2003, Schulz & Jobe 2001, Nonaka & Takeuchi 1995, Boisot 1995).

As noted, we have advocated for including additional data and information in this discussion even if the field doesn't generally recognize them as "knowledge." This preknowledge, in enterprise systems, customer relationship management systems, and similar IT structures, can also provide insights, especially to competitors trying to discern the strategic and tactical direction of a firm (Rothberg & Erickson 2005). This stance, of course, leads directly into advocating all of big data as a potential store of value that can be turned to competitive advantage.

The entire process of identifying, codifying/capturing, and sharing preknowledge and knowledge in digital form throughout a firm's network, however, makes it much more vulnerable to competitors employing CI techniques. Competitive intelligence involves the collection of a wide variety of inputs, including publicly available data/information/knowledge, human intelligence, and active gathering, then processing the resulting inputs to better understand and predict competitor strategies and actions (Rothberg & Erickson 2005, McGonagle & Vella 2002, Fleisher & Bensoussan 2002). In a number of ways, CI actually anticipates interest in big data more than KM does. CI has always had a broader view of what pieces of data or information might be of use, and CI operations have typically been more focused on analysis of knowledge and preknowledge assets, looking for insights through correlation and combination. Digging through data to discover unexpected insights is second nature to CI professionals.

In combining the fields, KM/IC and CI, the focus is on how much to develop intangible assets, benefiting from better utilizing scarce and unique knowledge assets, versus the risks of leaving them vulnerable to CI activity from competitors (and surrendering valuable, proprietary knowledge or preknowledge assets). The optimal balance is going to be dependent on circumstances. Reading the environment and discerning the best strategy for KM (full development to minimal investment) and protection from CI (full set of safeguards to no investment at all) is the challenge. Early indications, in line with our research findings, are that big data initiatives will face the same choices.

BIG DATA

As noted at the beginning of this chapter, and as should be obvious from this entire book, big data has a variety of representations. This diversity of understanding and approaches actually makes the point of strategic choice even more important. There isn't necessarily a single optimal path, but a variety of options. And, again, we believe the specific choice or choices made should be made depending on the environment faced by a specific organization.

Our perspective on big data recognizes the advent of low-cost data processing in the last few years. This increase in power and drop in price has allowed virtually anyone to collect substantial amounts of data and subject it to increasingly sophisticated, in-depth analysis, either through investment in their own systems or by using readily available computing power in the cloud (Vance 2011b). The latter is often provided by some of the bigger services providers on the web, such as Amazon, Google, and Microsoft. The availability of computing-on-demand from such providers allows even small players to participate, as data processing power can be rented as needed (Bussey 2011). At the same time, surrendering control over data to a third party raises other issues (*Economist* 2011, Ricadela 2011). Security, of course, is a topic of interest, especially due to the competitive intelligence environment we've been describing. With cloud computing, however, the issue is even more complex as a big processing provider is quite likely to have more advanced and more effective security procedures than a smaller, less-IT-proficient firm that rents capacity from it. In other cases, the provider may have less-effective procedures (or may be a bigger, more obvious target).

A lot of the attention paid to big data has had to do with marketing and operations applications, essentially uncovering and understanding more about customers (especially consumers) and about how an operation, supply chain, or distribution channel performs (Vance 2011a). But there are additional applications. Competitive intelligence can clearly be employed in this manner, adding even more data and information to the process while using ever more processing power and tools. Again, smaller firms may now be able to mount more sophisticated operations and analyses by employing partners in the cloud. Security alternatives can also be explored in greater detail in the cloud, arriving at better solutions whether managed in-house or out (Vance 2011b). Further, the security of the data used and the results needs to be a consideration in this environment as "data is the ultimate proprietary asset" and protection should be explicitly addressed (Karabin 2012).

So a variety of questions exist in exploring the potential for a big data approach. Should the process be in-house or in the cloud? What parts of the business should be improved by means of big data? Who should be responsible for security and to what degree? Should competitive intelligence efforts be used and enhanced by big data?

The answers to these questions will depend on circumstances and so should be subject to a strategic approach. The application of big data already shows some signs of differences depending on industry. Consumer goods and services are obvious areas for use and have been widely reported. Similarly, there appear to be considerable possibilities in financial services (*Economist* 2012). In the same way, security concerns can vary. Legal service providers, for example, have special concerns about cybersecurity (Smith 2012), while a defense provider like Northrup Grumman is one of those reportedly excited by the possibilities of even better security through applications of big data (Vance 2011b).

The question, then, is how decision makers are to assess their own situation. What does one look at to determine whether to invest in big data (and how much) and whether to do it in-house or in the cloud? How much does one invest in security? What access does one allow to the data being processed and to whom?

STRATEGIC PROTECTION FACTORS AND BIG DATA

As a first cut, we offer our framework for assessing knowledge development versus knowledge protection. In our research, we've found a theoretical justification and empirical support for treating this choice as a strategic reaction to competitive conditions mandating aggressive knowledge development (or not) juxtaposed with substantial investment in knowledge protection (or not) (Erickson & Rothberg 2012, Rothberg & Erickson 2005). These conclusions come from analysis of 2,000 firms and five years of financial results combined with data on competitive intelligence activity gathered from a proprietary benchmarking survey conducted by a leading CI consultancy, Fuld & Company. We also conducted a series of in-depth interviews with KM and CI practitioners from a variety of fields. If one begins with an assumption that interest in big data may be related to interest in knowledge management, it's a short step to a connection between our framework and some preliminary guidelines for assessing how to pursue big data. If we do see reasons for divergence between KM and big data, those can be dealt with as adjustments to the overall framework.

In our framework, we construct four broad categories:

- Strategic protection factor (SPF) 45, Cold War, with competitive pressure to develop knowledge assets as well as intense competitive scrutiny and a need to protect those same assets. A high-KM, high-CI environment.
- SPF 30, Glass House, with little competitive pressure to develop knowledge assets but still intense competitive scrutiny. A low-KM, high-CI environment.
- SPF 15, 800-lb. Gorilla, competitive pressure to develop knowledge assets but little competitive scrutiny. A high-KM, low-CI environment.
- SPF 5, Brilliance, little competitive pressure to develop knowledge assets, and little competitive scrutiny. A low-KM, low-CI environment.

Below we consider each in turn, including the specific implications for big data pursuit and protection.

SPF 45 refers to an environment in which knowledge assets are important to the firm to remain competitive and are also of interest to its competitors. Consequently, firms should invest in KM systems to keep up with competitive knowledge development efforts. They must also take steps to protect their proprietary knowledge from competitors. The nature of the knowledge (and preknowledge) assets is such that they are of considerable value to both the originating firm and its competitors.

Our research indicates that this category is filled with industries containing firms with complex operations, where knowledge is important at multiple points along the value chain, sophisticated marketing, and other factors that result in competitors benefiting from aggressive knowledge generation. Based on financial results, industries in this category held firms with an average market capitalization well above the value of physical assets, demonstrating considerable intangible assets. These industries also typically held multiple firms practicing competitive intelligence at relatively advanced levels. CI operations were experienced and plugged into the decision-making hierarchies of numerous firms.

Examples of industries in this category include

- Software
- Pharmaceuticals
- Semiconductors
- Food-based industries (restaurants, grocery retail, processed fruits and vegetables)
- Complex manufacturing (aircraft, communications equipment, guidance systems)

Firms in these industries will have an imperative to develop knowledge assets as their competitors will be building advantage by aggressively compounding their own intangibles. These organizations will also likely need to develop competitive intelligence capabilities of their own while taking steps to secure their proprietary knowledge.

For a number of reasons, we believe these strategies will extend to big data. These sorts of firms appear to possess considerable operational and transactional complexity, generating reams of potentially useful data. Although many are business-to-business rather than business-to-consumer manufacturers or distributors, their businesses are of a type to benefit from deep consumer knowledge further down the line (e.g., software, pharmaceuticals). These scenarios also suggest complicated marketing functions with multiple sales targets and marketing challenges, where deep data analysis could again contribute.

As with KM, however, there are protection issues. Databases from these sorts of firms would be of considerable interest to competitors, so advanced security systems and procedures are required, especially since the networks in which these firms participate can be so extensive and include so many data partners at different levels. One specific recommendation is to install levels of access and exposure to databases. Again, consider the case of pharmaceuticals with independent research partners, healthcare providers, insurers, benefit management firms, regulators, and others all directly involved with their businesses and data-sharing networks. Firms in these industries, however, would often be able to conduct big data analysis in-house, already possessing experience in both processing and protecting such intangible assets. Legacy systems will already exist in many cases as well, providing an additional justification for in-house processing. These firms shouldn't need to rely as much on the security expertise of cloud computing partners.

SPF 30 firms find themselves in industries in which knowledge assets are apparently less important but competitive attention is intense. While this may seem a contradiction, it can be the case that valuable knowledge is of a type that is difficult to manage or share (highly tacit, individualized insights) but that once realized and incorporated into products or practices can be easily and effectively copied by competitors. There is often very little new under the sun, but when there is, competitors are quick to recognize and react.

We identified industries in this category as those with market capitalizations less than or equal to their physical asset value. Intangible assets were worth very little, if anything. While there was undoubtedly valuable knowledge in the heads of employees in these firms, as with all organizations, in this case the knowledge was of a sort that was very difficult for the firm to capture or manage effectively. Hence, heavy investment in KM or advanced KM systems makes very little sense for these types of firms. Gaining an advantage through intangibles may be possible but not to any scalable degree, as with firms possessing more manageable explicit knowledge assets. At the same time, firms in these industries typically face multiple competitors with advanced CI operations. Consequently, these organizations are well advised to mount their own CI effort. They will also benefit from substantive security measures.

Examples of industries in this category include

- Financial services (banks, various insurance, security brokers)
- Mature manufacturing (plastics, inorganic chemicals, miscellaneous chemicals, steel, nonferrous metals)
- Natural resources processing (petroleum and natural gas, lumber and wood)
- Entertainment and communication (cable and other pay television, amusement and recreation, telecommunications)
- Autos (motor vehicle bodies, motor vehicle parts, auto dealers)
- High-level services (advertising, hospitals)

There is some question as to how effective big data approaches might be in these types of industries. Operations and processes are often mature. Customer relationships are also mature and settled. There is very little new under the sun. Although there will be new insights and new initiatives (battery development and hybrid autos, for example), these are not regular enough to justify large-scale investment in either KM systems or in big data, except perhaps on a case-by-case basis. Similarly, when there are flashes of creative insight (advertising, entertainment), these are often highly tacit, specific to a single individual, and hard to extend to others throughout the company. These insights could come from processing and analyzing the massive databases we are discussing in relation to big data, but it is much more hit-and-miss and subject to serendipity.

As a result, firms in these types of industries would be well advised to pursue big data initiatives on a more limited basis. A structure and/or schedule may make sense, but probably still focused on particular projects or particular individuals with precise objectives in mind. Almost certainly, these organizations would want to avail themselves of the cloud rather than build their own processing capacity. Similarly, while firms of this ilk may be accustomed to utilizing security measures, they don't necessarily have a lot of experience protecting knowledge or preknowledge development processes. So employing the cloud, but choosing storage and processing providers with advanced security processes and procedures, would be extremely important. As quickly as insights are copied, the months or weeks gained from utilizing an experienced provider would be worth any additional expense.

SPF 15 industries include firms with considerable potential for developing knowledge assets but very little fear of competitive acquisition and use of the knowledge. Again, this may seem somewhat counterintuitive that knowledge is valuable to one party, the originator, but not others. But we found that firms in this group were often in situations where other factors got in the way of effective competitive intelligence. Scale, an established base, brands, or other such matters could present a challenge to full copying of any insights that may be gained from CI. The classic case is Walmart, where all their competitors know what they do, but the size, scale, relationships, and supply chain–installed base make the firm extremely difficult to copy effectively.

Industries in this category hold firms that, on average, have market capitalizations above, sometimes far above, their physical asset values. So there is direct evidence of valuable intangible assets within these organizations.

But there is little evidence of any organized competitive intelligence activity. If any firms at all are pursuing CI in a given industry, they are doing it at a low level, usually as a side job for someone with responsibilities elsewhere.

As a result, firms in these industries pursue knowledge development rather aggressively and with little fear of copying. Industries are often characterized by differences in the size and dominance of competitors, resulting in knowledge developments hard to duplicate because of scale differential or because a move by a smaller firm isn't worth the bother by a larger one. Competitive intelligence is certainly possible, but what might be discovered is either already right in plain view or impossible to replicate, so a substantial and expensive effort isn't worthwhile. Details will vary by situation, but the end result is a potentially great payoff for knowledge development and a small one for CI, lessening the need for a CI operation or for protection from one.

Examples include

- Branded consumer products (sugar/confectionary, fats/oils, beverages; soaps, perfumes, cosmetics; apparel)
- Fashion retail (all types of apparel, home furnishings)
- Distribution and logistics (variety of wholesalers, freight transport, catalog and mail order, trucking)
- Specialty manufacturing (lab, optical, measuring instruments; special industrial machinery, metalworking machinery, oil and gas field machinery/equipment)
- Mining (metal, coal) and heavy construction
- Specialty retail (drug, auto, and home supply)

A big data approach should be very appealing in these industries. Quite a number are based on operations including some element of logistics, so understanding data is at the core of effective performance. Indeed, the value of knowledge in many of these industries comes from tacit insights concerning logistical and operational details. Big data fit right into this environment. Further, the lack of concern over security is an additional plus. While every firm would want to evaluate its own security situation and vulnerability to competitive intelligence, if it is in an environment with minimal CI arrayed against it, big data can be freely and aggressively employed, in the cloud or in-house. Decisions on where to house the data and analysis can be made on the basis of analytical effectiveness without the security complication. In a number of ways, firms in this category will often have the greatest potential upside from a big data approach.

SPF 5 includes industries in which firms see little benefit from knowledge development and little threat from competitive intelligence. Knowledge assets have relatively little value for either the potential developer or for competitors. Again, there are certainly exceptions and there may be important knowledge, but it is likely to be highly tacit and individual, hard to share or transfer, and therefore of little use in KM or CI systems.

In our research, we grouped industries into this category that held market capitalizations worth less than their physical asset values. And, as in the previous category, if there was any competitive intelligence activity within the industry, it was at low levels. There is very little value assigned to knowledge in these industries, principally because there is little new under the sun and/or new ideas are flashes of individual brilliance that are quite difficult to replicate. Industries tend to be old-line, mature manufacturers and service providers, often regulated. Examples include

- Energy distribution (natural gas transmission, distribution, and transmission/distribution; petroleum bulk stations and terminals; electric services; cogeneration services)
- Transportation (railroads, deep-sea freight transport, air transportation)
- Assorted manufacturing (electric transmission/distribution equipment, industrial organic chemicals, engines and turbines, miscellaneous plastics, printed circuit boards)
- Wood products (paper mills, paperboard mills, lumber wholesale)

Big data would likely have a minimal impact on firms in these industries. Exceptions are always possible, but many of these industries are established, quite mature operations. While a deep database of operational and transactional details is likely available, it's not clear that many valuable insights could be gained from advanced analysis. There is little if any contact with consumers and so little relevant data on their behavior, even far down distribution channels. Further, much of the most valuable knowledge in each industry is already known by major competitors, so there is little point of investing in an aggressive CI operation or worrying about how to guard against one. Given the low cost of outsourcing a big data initiative to the cloud, there may be little downside to starting one at a basic level, but again, there will also be minimal upside for firms in industries with these characteristics.

CONCLUSIONS

The framework laid out in this chapter clearly provides only very broad suggestions. As reiterated several times earlier, any individual firm will need to evaluate its own circumstances to balance the benefits and costs of initiating a big data approach. Similarly, the specific operating environment will also influence choices about how and where to process big data, whether to complement it with a competitive intelligence effort, and how much security will be needed to keep results proprietary.

But we come at this question with a data-driven framework that can serve as a first step in understanding the competitive environment in which data, information, and knowledge are managed and protected. The classifications provide some distinctive results as seen in the commonalities readily apparent within groups and the visible differences across groups. We have worked on analyzing the reasons for the groupings (what explains why semiconductors are in SPF 45 and paperboard mills in SPF 5?) and will continue to do so. Including the variable of valuable proprietary preknowledge, such as that analyzed in big data approaches, can only add to the depth of our understanding.

And, again, if applied as a first look in assessing a firm's data analytics initiative, we believe this approach can be useful. When a firm understands the nature of its industry regarding average and above-average results from knowledge development, it provides an entry to deeper evaluation of its own capability to employ knowledge management tools and what the possibilities are. This can be extended to managing data and data analysis. An industry should reflect the value of intangible assets such as knowledge, information, and data in financial results if they truly help performance. An individual firm can then benchmark its own abilities in these areas against those with which it competes.

Similarly, an industry will reveal a standard level of activity and sophistication of competitive intelligence efforts. Because CI is usually just as interested in preknowledge as in knowledge assets, these metrics shed light on its threat to proprietary data and proprietary knowledge. To be competitive, firms will look to both install CI operations themselves, up to the level of other industry participants, and take security precautions to better protect valuable data assets from threats typical of the industry.

Thus, we see these guidelines as broad and preliminary but also quite useful as a first pass. As we continue to employ them, more and deeper insights should become available, including from those evaluating their approach to big data analytics.

REFERENCES

Boisot, M. (1995), Is your firm a creative destroyer? Competitive learning and knowledge flows in the technological strategies of firms, *Research Policy*, 24: 489–506.

Bontis, N. (1999), Managing organizational knowledge by diagnosing intellectual capital: Framing and advancing the state of the field, *International Journal of Technology Management*, 18: 5–8, 433–462.

Bussey, J. (2011), Seeking safety in clouds, *The Wall Street Journal*, (September 16), B8.

Choi, B., & Lee, H. (2003), An empirical investigation of KM styles and their effect on corporate performance, *Information & Management*, 40: 403–417.

Davenport, T.H., & Prusak, L. (1997), *Working knowledge: How organizations manage what they know*, Boston: Harvard Business School Press.

Economist (2011), Online reputations in the dirt, (April 30), 65.

Economist (2012), Crunching the numbers (Special report on international banking), (May 19), 11–14.

Edvinsson, L., & Malone, M. (1997), *Intellectual capital*, New York: Harper Business.

Erickson, G.S., & Rothberg, H.N. (2012), *Intelligence in action: Strategically managing knowledge assets*, Houndsmills, UK: Palgrave Macmillan.

Fleisher, C.S., & Bensoussan, B. (2002), *Strategic and competitive analysis: Methods and techniques for analyzing business competition*, Upper Saddle River, NJ: Prentice Hall.

Karabin, J. (2012), Big data, bigger risks, *Technology Spectator*, http://technologyspectator. com.au/big-data-bigger-risks, accessed August 29, 2012.

McGonagle, J., & Vella, C. (2002), *Bottom line competitive intelligence*, Westport, CT: Quorum Books, Inc.

Nonaka, I., & Takeuchi, H. (1995), *The knowledge-creating company: How Japanese companies create the dynamics of innovation*, New York: Oxford University Press.

Ricadela, A. (2011), Raining on the cloud's parade, *Bloomberg Businessweek*, (September 5), 54–56.

Rothberg, H.N., & Erickson, G.S. (2005), *From knowledge to intelligence: Creating competitive advantage in the next economy*, Boston: Elsevier Butterworth-Heinemann.

Schulz, M., & Jobe, L.A. (2001), Codification and tacitness as knowledge management strategies: An empirical exploration, *Journal of High Technology Management Research*, 12: 139–165.

Smith, J. (2012), Lawyers get vigilant on cybersecurity, *The Wall Street Journal*, (June 25), B5.

Vance, A. (2011a), The data knows, *Bloomberg Businessweek*, (September 12), 70–74.

Vance, A. (2011b), The power of the cloud, *Bloomberg Businessweek*, (March 7), 52–59.

Zack, M.H. (1999), Managing codified knowledge. *Sloan Management Review*, (Summer), 45–58.

7

Saving Lives with Big Data: Unlocking the Hidden Potential in Electronic Health Records

Juergen Klenk, Yugal Sharma, and Jeni Fan

CONTENTS

What if you could be alerted, perhaps through your smartphone, that you may be about to have a heart attack, stroke, or some other medical event—well before its onset? And that this warning would be based not on commonly recognized symptoms but on a sophisticated data analysis of your vital signs and other health information. In such a scenario, your medical data would be continuously monitored and scanned by powerful computers searching for complex patterns—the patterns of thousands of heart attack or stroke victims, for example, whose pre-event data looked just like yours do now. Alerted to the danger in real time, you could seek emergency medical attention.

While this capability is not yet at hand, advanced research by teams of physicians and data scientists is yielding promising results. In a significant collaboration, Booz Allen Hamilton and a large hospital system in the Midwest set out to find whether a data analysis of past patients' medical records could help hospitals deal with dangerous, hard-to-treat infections. Their research discovered previously unknown patterns in the historical data that could predict when such infections might suddenly become particularly life threatening.

This is big data—but with a twist. While most analytics rely on the latest available information—to look for emerging business trends, for example—this kind of analysis instead looks backward with big data to try to predict the future. The U.S. government is now at the cutting edge of this approach, developing highly sophisticated techniques to find patterns in past activity that might anticipate threats such as terrorism and cyberattacks on our nation's infrastructure. Other sectors may well find benefit in this approach. Government financial regulators trying to prevent another meltdown, for example, might look at the historical data patterns of banks that failed and see whether similar patterns are emerging in banks today.

In medicine, such an approach could be applied to a host of diseases and conditions—with the potential to save many lives. Just a few years ago, that would not have been possible. But with the rapidly growing transition from paper to electronic health records, vast amounts of medical data are now becoming accessible to researchers. At the St. Louis–based Mercy health system, which collaborated with Booz Allen on the study, Dr. Thomas Hale says that until about five years ago, all of Mercy's patient records were on paper. And collecting data for research was difficult. "To get the data, I had to hire a nurse—and we were lucky if we could collect data on a hundred patients." With the move to electronic health records, he says, "We're now collecting data on three million patients."

Such a wealth of current and historical patient information is one of the key requirements in using data analysis to predict future medical events. If health data analysts are to find critical hidden patterns—if they are to pinpoint clear signals through all the noise—they need as rich a data source as possible.

This search for patterns in data from electronic health records represents a new but valuable tool for physicians. Dr. Hale, the executive medical director of Mercy's Center for Innovative Care, says that traditionally, "Someone comes into our office and gives us symptoms, and we know what the disease is. What we're saying now is, what else is the data showing us that we need to explore? This is entirely different from what we're used to doing as physicians."

Dr. Hale compares the process to that in *Moneyball*, the popular book and movie in which the Oakland A's baseball club achieved success by using computer analysis to find undervalued players. "You take the data and find data points you would not have traditionally suspected," says Dr. Hale.

SURVIVING SEPSIS

The project had its origins in an annual employee ideas contest at Booz Allen, the strategy and technology consulting firm. Among the winning entries of the 2010 contest was the notion that electronic health records might be leveraged to improve the quality of healthcare and patient outcomes. Booz Allen agreed to fund the idea, and the company reached out to Mercy. Booz Allen had previously worked with the 31-hospital system and knew it had large numbers of electronic health records that might be suitable for the research project. Mercy was interested.

The next step was to settle on what disease or condition to research. Booz Allen wanted to pick an area that would have a major impact on Mercy and would provide insights that could be used right away. Clinicians at Mercy suggested studying severe sepsis and septic shock, which are conditions that kill hundreds of thousands of patients at hospitals nationwide each year. Severe sepsis occurs when a localized infection spreads throughout the entire body, causing vital organs, such as the lungs or kidneys, to shut down. Often such infections are hospital acquired, originating when the body's primary barriers are compromised. And because the microorganisms causing the infection may be resistant to common treatments—often due to the widespread use of antibiotics—severe sepsis is notoriously hard to treat. According to the Surviving Sepsis Campaign, a global collaboration by healthcare organizations and professionals, 30 to 35 percent of severe sepsis patients do not survive. Even more deadly is septic shock, which occurs when the organ that fails is the heart. At that stage the patient is typically receiving active treatment in the intensive care unit (ICU)—yet even so, the death rate is about 50 percent.

Dr. Hale likens the progression of sepsis to pouring water into a glass, with severe sepsis occurring when the glass is almost full, and septic shock occurring when the water overflows. The key, he says, is catching sepsis early. "Once you're septic, you start showing signs and symptoms, and the problem is they're not always picked up in time," he says. "The reason you have such a high morbidity is that you may not catch it in the early stages, when it is tissue inflammation and not organ failure."

Mercy initially wanted to use the data analysis to find out how well its hospitals were complying with treatment "bundles," or protocols, developed by the Surviving Sepsis Campaign. The protocols call for taking certain lab tests and administering antibiotics and fluids—all in a particular order and within a specific time frame. Sepsis treatment is generally not standardized in hospitals across the country. Physicians might order one test but not another, or they might prescribe the antibiotics but not the fluids, or they might take the individual steps out of order or outside the time frame.

Mercy also wanted to know the correlation between compliance with the protocols and patient mortality. That question was critical, because although the protocols had been compiled as best practices by healthcare experts, they had never been systematically tested on a large scale. Such a task would have been extremely difficult with paper health records, because of the need to track the relationship between a number of individual steps that may or may not have been applied to each individual patient.

A second major goal of the research with Mercy was early detection. The analysts wanted to see whether an analysis of data from previous patients, whose conditions had worsened into severe sepsis, might reveal previously unknown patterns in vital signs and other readings. If so, those patterns might be used to identify current patients who were at high risk for severe sepsis.

While both parts of the project called for extracting data from electronic health records, the search for patterns represented new ground for the Booz Allen–Mercy study team. As far as could be determined, this would be one of the first times a data analysis had been performed on electronic health records to try to predict the onset or worsening of a condition or disease. Similar research has since been conducted or is now underway at other facilities, but at the time, the Booz Allen and Mercy analysts and clinicians were on their own.

Although electronic health records offer valuable opportunities for data analysis—they are a far cry from paper records—they offer their own substantial challenges. Most electronic patient records are intended to be read by people, not computers, and do not naturally lend themselves to data analysis. In addition, the sheer volume of information in electronic health records is daunting—each one used by Mercy, for example, has about

8,000 fields in which information can be entered. These fields catalog every last detail of a patient's hospital stay, from symptoms and vital signs to tests, treatments, medications, and a host of other factors that are duly noted along the way. To complicate matters, vendors of health-records software typically establish their own sets of information fields and design particular ways that medical professionals can view the data—such as bar graphs that show the number of patients with a certain diagnosis. This lack of standardization among vendors can make it difficult to compare records among hospitals that are using different systems.

NEW APPROACHES TO GATHERING DATA

To solve such problems, the Booz Allen–Mercy team gathered information from the electronic records in an innovative way. Their approach was drawn from work conducted by Booz Allen in collaboration with the U.S. government. Intelligence analysts searching for terrorists and other threats need the ability to paint a comprehensive picture that considers all kinds of data at once. Booz Allen and the government addressed this problem by developing what is called a *data lake*—a new kind of information repository that is beginning to change the shape of data analysis.

Data lakes represent a completely different mindset from current advanced analytic techniques like data mining. Users no longer need to move from database to database, pulling out the specific information they need. With a data lake, the information from any number of databases is essentially dumped into a common pool, making it easier to ask bigger, more complex questions.

Just as important are the new ways that all of this pooled information can be used. Analysts now typically search for answers by creating limited datasets and then asking specific questions based on hypotheses of what the data might show. A keyword search of a database is a simple example, though the questions can become extremely detailed. If users want to ask different kinds of questions, they often have to reengineer both the databases and the analytics involved—a process that can be prohibitively long and expensive. This tends to limit the complexity of the questions that are asked. Not so with the data lake, which frees users to easily tap all of the data in a variety of constantly changing ways.

Perhaps the most transformative aspect of an analytics architecture that incorporates a data lake is that users do not need to have the possible answers in mind when they ask questions. Instead, they can "let the data talk to them." The ability to make complex inquiries, easily switching in and out any number of variables, allows users to look for patterns and then follow them wherever they may lead. This is particularly important in predictive analytics, when people may not know exactly what they are looking for.

The Booz Allen–Mercy team adopted several of these techniques, though their task was simplified because all of the information used in the study came from a single source, Mercy's electronic records. As similar studies become more complex—using electronic health data from many different sources in all types of formats—comprehensive data lakes will be essential. It would be impossible otherwise to analyze so much varied information—and find the critical patterns within it.

A QUESTION OF TIME

Although the data for the sepsis study came from only one place, there was a great deal of it. The study team collected anonymous data from the electronic health records of 27,000 Mercy sepsis patients from four hospitals over a two-year period. Most had a mild form of the condition, but about 6,000 had advanced to the more life-threatening stages of severe sepsis and septic shock. Of the data fields available in the electronic records, the team chose the most relevant 4,000 for the study—giving them more than a hundred million separate pieces of patient information to work with.

But it was not enough to simply collect the information. Before the analysis could begin, the team needed to establish an *ontology*—or set of organizing principles—for the data. This was needed so that the team could ask questions of the data and get answers in a way that would make sense for the study. Essentially, an ontology gives the raw data its needed context for analysis. This was particularly important here because electronic health records have no inherent organization or context. Each record is just a collection of disparate and often loosely related information about an individual patient.

The study team ultimately chose as the primary organizing principle one that cut across all of the data—time. Each bit of patient information—each test, each vital sign, each treatment—would be put in chronological order. Such an *event-centric ontology* was a natural choice for the study's goals. Determining whether Mercy's hospitals followed the treatment protocols for sepsis—which called for taking certain steps in the right sequence and time frame—dictated organizing the data by time. The same was true if the team was to determine whether a certain action (precisely following the treatment protocols) led to a certain outcome (a lower mortality rate). And, of course, the team needed to see the data in chronological order to determine whether progression of the condition could be predicted.

Electronic health records themselves are not organized by time. A list of tests given to a patient, for example, will not necessarily be shown in chronological order. However, organizing the data for analysis in this manner was possible for the team because of a key feature of electronic health records—every item entered into a patient's file is electronically stamped with the date and time. Or at least should be, in theory—a small percentage of the data did not have a stamp. A larger challenge lay in dealing with time stamps that were inaccurate. It was not uncommon to see events occurring in an illogical order—time stamps might show blood being drawn, for example, after the patient left the hospital.

The team discovered several reasons why time-stamp problems occurred, including that clocks in different computer systems were not synchronized, or that there was too big a gap between the time that tests and medications are administered and when the information was entered into the system. Such gaps in time logic were flagged automatically during the process of preparing the millions of pieces of data for analysis. Team members resolved some of the discrepancies by talking to the doctors and nurses who had treated the patients, though in other cases information had to be left out. While the study would have been stronger had all the information been usable, the team concluded there was enough data available to have confidence in the study's conclusions.

In preparing the data, one other task was necessary—standardizing the medical language so that drug names, units of measurement, test results, and other information were expressed in a consistent manner. For that, the team leveraged an open-source medical vocabulary software known as SNOMED CT.

The entire process of collecting, preparing, and integrating the data—all before it could be analyzed—consumed the lion's share of the time the team spent on the study. This is typical in data analysis, where many of the most difficult challenges lie in the preliminary spadework.

EVALUATING COMPLIANCE

The study team then began its analysis. The first task step was to determine how well Mercy was following the severe sepsis protocol bundle. Using data from the four hospitals, the team looked at how often all the elements of the bundle were adhered to—that is, whether doctors ordered all the lab tests and treatments, and whether they did so in the prescribed order and time frame. The analysis revealed that this compliance occurred with about 17 percent of sepsis patients. That figure was in line with estimates that compliance at hospitals nationwide is generally under 20 percent.

This part of the analysis also examined the impact that compliance had on patient mortality rates. It found a direct correlation—the greater the compliance with the protocols, the fewer patients died of severe sepsis or septic shock. For example, at the hospital with the lowest compliance—just 10 percent—nearly 60 percent of patients died. At the hospital with the highest compliance, where the protocols were precisely followed about half the time, only about 20 percent of the patients died. While the results were perhaps not surprising, they marked the first time the severe sepsis bundle had been tested through data analysis using electronic health records. What ultimately made this possible was the unique ability to analyze large amounts of patient data in chronological order.

The results had an immediate impact on Mercy. Officials quickly began an initiative to make sure the sepsis protocols were implemented at its hospitals. "When we saw the numbers, it was a wake-up call," says Dr. Timothy Smith, vice president of research at Mercy. "We didn't waste any time—people's lives were at stake."

Smith says one reason for low compliance is that the doctors most familiar with sepsis bundles tend to be in intensive care units, where patients with advanced stages of the condition, severe sepsis and septic shock, are typically treated. Doctors on the hospital floor or in the emergency room do not typically manage advanced cases and so are less familiar with the protocols. However, says Dr. Smith, it is critical that sepsis be recognized and treatment initiated in the condition's earliest stages—before it becomes life threatening and the patient is transferred to the ICU.

In a pilot program at its St. Louis hospital, Mercy educated doctors and nurses on sepsis and the sepsis bundles and took steps to make sure the protocols were implemented in a timely manner—for example, expediting the delivery of antibiotics from the hospital pharmacy.

The results of that effort have been remarkable. Because the protocols are being used earlier and more often, many more patients are surviving the dangerous advanced stages of sepsis. During the first nine months of the pilot program, the mortality rate for patients at the hospital with severe sepsis was cut almost in half—from 28 percent to 14.5 percent. The results for patients with septic shock, which causes heart failure, were even more significant. Prior to the initiative, about 47 percent of septic shock patients died, slightly below the national average. That figure dropped to just 18.5 percent. Mercy estimates that in this initial period alone, the pilot program saved nearly 100 lives. Says Dr. Smith, "We anticipate lives saved to be in the thousands once the program is generalized to all our hospitals."

EARLY DETECTION

Those kinds of outcomes were just what Booz Allen was hoping for when it set out to study how applying data analysis to electronic health records might positively impact patient care. But the research team wanted to take it a step further and see whether even more lives could be saved by actually predicting the severe worsening of sepsis—so that patients could be treated before the condition got out of hand.

For this part of the study, the team examined the data of septic patients whose condition had worsened into severe sepsis. The hope was that advanced data analysis might reveal certain patterns in the data that could serve as red flags. It was here that the team members were asking that the data "talk" to them. Since the analysts didn't know in advance what those red flags might be, they needed to see whether patterns might emerge on their own. This required an entirely new level of data analysis, one more sophisticated than the examination of compliance with sepsis protocols.

The study focused on three key vital signs—heart rate, respiratory rate, and temperature. Here again, the organization of the data by time was critical. A single reading of a vital sign may or may not mean anything. But how vital signs change in combination over time can be far more revealing—that is where crucial patterns begin to emerge.

The team analyzed the progression of the three vital signs of about 1,500 patients who started out with uncomplicated sepsis. About 950 of those patients went on to develop severe sepsis. Were there differences in the progression of vital signs between the patients whose conditions worsened and those who did not worsen? Could those differences reveal previously unknown red flags that might lead to earlier diagnosis?

During the analysis, several important patterns did in fact emerge. And these enabled the study team to create a computer model that could predict when a patient is at high risk of moving into severe sepsis. The model was preliminary, requiring further development and testing. But it demonstrated that advanced analytics applied to electronic health records could provide insight into the progression of many diseases and conditions.

In practice, patients diagnosed with uncomplicated sepsis are typically already receiving the necessary treatment, and knowing they are at risk of developing severe sepsis may not prompt a different course of action. But the value of the study was that it found indicators the patient might be *worsening,* at no matter what stage of sepsis—that the glass of water, in Dr. Hale's analogy, is steadily filling. Such information is critical for early diagnosis and treatment.

THE NEXT PHASE: CONTINUOUS MONITORING

Early warnings—of sepsis or any other condition—can be fully effective only if patients are continuously monitored. While such monitoring does occur in intensive care units, the vital signs of non-ICU patients around the country are typically taken only once every eight hours, or perhaps once every four hours for patients who need closer observation. One of the frustrating challenges of sepsis is that those time frames are often not enough to catch the condition before it rapidly spins out of control.

Until recently, continuous monitoring on all hospital floors was not practical. However, new technologies, including inexpensive, noninvasive monitoring strips, are now becoming widely available. As part of a new "virtual sepsis initiative," Mercy is beginning to use these monitoring strips to capture real-time, continuous biometric data on patients receiving care in non-ICU beds. In this project, patients hospitalized with simple sepsis or considered to be at risk for sepsis are being monitored for signs that they might be progressing to severe sepsis or septic shock. The idea, says Dr. Smith, is to try to detect such a progression as early as possible and speed the implementation of all the sepsis bundle elements. The patients' doctors are looking not only for the previously known symptoms of sepsis but also for several of the new indicators that were uncovered by the Booz Allen–Mercy study.

For example, says Dr. Smith, the data analysis revealed that an important indicator may be when the heart rate and respiratory rate go up at the same time—something doctors had not been fully aware of. Although the simultaneous rising of the two rates doesn't by itself indicate sepsis, he says, it does show that the patient is experiencing the kind of distress that sepsis can cause. And it can help alert doctors that a patient not known to have sepsis might have the condition, or that a patient already diagnosed might be worsening into a more severe state.

Advanced analytics does not supplant the doctor's traditional approach, but rather aids it by providing new and perhaps critical information. As Dr. Hale puts it, "We still want to look at the patient heuristically and use our experience. But now here's more information about a patient that will help us make our decision."

INTERPRETING DOCTORS' AND NURSES' NOTES

While the Booz Allen–Mercy study was limited in scope, it laid the foundation for several areas that will require further study. One was the thorny challenge of doctors' and nurses' notes. Such notes often contain important information about patients that do not necessarily appear in one of the data fields—for example, a doctor might write that a patient was sweating profusely or had significant pallor. This kind of "unstructured" information could be valuable to data analysts looking for patterns in patient symptoms, and it often may be needed to gain a full picture. What this means is that if electronic health records are to be used to their full potential, researchers will have to find a way to turn those notes into a format that can be analyzed.

The common approach to translating prose into computer speak is known as natural language processing, but notes from doctors and nurses do not easily lend themselves to this technique. Most natural language processing is designed for complete, properly ordered sentences. Doctors' and nurses notes, in contrast, are typically filled with sentence fragments, medical shorthand, and other quirks such as the framing of patient conditions in the negative—as in, "The patient was *not* sweating."

The study team attacked this challenge by bringing together a variety of natural language processing techniques, many of them developed at academic institutions and placed in the public domain. Team members selected the most suitable techniques and then customized them specifically for use on electronic medical records. Because of the study's time constraints, the team was not able to incorporate enough information from the doctors' and nurses' notes to have a significant impact on the study results. However, the progress made by the study team will help point the way for further research.

TOWARD THE FUTURE

The study's success in finding predictive patterns in historical medical data has important implications for the future of healthcare. As electronic health records become commonplace, large amounts of patient data on virtually every condition and disease will be available for analysis. While initial research is likely to continue to focus on identifying infections in hospitals, data analysts and doctors will eventually be able to aim their sights in almost any direction.

An area that holds particular promise is mobile patient monitoring, which frees doctors to keep an eye on patients out of the hospital setting as they go about their daily lives. Although several forms of mobile monitoring have been widespread for years, they currently do not leverage the kind of data analysis of historical electronic health records that was explored by Booz Allen and Mercy. Matching historical patterns with a patient's continuous readings would greatly expand the ability of doctors to catch and even predict worsening conditions before they turn dangerous.

New kinds of mobile monitoring devices to make this possible are emerging, from wristbands to skin patches to pills that send out data from the gut. The opportunity lies not only in providing better care to the individual patients being monitored but also in analyzing all of these new streams of information—to constantly build and refine even better predictive models.

There are limitations, of course, on the ability to anticipate how and when a patient's condition may change. The further in advance one tries to predict, the lower the accuracy will be. It may not be possible to look around 10 corners, but advanced data analytics may help doctors look around one or two. And having crucial information about that short time frame may be all that is necessary to save a patient's life, whether in a hospital setting or on the street.

The application of advanced data analytics to electronic health records is just beginning, but early studies, such as the one by Booz Allen and Mercy, show great promise. The healthcare community, which has been adopting electronic records, now faces a new challenge—how to take full advantage of them to benefit patients and reduce medical costs. This challenge was reflected in a provision of the federal stimulus legislation that gives medical care providers financial incentives for the "meaningful use" of electronic health records. The Booz Allen–Mercy study demonstrated how data analytics can help achieve that goal.

It also suggested how the meaningful use of data might be considered in other areas of business. As in healthcare, just amassing big data is not enough—it is what you do with it that counts. "From my standpoint," says Dr. Hale, "if you take the clinical aspect out of it, these are all the various things one wants to do in business." The key, he says, is in "finding data points that are easy to monitor, but that you didn't realize actually had an impact on your business. You use that to improve your business practices and make a positive change."

8

Innovation Patterns and Big Data

Daniel Conway and Diego Klabjan

CONTENTS

INTRODUCTION

Big data is often generated by devices configured for collection based on the occurrence of events. Events can occur based on scan rates (collect yield from a combine every five seconds), from status change (pitch is a strike, count is now 3-1), or from rule execution (S&P 500 VIX > 24.5). Domains such as finance and physics, where big data was first collected and analyzed, were the first to create new theories and innovative new markets, and those innovations are now finding their way into domains where data collection has recently become feasible. For example, the financial options pricing method known as Black–Scholes is now used to estimate the future value of baseball players. These innovations are often the answer to questions formulated with innovation theory. Innovation theory would suggest new domains where big data is now available, and it should allow for the creation of new markets based on predictive analytics applied over robust event histories. We look at these innovation patterns and apply them to the important area of global food supply with particular focus on the opportunities the agricultural market participants will encounter while moving from traditional manufacturing and distribution to competing on analytics over big data.

Big data is a hype peddler's dream come true. *Big* is somewhat ambiguous and modestly confident, yet invokes a sense of challenge. What's big to me might not be big to you, and what's big to you today might not be big to you next month. It is a fairly versatile term and thus likely enduring. *Data* is somewhat dormant and passive, yet invokes a sense of opportunity. Data can be dense with value or sparse. It can be meaningless unless combined with other data. It can be useful at one time and useless at another time. Perhaps Yogi Berra might have given clarity to the term as well as anyone: Data ain't big until it's big.

An economic approach might require coupling big data with analytics and thus attempt to measure the derived value based on the computational effort expended. The cost side of this effort is often estimated with the usual suspects of CPU/cluster cycles, storage costs, labor, and utilization rates for cloud services, for example. If we consider the three Vs of big data (velocity, volume, and variety), then our traditional measures primarily address velocity and volume. The variety of data implies the need for integration, and while we have improved data integration in practice, it remains an endeavor with domain-specific challenges.

The value side of the economic approach involves a transformation from digital assets into actionable insights. The difficulty in measures of value is that one often doesn't know how the assets will be leveraged in the future if at all. In this chapter, we examine how process innovation can help guide this transformation with particular emphasis in the agricultural production domain.

CONTEXTS FOR UNDERSTANDING BIG DATA

Big data has been described in several ways in this text alone, so we will instead examine the context in which the term exists. Below, we briefly discuss some of the more popular contexts in use today.

Big Data as a Natural Resource

IBM has described big data as a new form of natural resource [1]. This is an appealing analogy as it associates a visual process such as panning for gold nuggets with something that is more difficult to conceptualize: terabytes, petabytes, exabytes, zettabytes, and yottabytes. It offers the lure of "hitting it big," untapped wealth, and new frontiers to those willing to partake in the romance of adventure.

Natural resources typically need to be mined and combined, which makes the analogy helpful, as data often has to be mined and combined to produce value. We often learn and improve our processes over time, making this extraction and transformation more efficient with physical as well as information assets. These efficiency improvements help make extraction of previously sparse resources worthwhile to undertake.

Natural resources are often associated with scarcity. Roughly 130,000 tons of gold are estimated to exist today, or roughly $1,000 per person on earth. Gold has perceived value partially because of this scarcity. Big data on the other hand is not scarce, nor is it of fixed supply. In fact, it has the potential to grow faster than our ability to store and process it. In that sense, natural resource is not a fitting label.

The term *natural resource* also implies a form of commoditization. Gold is gold in every context. With big data, this is often not the case. Some data is simply more valuable than other data. Certainly all data is not the same in terms of sensitivity and ownership. Natural resources have sophisticated marketplaces for buying and selling product due to this commoditization, and perhaps big data has similar markets emerging for trading particular types of somewhat commoditized data.

Big Data as Big Digital Inventory

By *digital inventory* (DI), we are referring broadly to digitized representations of system states and persisting in storage including databases, blogs, images, videos, chats, logs, e-mail, transaction data, click traffic, and so on. Information, as described by Varian and Shapiro's *Information Rules* [2], has the property that it is expensive to produce and inexpensive to reproduce. Examples of this include the Windows operating system, the Beatles' White Album, and the latest *Batman* movie. To be fair to Hal Varian, his study was the economics of information and not the economics of data, though much of his thinking applies to both. Varian's work became the blueprint for Google of course, and his economic predictions regarding software pricing continue to play out as he suggested years ago.

DI differs from our standard concept of physical inventory (PI) in several other ways. The cost of maintaining, duplicating, moving, and accessing DI is typically lower than its PI counterpart, and the speed at which data manipulation occurs implies a different risk profile. PI is often viewed as a manifestation of a process problem, and methodologies such as Quick Response Manufacturing [3] and Just-in-Time approaches tend to categorize PI as an undesirable asset. Physical inventories rarely inspire innovation the way digital inventories do today.

Within the context of inventory, how does DI differ from big DI? In some ways, big DI moves us closer to the PI paradigm. Big DI is not easy to transport, and the storage costs are not trivial. Big DI is not easy to duplicate compared to the White Album. Big DI exposes bottlenecks in bandwidth, which is not a uniformly available resource, especially in agricultural infrastructure.

In some ways, big DI is partially a return to centralized computing of the 1960s and 1970s, before we distributed our data to personal productivity tools such as spreadsheets. As for a centralized data store, we have returned to the model where we send the software programs to the data rather than the data to the programs. The programs use less bandwidth. Centralization of data has many positive features that were lost when data became distributed, including enforceable data access control, version control (integrity), and disaster recovery/business continuity. Of course, Microsoft Excel is an easier tool for most users than Hadoop, so there is a reason we moved toward distribution in the first place.

All in all, big data does have a different set of economic realities than data that we commonly manipulate with workstations. In the context of inventory management, big DI is more closely aligned with DI than with PI.

Big Data as a More Granular View of the Past

Eventually, we ask what data is being captured, and most often the simple answer is that big data represents a more granular view of the past. We would thus expect the most potential value-add for big data analytics to occur in efforts that leverage information about the past to help drive decisions about the future.

Better granularity about the past would include data from automated sources, such as sensors, radio-frequency identification readers, and telecommunications infrastructure. For example, a combine is very similar to a process control plant, with the onboard computer system generating machine data (pressures, temperatures, flow rates, fuel usage) and agronomic data (geospatial yield) with as much granularity as the system configuration requests. That could be every second or every square foot of a worksite. The ability to generate big data in this context far exceeds the storage and bandwidth capacities. This is true in many contexts. Like other industries, the value proposition is just emerging to drive the capacity enhancements.

Big data is also generated from media such as images, audio, video, transactions from enterprise resource planning systems, logs from web products and GPS devices, and many other sources. They represent both past events as well as reactions to those events. A more granular record of the past can provide more accurate inputs for existing forecasting models. More granular data can also drive more robust postanimations in domains where visualization can be of value.

Big Data and Organizational Challenges

One of the more interesting Vs of big data is variety, and that variety might mean data sources are beyond an organization's boundaries. Interorganizational systems have never been trivial to design, negotiate, or manage, and we don't expect interorganizational systems leveraging big data to simplify any of those issues.

Consider the granular data describing the life cycle of a corn plant. A seed is planted and the planting device can record the depth, soil moisture, soil composition, below- and above-ground temperature, seed type, geospatial (longitude, latitude, altitude), and other features. Upon harvest, the real-time yield can be transmitted to a farm management information system or a distant location. Parties interested in the success of this process include the seed company; the equipment manufacturer; the Department of Agriculture; university researchers; commodities trading firms; food storage, distribution, and processing facilities; and even international food distribution charities. In essence, a real-time view of the global food supply chain could present tremendous opportunities for efficiency gains in practice and substantial reduction in production variance in poor world regions, but also present huge risks that accompany complex financial risk taking. It is an important problem.

Big Data as a Role in Process Innovation

A decision process is composed of a set of activities, an order of execution of those activities, and decision rules to determine path choices. Innovation can occur within the activities of the process, as a driver for process redesign, or within the rules. Innovation can be done individually or through collaboration. Big data can have a role in each element of the process.

A common procedure is to first map the process using a flowcharting tool such as Business Process Modeling Notation (BPMN 2.0 specification can be found at http://www.omg.org/spec/BPMN/2.0/). Figure 8.1 is an example of a BPMN mapping for a harvest process containing both user tasks and information tasks. The swim lanes represent different roles in the process, here National Weather Service, farm management information system, big data services, and market. The swim lanes represent participant roles. The details are unimportant.

If one were going to determine how big data might participate in the above service-oriented process description, one would go through each of the information tasks (weather forecast, yield forecast, market price forecast) and ask if having big data would improve the accuracy of the prediction. One might next ask how big data might change the order of activities or eliminate the need for other activities. Finally, one might ask if big data might change the rules driving the decisions. This could be done collaboratively or individually.

There are many process flowcharting languages, but determining the impact of big data should follow a similar procedure:

1. Map the process using a visual tool.
2. Partition the process into the artifacts of rules, activities, and sequencing.
3. Determine how big data might impact the artifacts.

By considering the most important organizational processes, we prevent the accumulation of big data for the sake of big data, and keep the focus on the competitive advantage, our business process.

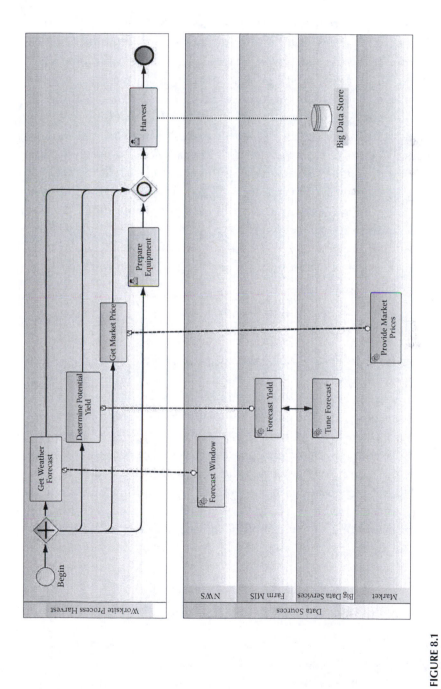

FIGURE 8.1

Example BPMN mapping for a harvest process containing both user tasks and information tasks.

P-TRIZ: REPEATABLE PROCESS INNOVATION

There are many process flowcharting languages because each has a particular strength. BPMN (used in the example shown above) is designed to be executable (zero code), which appeals to many who are interested in process agility. Event-driven process-mapping languages such as SAP's event process chain are useful for visualizing transaction-oriented processes driven by events. Howard Smith introduced a process flowcharting technique [4, 5] based on a cause–effect mapping, which is particularly well suited to innovation. It is based on TRIZ, a theory of inventive problem solving introduced by Russian researchers who studied the patterns of how patents evolve and what question patterns they seem to answer. TRIZ is one of many innovation theories but has the appealing feature of simplicity, allowing innovation on the fly without the need for computation assistance. Readers familiar with the process form of TRIZ may want to skip to the applications section as we cover the notation and some basic innovation option patterns.

Notation

Activities (functions, operations, processes) in P-TRIZ are characterized as being either useful or harmful. Figure 8.2 shows useful and harmful activities. Figure 8.3 shows activities related by arrows, which signify inputs, outputs, causes, and effects. Figure 8.4 shows an example of a process pattern using the above mapping notation.

We can give several examples of process-pattern mapping using BPMN. For example, enterprise resource planning systems standardize processes but stifle innovation. Cloud computing simplifies IT operations but reduces the effectiveness of an internal IT audit. RFID sensors offer a real-time view of a supply chain but introduce additional IT management complexity. It may be difficult to come up with an IT function that

FIGURE 8.2
Useful activities are in light gray and harmful are in dark gray.

Produces a useful function	
Counteracts a harmful function	
Produces a harmful function	
Counteracts a useful function	

FIGURE 8.3
Activities are related by arrows, which signify inputs, outputs, causes, and effects.

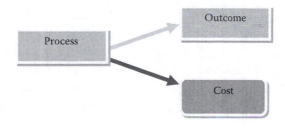

FIGURE 8.4
A process pattern using P-TRIZ mapping.

doesn't have both a useful outcome and a harmful cost. Smith provides many additional patterns of varying complexity for the interested reader.

For each pattern, a set of questions is generated based on the pattern. For the above pattern, we would generate the following *primary options* [5]:

1. Find an alternative way to obtain (Process) that offers the following: provides or enhances (Output), does not cause (Cost).
2. Try to resolve the following contradiction: The useful factor (Process) should be in place in order to provide or enhance (Output), and should not exist in order to avoid (Cost).
3. Find an alternative way to obtain (Output) that does not require (Process).
4. Consider replacing the entire system with an alternative one that will provide (Output).
5. Find a way to eliminate, reduce, or prevent (Cost) under the conditions of (Process).

Smith also provides several *secondary options* for the pattern given above:

- Find a way to increase the effectiveness of (Process).
- Find additional benefits from (Process).
- Find a way to obtain (Output) without the use of (Process).
- Find a way to decrease the ability of (Process) to cause (Cost).
- Find a way to increase the effectiveness of (Output).
- Find additional benefits from (Output).
- Consider transition to the next generation of the system that provides (Output), but which will not have the existing problem.
- Consider enhancing the current means by which the primary useful function is achieved, to the extent that the benefits will override the primary problem.
- Consider giving up the primary useful function to avoid the primary problem.
- Find a way to benefit from (Cost).
- Try to cope with (Cost).
- Consider ways to compensate for the harmful results of (Cost).
- Consider creating a situation that makes (Cost) insignificant or unimportant.

EXAMPLES OF P-TRIZ AND TECHNOLOGY

EXAMPLE 8.1

Consider ordering food from a fast-food drive-through window, an activity that was basically unchanged for 30 years until recently (Figure 8.5).

Here are some recent innovations made possible by Internet and mobile technologies and by the recognition that placing an order is a pure information activity resulting in a piece of information. There is no exchange of physical goods.

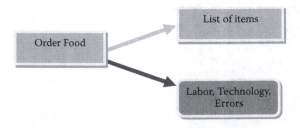

FIGURE 8.5
Ordering food from a fast-food drive-through window.

Primary option 1: Find an alternative way to *order the food* that offers the following: provides or enhances *list of items*, does not cause *labor, technology, or error costs.*

- Have a call center take orders, thus one person can scale to cover up to 5 stores during busy times and up to 10 stores during slower times. McDonalds currently uses call centers in Colorado Springs, Colorado, to perform this activity.

Primary option 2: Find an alternative way to obtain the *list of items* that does not require the *order food* activity.

- Allow for orders online or mobile apps (push labor and technology costs to user).

Secondary option 2.1: Find a way to increase the effectiveness of the *list of items*.

- Present a screen to verify the order (reduces cost of errors through process variance reduction).

Secondary option 2.2: Find additional benefits from the *list of items*.

- Collect the list of items with corresponding geospatial information and best guess of customer demographics to drive better forecasting.

EXAMPLE 8.2

Consider education. Again, learning requires no exchange of physical goods (Figure 8.6).

Primary option 1: Find an alternative way to *take a course* that offers the following: provides or enhances *learning*, does not cause *cost of facilities, faculty, and travel.*

- An obvious solution is online education, such as that offered from Udacity.com or MITx.

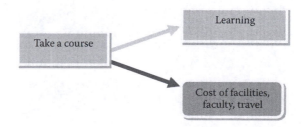

FIGURE 8.6
Education example.

Primary option 2: Find a way to eliminate, reduce, or prevent the *cost of faculty* under the conditions of *taking a course*.

- Udacity provides an infrastructure where students can "rate" student questions for quality as well as rate student solutions. Highly rated submissions generate "karma points," which can be used in assigning collaboration scores to students. Students performing the activity of answering their own questions reduce the faculty time commitment to that activity, allowing a faculty member to scale better (bigger classes).

In this case, we could generate a set of options and solutions from the various perspectives, including students, incumbent institutions, faculty, hiring organizations, loan agencies, and so on. Perspective is important in TRIZ.

EXAMPLE 8.3

Consider harvest of corn, producing big data consisting of both machine telematic data as well as agronomic data (Figure 8.7).

The harvest activity above has the benefit of producing useful data, as combines are data sources in a food supply-chain information architecture. Precision farming was designed to enable a worksite manager to visualize the crop yield with the help of a GIS tool. The original purpose of collecting this data was agronomic only and meant to assist the manager with planning the distribution of field care the following year.

The potential big data that is available through precision farming would be of interest to a number of participants in the food production supply chain. We consider several perspectives as we address particular TRIZ options that are being considered today. Currently, the data is generated by the equipment makers using a proprietary format, though the equipment manufacturing industry is moving toward an open systems interconnection (OSI) XML standard for the generation and storage of this data. The owner of the data is the operator. A small subset of innovation options is presented below.

Seed Company

Companies such as Pioneer or Monsanto compete on information, using it to provide guidance into their genetic research. The information of what

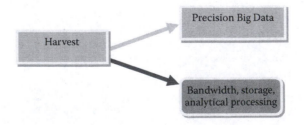

FIGURE 8.7
Harvest of corn.

hybrids do well in what conditions (soil type, moisture, altitude, etc.) is very desirable. Most seed bags contain RFID tags and many harvesters contain RFID readers to facilitate the automated collection of this type of data, though the OSI standard data structure is not explicitly supportive of this type of information. It is extensible (XML) though, so we would expect extensions as the value proposition plays out. From this perspective we have the following possible options.

Primary option 1: Find an alternative way to obtain *the harvest* that offers the following: provides or enhances the big data, does not cause *costs*.

- Seed companies should actively participate in information standards of agricultural equipment manufacturers, such as ISO 11783 [6]. That way they can help drive standards determining what types of information are captured.

Primary option 2: Find an alternative way to obtain the *big data* that does not require the *harvest activity.*

- Because of the economics of information, this data is expensive to generate but is inexpensive to duplicate. In our experience, most worksite operators are willing to share this data with researchers upon request.

Primary option 3: Find a way to eliminate, reduce, or prevent *the cost* under the conditions of *the harvest.*

- Part of the cost is data integration at a later date. Participation in data capture design would reduce these costs.

Secondary option 3.1: Find a way to increase the effectiveness of *the harvest.*

- What other types of information would be useful for a seed company to obtain during both planting and harvest?

Secondary option 3.2: Find a way to increase the effectiveness of the *big data.*

- By aggregating millions of acres of data from around the world, a seed company can better position its product in environmental settings where its product outperforms and attempts to identify causes result in gaps in performance elsewhere.

Equipment Manufacturer

Companies such as John Deere and Company and Caterpillar are best positioned to design solutions to architect and capture big data from equipment sensors. However, engineers rarely produce products that do not explicitly support their well-defined scope. Adding the capacity to capture additional agronomic information without explicit design instructions would simply not occur. However, equipment manufacturers are very interested in the resulting data.

Primary option 1: Find an alternative way to obtain *big data* that does not require *the harvest process*.

- Through a simulation context with some historical data, very accurate agricultural models can be produced. For example, plant growth is fairly well understood, following ordinary differential equations with inputs of moisture, light, fertilizer, and other common inputs. Historical weather data exists, which can drive simulations for the purposes of measuring operational risk over variations of practices. Simulations can create big data even faster than combines.

Secondary option 1.1: Find a way to increase the effectiveness of *big data*.

- Telematics data can provide worksite managers with insights as to how the equipment is being used. Similar to automobiles, different levels of operator aggressiveness will result in quite different fuel economy performance.
- Telematics data can provide usage summary statistics, which could provide engineers with information about component failure rates.
- Airlines and movie theaters perform market segmentation based on many factors. Agricultural marketing efforts would find this big data valuable to assist in this endeavor.
- Warranties are often established based on engineering designs and known structural properties. Big data would help in better understanding failure causes and failure rates and even help with positioning parts for repair or remanufacture.
- Data regarding changes to soil type and temperature over time could give better insights into global climate changes. It is likely only the planters and harvesters know the full truth about this.

Owner and Operators

The owner of big data under current contracts is the owner of the equipment. We would expect some changes to this in the future along the lines of how other forms of intellectual property have developed.

Primary option 1: Find a way to eliminate, reduce, or prevent *the cost* under the conditions of *the harvest*.

- The environment in which this type of data is produced is generally characterized by poor bandwidth, temperature and humidity variation, and vibration, all of which impact the creation, storage, and transmission of big data. As there are many external parties interested in this data, the worksite operator could ask for cost subsidies in exchange for data sharing.

Secondary option 1.1: Find additional benefits from *big data*.

- Sell to interested parties.
- Determine which equipment performs best in which operating environment. For example, there are over 35,000 possible combinations of wheels and tires alone. Which combinations seem to produce the most efficient and thus profitable yield?
- Use visual optimization tools such as SAS driven by big data to get a bird's-eye view of complex logistics operations.

Commodities Trading Firms

Commodity trading is an information business driven by estimates of global yield, which are often driven by other estimates (weather, sunshine, logistics costs). Such firms have interests in agronomic data more than telematic data, though like seed companies they are not as well positioned to drive the data generation effort. An innovation option might include the following.

Primary option 1: Find an alternative way to obtain *big data* that does not require *the harvest*.

- Satellite imagery provides a wealth of big data opportunities for trading firms. Subtle difference in crop color at particular times of a crop life cycle can be combined with weather forecasts to generate reasonably accurate yield models.

We presented select options with several others being possible. In summary, there are few groups who do not have some interest in the global food supply chain. Companies such as Walmart and UPS have achieved an analytical maturity in supply chain, and they have also repurposed this information for additional value. Walmart competes analytically on big data, and even pushes big data to customers such as 3M and other suppliers to gain their analytical insights. UPS has created an entire insourcing operation based on their supply-chain information. The agricultural supply chain represents enormous opportunities for new business models driven by big data, and we should expect dramatic improvements in efficiencies as this data becomes available to market participants.

SUMMARY

Big data and innovation are integrally related. Big data plays a role in improving processes through rules, process structures, and process innovation. Howard Smith's TRIZ offers a process mapping technique that is particularly well suited to innovation, simple in syntax, inherently collaborative, and repeatable.

The food supply chain is among the most important issues facing the world today, and potential efficiencies resulting from mining massive data, integrating it with genetic information, logistics information, engineering analysis, and market analysis will drive substantial changes to the industry as data infrastructure is built out. This data also has the potential for egregious misuse, to the point that many conversations conclude with a Pandora's Box analogy. These issues will eventually be worked out, as the economic drivers and increasing food demand will eventually induce innovation upon both incumbents and those seeking new opportunities.

REFERENCES

1. Kenneth N. C., "The Age of Big Data." Special to CNBC, http://www.cnbc.com/id/46683673, March 16, 2012.
2. Varian, H., and Shapiro, C. "Information Rules: A Strategic Guide to the Network Economy." *Harvard Business School Press*, Boston, MA, November 19, 1998.
3. Suri, R. *Quick Response Manufacturing*. Productivity Press, a division of Productivity, Inc., 1998.
4. Smith, H., and Fingar, P. *Business Process Management: The Third Wave*. Meghan-Kiffer Press. 2006.
5. Smith, H. "Process Innovation, Introducing P-TRIZ." *BP Trends*, February 2006.
6. Stone, M., McKee, K., Formwalt, C., and Benneweis, R. "An Electronic Communications Protocol for Agricultural Equipment." ASAE (The Society for Engineering in Agricultural, Food, and Biological Systems), February 10, 1999.

9

Big Data at the U.S. Department of Transportation

Daniel Pitton

Within government circles, big data is well positioned as an administration initiative that is supported by the Office of Science and Technology Policy (OSTP). Called the Big Data Research and Development Initiative, it commits a $200 million dollar investment into big data among six federal agencies, including Defense Advanced Research Projects Agency's (DARPA's) XDATA Project that is chartered to

1. develop scalable algorithms for processing imperfect data in distributed data stores, and
2. create effective human–computer interaction tools for facilitating rapidly customizable visual reasoning for diverse missions.

Within the U.S. government, the Department of Transportation (DOT) is a significant holder of information assets across a number of internal modal organizations, consisting of some 14 administrations, all of which attribute their reason for being as integral to the transportation safety mission. The largest of these is the Federal Aviation Administration (FAA), which in turn performs numerous administrative functions on behalf of the entire department. The department organizes its big data holdings around the central idea of documenting its publicly releasable data sets within an internally developed tool called the Metadata Repository (MRTool). This tool performs a number of functions in the management of DOT data that are targeted for release via data.gov. The primary rationale for this tool is to ensure that the DOT must be able to assert that data it has released to the public is identified and managed as a big data resource. The management thereof falls under three separate management domains.

The first management domain is the idea of identifying, at the data-field level, which datasets may or may not be subject to Freedom of Information

Act (FOIA) exemption. This capability would allow the department to categorize certain data as falling under one of nine FOIA exemptions that preclude release, so that we do not exceed the authority of releasable data. A key driver in this requirement is the prevention of release of personally identifiable information (PII), which falls under Exemption 6. The release of PII, accidental or otherwise, is a notorious example of an Exemption 6 violation. By flagging potential data fields within the MRTool as a FOIA exemption, the department can proactively prevent the unintended consequences of critical unclassified information release.

The second management domain is establishing which datasets are authoritative in the event a conflict arises between data found in two or more datasets published by one or more modal administrations. This approach would allow DOT to know, beforehand, where contradictory data might possibly exist and, where extant when found, creates a forum leading to a management decision declaring one or the other authoritative. An example of this inconsistency is traffic fatality data released by both the National Highway Traffic Safety Administration (NHTSA) and the Federal Highway Administration. Being able to understand the context of an inconsistent fatality count assumes the department is even aware of such a condition. That is what the MRTool helps us identify.

Last, the department wanted to explore the feasibility of embedding National Information Exchange Model (NIEM) metadata within the MRTool application so that we have a central repository in which NIEM progress can be recorded as a matter of practice, when applied to releasable data. NIEM success is defined as the Information Exchange Package Documentation (IEPD), itself created and ready for jurisdictional approval by the NIEM PMO (Program Management Office). In that regard, the department's big data (both structured and unstructured) holdings need to aggregate sufficient metadata structures that include NIEM IEPDs for the purpose of creating the NIEM Transportation Domain. This domain does not yet exist; however, it is considered a data management priority within the department.

The MRTool is administered by the Services/Data Architecture Group (SDAG), which is a deliberative body composed of the department's chief architects. The SDAG meets every other Friday and focuses on the status of known datasets that are in various stages of release maturity. The MRTool gives DOT the ability to analyze and report on what data has been released, which modes are authoritative for potential conflicts, and where the department is in terms of NIEM maturity. The very idea of big data at DOT is therefore considered an aggregation of some 130 smaller managed datasets, which form the heart of our Data Reference Model. Contrary to many enterprise architecture shops, using a tool to implement a reference model is a significant step beyond the common practice of a theoretical PowerPoint deck implementation. Using the MRTool to document and manage big data in this way gives us a collective grasp of what is in the public domain. The theory is that if we have no clue what is circulating in the public domain, the idea of managing all internal-only data at a departmental level across 14 modes significantly fails the laugh test.

Beyond the aggregation of smaller data.gov data sets, there are instances of massive data sets within DOT surpassing petabyte levels. One such example is the data assembled by the Naturalistic Driving Study under SHRP2, the second iteration of the Strategic Highway Research Program, operated by the Transportation Safety Institute at Virginia Tech. This dataset encompasses every sort of structured and unstructured data type imaginable, largely gathered from instrumentation apparatuses installed in all manner of test vehicles. Numbering some 3,100 cars, trucks, and motorcycles across six states, the telemetry comprises massive quantities of captured and stored video feeds, as well as analog and digital data that measure anything and everything behavioral. Because these videos identify test subjects, the presence of PII is a given, and general release of the same to the public is not feasible. Use of SHRP2 data is therefore limited to research-oriented, government, and nongovernmental organization safety analysis domains.

Within DOT, there are instances of large datasets acting as data warehouses that implement corporate information factories (CIFs) that support business intelligence activities. CIFs sometimes assimilate a great deal of organizational data and, architecturally, are great for interactive data mining and BI analysis activities. At NHTSA, a CIF supports a number of enterprise-wide big data initiatives designed not only to support the NHTSA mission, but also to serve as a centralized publishing mechanism that anchors NHTSA's contributions to safety.data,gov. As a subdomain, there is intense interest in the transportation aspects of the safety mission, and the department expects to contribute heavily over the coming years. As a managed process, submissions to data.gov will be heavily scrutinized to prevent the release of FOIA-exempt datafield classes identified as such in the previously described MRTool.

Other potentially huge big data challenges for DOT are ventures to offload e-mail into a cloud environment that can better unify the features and challenges of petabyte-level messaging stores that aggregate about 100 terabytes of archives annually across 50,000 users (incrementing at 2 gigabytes annually each). Searching such masses of big data for e-discovery purposes, for instance, will require significant technology optimization to support search efforts in a timely manner. The world standard of such search optimization is the original Google technology developed in the early 2003 time frame, when Google perfected the MapReduce concept and ported it to their Hadoop Tool Set ecosystem. This architecture drives the amazing search query times returned to any user on the Internet, for any conceivable search string, answered in a matter of milliseconds. Hadoop technology is what made Google the largest revenue generator on the Internet, approaching $100 billion annually. Although Hadoop is an amazing technical feat, it is now considered first generation and is already technically obsolete. It is known that Google has improved upon it already and is fielding the next generation of its database engine called Dremel to replace Hadoop as their new world standard. Hadoop, however, is now open source, mature, and far from obsolete. When coupled to enabling services like Cloudera, it is still a viable search engine architecture capable of immense duty.

Security is always an issue when huge collections of data are released to the public. It might seem counterintuitive to reason why information security is any issue at all, since confidentiality is not even the issue anymore; however, the major security issue facing big data is the potential for privacy breaches. This is very apparent when PII is inadvertently released and litigation invariably ensues. Therefore, the security controls around dataset releases are far more mindful of NIST 800-53 Appendix J, since that is where privacy controls are described that are meant to maintain information privacy, if not information security. The principles espoused in Appendix J follow a framework described in the Privacy Act of 1974 and elaborated upon in the E-Government Act of 2002, hence christened the Fair Information Practice Principles. The controls described in Appendix J are mean to inspire public trust, assuage litigation, and limit damages arising from privacy incidents. Unstructured data is especially subject to these controls, since videos are notorious for revealing unintended PII, including faces, license plates, and residential streets and addresses.

Security controls that protect big data can themselves generate enormous amount of big data when coupled to intrusion detection apparatuses that capture web traffic at petabyte levels. Such architectures are well understood and are actually feasible in cloud environments. At DOT, an intriguing project at NHTSA involves a cloud trust model worth evaluating. Much of the reluctance of many federal organizations to move to the cloud is rooted in trust issues with managed cloud services. When cloud capacity is purchased, it is understood that the infrastructure is already secure. Additional managed security services can be purchased that enhance security even more. Even in the FEDRAMP cloud security model, security controls are baselined in such a way that inheritance occurs between the cloud service provider (CSP) and the application owner. Trust is simply assumed. Every single one of the inherited security controls is managed by the CSP. The fundamental problem with managed security services by a CSP is a classic conflict-of-interest scenario of the fox guarding the chicken coop.

This single-ended web of trust is, in the eyes of most security practitioners, unsustainable and ill advised. What is needed is a better trust model that introduces an IV&V (independent validation and verification) element into the equation. NHTSA is working with its CSP to embed an IV&V capability where government-furnished equipment (GFE) is integrated into a COLO rack at the CSP data center. This GFE is in turned cabled into the hubs and routers of the cloud infrastructure so that a span port is leveraged to route web traffic through a Cloudera instance that is in turn operating a Hadoop matrix of big data tools. The datasets generated are in turn parsed through a SNORT engine that detects intrusion detection events. As a trust model is the ultimate goal of this managed COLO (MOLO) architecture, comparative analysis needs to occur between what the GFE MOLO detects and what the CSP managed security service reports. This gap analysis is what the trust model provides and is meant to highlight the disparity between what the GFE sees and what the cloud sees. If disparity is nominal or nonexistent, then trust is established. If the gap analysis is wildly pejorative, then the government can launch inquiry and seek redress via mitigation.

The MOLO Trust Model can be used for purposes far beyond simply IDS validation. Other GFE devices assist in rendering services that the CSP does not even offer as a managed service. Routing big data instances through such localized services are a cloud advantage that the MOLO provides, over other models that might require route backhaul or other inconveniences. One such service being provisioned in the MOLO is PII identification. XML data being served up as conventional web content does still need to be checked for PII instances, and privacy mechanisms exist that meet the intent of NIST Appendix J. Such a mechanism is part of the MOLO concept, which supports XML detection of PII and firewalls it before ever leaving the cloud.

Big data in the cloud is another venue that has exciting implications to the concept of business intelligence. Federal organizations that make the move to cloud infrastructures have the potential of applying their vast dataset collections as neural network feeds that search out hidden patterns and other informatics that can yield new insight into data mining efforts that only a vast number of data points can provide. The lower storage costs of cloud venues make such data mining an attractive option to cash-strapped organizations seeking to get out of the hardware business and who are willing to adopt massively parallel commodity servers with Hadoop-like processing power as an alternative to owning their own hardware-operating conventional relational databases. With upcoming advances in quantum computing and ever faster chip architectures, the surge in big data collections that process petabyte-level datasets will help spur the knowledge explosion that can lead us to a future prosperity that is far closer than can be imagined.

10

Putting Big Data at the Heart of the Decision-Making Process

Ian Thomas

CONTENTS

With all the many challenges of capturing, storing, transforming, and delivering big data to business users, it's easy to overlook one vital aspect: how to get those users to incorporate data-driven insights into their daily decision making. This chapter will focus on several important techniques for achieving this, including organizational design and staffing, the creation of robust processes around data publishing and the evolution of data assets, and delivering technology solutions that address the needs of a diverse user base.

CONTEXT

My own entrée into the world of big data began in 2000, when I joined a tiny software start-up in the UK that specialized in web analytics tools. The web analytics industry was very different from how it is today. Back then, dozens of technology vendors strove not just to convince potential customers to buy their solution, but to convince organizations that web analytics was worth investing in at all. Of course, in those days, big data meant megabytes or possibly gigabytes of data per day, rather than the terabytes and beyond of today's world. But in many ways, the web analytics industry at the turn of the millennium was not so different from the big data industry of today.

In 2000, the dialog with web analytics customers (and within the industry itself) was almost exclusively focused on *technology*. The available tools rapidly gained new features, and these features were paraded in front of potential buyers: funnel reports, 3D visualizations of traffic patterns, heat maps. The total number of out-of-the-box reports provided by each product became a competitive differentiator, until it reached such a ridiculous extent ("We have over 300 prebuilt reports!") that it became an object of parody.

For their part, the industry's customers were on an incredibly steep learning curve. Many of them had only recently made a decision properly to invest in the web, and it was still very much seen as an IT function in many organizations. For many, the only key performance indicator (KPI) attached to the website was a simple yes/no answer to the question "Do we have a website?"

Since IT people are used to evaluating tools based on features, many purchasing decisions were made, and later regretted, based on whichever tool had the flashiest demo. Our own little company wasn't immune to this phenomenon—I remember several features that we shipped specifically because they looked good on the screen.

What many of these early adopters (and the vendors that supplied them) discovered, however, is that getting value out of an investment in web analytics was not a simple case of installing some software, setting up some logging, and then waiting for the insights to come rolling in. Most organizations simply didn't have any staff with either the skills or the time to spend analyzing website traffic. As the decade progressed, organizations like the Web Analytics Association (now the Digital Analytics Association) would spring up and champion the role of the web analyst—but then, hard-pressed IT staff or marketing managers were expected to take on web analytics in addition to their normal duties. The vendors themselves had yet to develop the full-service implementation and analytics capabilities that they have today, and no third-party analytics services companies existed.

Not surprisingly, this combination of an overemphasis on technology, unsophisticated buyers, and a shortage of implementation and analysis skills meant that the early days of web analytics were bumpy for many. At the heart of the problem was the fact that customers simply weren't getting a return on the investment they were making. Once implemented, many tools (including our own in several cases) gathered metaphorical dust as they were largely ignored or forgotten about by users.

Of course, the web analytics industry grew up. Substantial vendor consolidation created a much-easier-to-navigate field of players for customers to choose from, who themselves became more sophisticated. Most importantly, a vibrant services industry grew up around the discipline. Nowadays the discussion at industry events like the eMetrics Summit is hardly at all about which technology to choose—it is about best practices and advanced analytical techniques like predictive modeling.

Today's big data industry is not as immature as the web analytics industry of 12 years ago, but it does share some of the same challenges. Many discussions of big data today tend to focus primarily or exclusively on the technology. This is partly because the technology landscape is currently changing very rapidly. It's also caused by the wide variety of vendors who are in the market with solutions that are not easy to compare with each other. As a result, making technology choices for big data is very difficult, and so a lot of energy is expended on these discussions.

However, as with the early days of web analytics, this focus on technology crowds out discussions about the real purpose of implementing big data systems, which is to enable people across organizations to rely on data every day as they make many large and small decisions about how to do their job and run their business.

THE TRIAD: SKILLS, TRUST, AND ACCESS

For users to really start relying on data to help them with their jobs every day, three conditions need to be met:

- Users need the *right skills and assistance* to be able to make sense of the data and draw meaningful conclusions.
- Users must *trust* the data and feel that it is *authoritative.*
- Users need to be able to *access the data they need* easily, at the right level of detail.

Satisfying only two of these conditions but not the third is insufficient to habituate the usage of data for decision making. For example, if data is easily available and trustworthy but users lack the skills to analyze it, they will not bother. On the other hand, if data is available and users do have the required analysis skills but they don't trust the data, they will not use it and instead will likely create their own sources of data, which will be inconsistent with any broader view of the business.

It takes a broader approach to the problem to ensure that the three conditions are met, but the core approach relies on the age-old triad of *people, process,* and *technology*:

- By providing the right *people*, a big data team or function can provide users with the help and education they need to utilize data correctly, as well as providing thought leadership on analysis techniques and focus areas to move the dialog forward.
- By publishing data according to well-defined *processes*, paying attention to the unglamorous spadework of tracking and reporting data quality issues, and championing standards and definitions, the data team can build trust in their data and make it users' first port of call for analysis.
- Providing the correct portfolio of *technology* to expose data to users, which caters to the broad range of user needs, will ensure it is easy for users to draw on data when they want to and reduce the risk of "rogue" datasets.

In the rest of this chapter, we'll examine each of these areas in greater detail.

PEOPLE

A question I have been asked many times by colleagues within and outside of Microsoft, especially those who are looking to set up a business intelligence or big data function themselves, is, "How big should the team be?" Being innately quantitative folk, I think they are hoping for some convenient formula to spring from my lips, perhaps based on some kind of ratio to the overall number of users, or total volume of data, or some other concrete number. Unfortunately, my answer almost always begins with the words "It depends ..."

The interesting thing about the "how large" question is that there is an assumption baked into it. This assumption is that is necessary to have *some* kind of centralized data team—or, to put it another way, that the size of said team should be greater than zero. This is an important assumption to be making, because it is possible to get data to users without a centralized team to manage it. This in fact was the case in Microsoft's Online Services Division until some years ago: No centralized team existed, and users accessed data by reaching out to individual contacts they knew within the engineering organization and brokering bilateral agreements to gain access to data. The typical form of these agreements was that the user of the data would persuade the provider to write a bit of code that would drop a CSV file onto a file share, or possibly populate a database table or view, and the user would then load the resulting file or whatever into Excel and build some reports.

The impracticality of such an approach is fairly obvious—before long, many, many such agreements will exist, with considerable overlap between them, while those engineers unlucky enough to be afflicted with what Dilbert cartoonist Scott Adams calls the "Curse of Competence"[*] soon end up inundated with requests to expose data to a broader and broader group of people. Eventually, the inevitable happens: two senior executives, relying on data that has been pulled from the same source but by two entirely divergent processes, encounter one another in a meeting. After they have spent 45 minutes of a one-hour meeting arguing about who has the "right" numbers, they realize that what they *should* be discussing is how come they have two sets of numbers at all. This kind of jolt is often what gets people started asking questions about how large a centralized data team should be.

Functions and Scope—The Goldilocks Principle

The key to answering this question is in fact to consider the functions that a business intelligence (BI) or data team actually provides to an organization. These functions are as follows:

---

[*] http://dilbert.com/strips/comic/2008-09-13/

- *Build*—Building out, maintaining and enhancing the data systems themselves
- *Product Management*—Handling internal customer demands and turning these into requirements for the data systems
- *Support and Operations*—Managing the publishing process, taking action when things go wrong, and providing support to users
- *Communications and Training*—Communicating about new system features or issues, providing collateral and reference material, and providing training resources to users
- *Data Quality and Governance*—Monitoring and managing data quality, including implementing data quality systems; championing data consistency and providing a governance framework for definition changes for key metrics and metadata
- *Ad hoc Analytics and Consultancy*—Performing "quick twitch" analysis activities in response to business requests; providing advice on interpretation of results
- *Reporting and "Rhythm of Business" (RoB) Support*—Publishing reliable reports of business performance; providing and defending an impartial view of progress in regularly scheduled review meetings, such as monthly business reviews
- *Data Sciences/Data Mining*—Performing deep analysis of long-term trends, customer behavior, or other multivariable datasets, either in response to inbound requests or proactively as a service to the broader business

In the absence of a centralized data team, many of these functions will be performed by existing parts of the business. In Figure 10.1 I have labeled these parts Engineering and Business, which is how many Microsoft divisions are organized—an engineering organization that builds products and technologies, and a business organization that takes these products to market through sales and marketing efforts.

In the figure, functions that are typically found in engineering or product-centric groups within an organization are placed on the far left side of the diagram, where the Engineering circle does not overlap with Business, while functions that are most commonly found in marketing-focused business groups are on the far right side, in the Business section. The middle section that overlaps contains functions that are frequently found in either type of organization, or (commonly) in both at the same time.

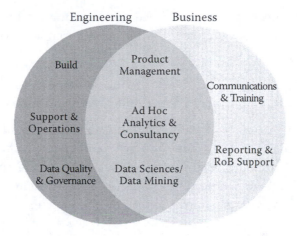

FIGURE 10.1
Typical location of common data team functions within the business.

Depending on your specific organization, you will find that these functions are being performed in various different places. In very product-centric organizations, such as technology companies, functions will be concentrated within the Engineering group, which will produce and consume data to drive product innovation. In this case, high-quality communications and training, together with good support for executive reporting, may be missing.

In more marketing-focused organizations, such as a consumer packaged goods firm, the center of gravity will be much closer to the marketing or sales teams, with data about customers and marketing effectiveness the focus. In these kinds of organizations, it is often the underlying quality and reliability of the data that suffers, since the marketing teams do not have access to skilled personnel to build and run such systems.

If one of these organizations is very dominant, then it may be possible or practical to house a data function within the existing organization structure—for example, as an outgrowth of a market research function in a marketing-led organization, or as a kind of platform service in a product or technology-led one. But such a structure will inevitably have a bias toward one side of the organization or another. In so many organizations today, the key to driving business value is to understand the complex relationship between the products being created and the impact and usage of those products by actual customers. So a mature data function really needs to unite these two worlds, which in turn leads to the conclusion that an independent group is required. But, to return to the question I am so often asked, How big should this group be? And how do you define its remit?

If You Want to Get There, I Wouldn't Start from Here

In an apocryphal story, a confused tourist accosts an old man in a small Irish village and asks him the way to Dublin (or Cork, or County Down—the destination varies by the teller). After giving the question some thought, the old man responds, "Well, if it's Dublin yer tryin' to get to, I wouldn't start from here." Likewise, the route to the destination of a well-functioning centralized data group may start from an unpromising location, with the component functions described earlier scattered across various teams. Organizational politics being what they are, people are very reluctant to hand over parts of their teams to a new organization without one or both of the following things: *Trust* that the new team can deliver, and strong *support* from executive leadership. In Microsoft, both are typically required, but trust is the essential element.

Building trust, whether in an individual or a team, is a cyclical process. An analogy is the process by which a teen driver convinces her parents that she can be trusted to borrow the family car. At first, the driver takes the car out on short trips during the daytime, perhaps to the mall, or to school. When she's demonstrated that she is reliable in this context, she can start taking the car out on longer trips and at the weekends, and finally she's able to go out at night and perhaps on even longer excursions. But if she wrecks the car, or even breaks an agreement (for example, promising to be back by nightfall, and then coming back at midnight), her progress toward total trust will be halted and even perhaps reversed.

The learning for a new data team is to start with modestly scoped deliverables within an existing area of expertise and move on from there in an iterative process to more and more ambitious goals. The nature of your organization will determine the best starting point. For example, imagine that there is a team of talented analysts working in a product group. The analysts have already developed a bit of a reputation among their peers and management for reliable, sensible work, but they have little control over the data systems they use. Rather than spinning up their own data tools without a proper mandate, the analysts would be better served by forming close links with their colleagues who are performing this function and starting to evolve deliverables that rely not just on analytical capability but also the development of new technology.

When these deliverables have been well-received, the analysts (or, in fact, the "v-team" of the analysts and their developer counterparts) can make the case that these kinds of deliverables would be much easier and more cost-effective to create if the two teams were combined, or at least had some formal alignment. Once the teams are combined, they should focus on deliverables that demonstrate the value of the combined team but are still achievable, such as collaborating with a similar team in the marketing function to deliver a combined project. Once this next level of credibility has been achieved, the two teams could make the case that they would function better as one. And so on.

Not Too Hot, Not Too Cold

In the telling of this example, I may make it seem that bigger is always better and that the goal for a consolidated data team is to be as big and as broad in scope as possible. But this is absolutely not the case. Again, the overall organization's dynamics and its level of maturity with respect to data will dictate the optimum size and scope for a data team. I call this principle the *Goldilocks Principle*. If the data team is too small, it will be too much at the mercy of the interests and vicissitudes of the other teams— it will not be able to impose discipline on the use of data, for example, and will not have the bandwidth to prevent "homegrown" solutions for data problems from springing up. Such a team will fail to build *trust* in the data, one of the three key pillars of effectiveness that I introduced at the start of the chapter.

On the other hand, a data group that is too large risks coming across as an overly bureaucratic entity that spoonfeeds numbers to its customers without taking their specific needs into account or giving them the freedom to explore the data themselves. This type of function fails users for a different reason, by disempowering them with regard to the data and reducing their sense of ownership and knowledge about the data.

At Microsoft, we have explicitly taken an interactive approach to building out the data organization in the Online Services Division, always seeking to find an operating model that delivers the benefits of centralized coordination of core assets and policies while retaining a level of empowerment for users. There's no such thing as the perfect organizational structure, of course, so we continue to tune and tweak our model as our business evolves. We have also been fortunate in the past few years to have the support of leadership who implicitly understand the value of data to the business and who are prepared to act as a tie-breaker for difficult organizational decisions.

If your executive leadership is not so bought into the strategic value of data, then, as well as building credibility and trust across the organization, you will need to build that trust with the executives. The experience that many senior leaders have with data is often one in which data makes things *less* clear rather than more so. This occurs when leaders are presented numbers that are inconsistent with one another or with themselves, or that are of poor quality. It is also very important to present only as many numbers as are needed to tell the story, rather than doing, as Avinash Kaushik memorably coined it, a "data puke." Over a period of time, if you can show a senior leader a consistent narrative about the business, backed up by easy-to-understand numbers that stay fairly stable and that enable actual decisions to be made, then you will be well on the way to turning that executive into a data convert.

PROCESS

Senior people aren't the only ones who need consistent and reliable numbers—everybody does. As you look to build the trust and credibility of your data team, *how* you produce your data is at least as important as what is in the data. This becomes particularly true as you look to expose a larger audience to your data. When you live and breathe data every day, it's easy to forget that most of the people who are actually consuming the data have demanding day jobs, which means they may spend only a few minutes with your data each week—or even each month. If the data isn't there when they look for it, has changed unaccountably, or is incomplete, they will become confused and angry in ways that to you may seem disproportionate. It's a bit like going to a 10-year class reunion having gained 50 pounds and shaved your head and then being hurt when people don't recognize you.

The *process* part of the business of data usually goes under the unexciting banner of *data quality*. To most people, data quality is, well, boring. It doesn't have the tinkering, making-something-new satisfaction of actually building the data systems, and it doesn't have the intellectual satisfaction (or the mystique) of hard-core analysis work. But all the data systems and smarts in the world are useless without it.

Data quality means many things to many people, but it breaks down into the following components:

- Publishing data on a reliable schedule
- Publishing accurate (or complete) data
- Keeping data self-consistent over time
- Providing high-quality business metrics and dimensions in the data

Regular as Clockwork

One of the best ways to ensure that data becomes embedded in day-to-day decision making is to ensure that data consumers can incorporate it into their business processes. For example, a sales team may meet on a Monday morning to review their progress against their quota in the previous week. If the data isn't there when they need it, they will have to postpone the meeting or muddle through on verbal accounts from salespeople (always a bad idea). Miss the deadline another couple of times and the sales team will look elsewhere for the data they need, possibly going to some "unauthorized" source (a colleague of a colleague who knows how to hack into the back end of the CRM system, for example), undermining the broader integrity of the data landscape in the organization.

If you're looking to get your data established as a ground truth in your organization, make sure you set a publishing schedule for the data that you are confident that you can meet *at least 90% of the time.* There will always be people asking for the data sooner, but discipline is essential— it's far harder to win unhappy customers back than it is to recruit them in the first place. One challenge we have faced at Microsoft is when we have sensibly applied this rule and communicated a conservative schedule (for example, "Data for the previous day will be available by 3:00 p.m.") but actually beat this schedule quite a lot of the time, for example typically publishing by noon. Despite the official schedule, users start to learn that they can typically find the latest data at around noon, and so on the occasions when it is a bit later, but still within the official service-level agreement (say, 2:00 p.m.), they get annoyed. Calm reminders that "we're still within the service-level agreement" don't have much effect. One solution to this problem is to actually *delay* publication until the scheduled publish time, but that seems a little perverse. So we do our best to remind users through our communications of the official publish schedule, and of course are constantly working to improve publish reliability to the point where we can move the schedule up.

Only Half the Story Can Be Worse than No Story at All

Possibly the thing that enrages users above all other is when new data appears but is incomplete. Some of my most professionally awkward moments have come when I have had to communicate to a large group of users that the data they just spent a couple of days working with and drawing conclusions from, for example, to prepare end-of-month financial reporting, was actually incomplete, and that they must now do that work all over again. The very worst of these moments have come when we were actually rushing to publish our data ahead of its normal schedule, in an effort to please those very same users who we then let down.

One of the very hardest challenges in data publishing is detecting errors and omissions in the data. The solution involves checks and balances all through the data-publishing process—checking that primary data sources exist; checking that those data sources were actually loaded; checking that the various stages of the publishing process completed successfully. These kinds of checks can be thought of as process or input checks—they check that what was meant to go into the publishing process was actually there, and also that it was there at the other end.

More tricky are problems within the data itself, either caused by problems with the source data or by bugs in the publishing code. Detecting these kinds of problems is hard. For example, it might be that traffic to a website from the UK has dropped by 30 percent since yesterday. Is that because the UK site was down for six hours, or because there was a domain resolution problem in the UK, or because of a bug in the reverse-IP lookup code that is incorrectly assigning UK IP addresses, or because it was a public holiday? The best thing that any kind of error-detection system can do in this kind of situation is to raise a flag about the anomaly and alert a human who can do a manual check.

For data with a high accuracy requirement (such as financial data), it can be advantageous to implement a two-phase publishing process, where the data is published to a nonpublic location where final checks can be run before it is made publicly available. If a problem is found at the last minute, a decision can be made whether or not to release the data or take remedial action (which might push publishing past its advertised schedule). Sometimes, though, it's better to publish late than to publish something that is incorrect.

Adding Value without Adding Problems

If you plan to deliver valuable data to business users, you will likely want to add some business logic to the raw data during the publishing process. A simple example of this is the "user country" example above—if you are capturing the IP address of visitors to your website, it is valuable to use an IP geo-lookup service to add country and city information to your data. This kind of augmentation makes it much easier for users to get value from the data in reports or analysis work.

Once you introduce these derived measures or dimensions, however, you have an obligation to keep them consistent and of a high quality. The users, after all, cannot tell the difference between the "real," or underlying, data and the new, "derived" data. In our example, if the IP lookup service goes down, it's not enough to shrug and say, "Well, the IP addresses are still there—just use those." Users will have built reports and analysis templates around the assumption that the derived data will be available and can't just change them at a moment's notice.

The creation of derived components in your published data will inevitably add complexity to the publishing process; and where there is complexity, there is an increased risk of failure. When considering whether to add more derived data, therefore, you should always consider the cost/benefit (or risk/benefit) balance—is the utility to users worth the extra cost of maintaining it and the extra risk of failure?

This calculus becomes even more important in the case of dimensions or measures that are derived via complex rules—for example, a customer segmentation model that combines multiple fields of source data. Such new dimensions may deliver a lot of benefit to users, but you should also consider whether such additions increase the *opacity* of the data by being hard to unpick.

Finally, the more complex your derived data logic is, the more temptation users will have to ask you to change the logic to suit them or a particular reporting/analytic scenario that they have—which will usually result in the logic becoming even more complex. For example, a customer segmentation model may classify a company as midsized based on various criteria, but a salesperson with a particular account may then say, "Well, this company is classified as midsized, but they're really a large account, for these reasons ..." If you implement every such request, before you know it, the boundaries of your segmentation logic will be as convoluted as the borders of a gerrymandered congressional district, which not only will be harder to maintain, but also is harder to defend against further requests for changes.

Ultimately, some of the derived data you create may become important enough that it needs to be managed through a formal change request process. In the Online Services Division at Microsoft, we are putting in place processes and metadata management technology to manage and govern changes to important measures and dimensions, with the explicit intent of creating stability and trustworthiness in these entities.

Rewriting History

As our ability to gather and manage data and our understanding of our business improves over time, we naturally want to make improvements to the data we publish. Users want to see these improvements, too, but a balance must be struck in terms of protecting the long-term consistency of the data. This is particularly true in cases where budgets or targets have been set against the data; any change that makes it hard for the business to reach these targets (or, for that matter, easier, since it would create a false impression of success) will generate discontent among users.

Whenever you make any change to the way data is processed, then for any data with a time element you have to decide what to do about historical data. You can leave it as it is, do a restatement (i.e., republish) of data back to a certain date, or do a full republish of all data. For aggregated data (such as user profiles) there is a similar choice—if you make a change to the aggregation rules, for example, you can choose just to apply that rule going forward, or re-create the aggregations from scratch with the new rule.

Not doing any kind of restatement or publishing is of course the easiest and cheapest option, but it will create a discontinuity in the data, which will make analysis (especially historical analysis such as year-on-year comparisons) harder and generate user dissatisfaction. On the other hand, full republishing or restatement can be a costly undertaking and will invalidate previously published reports, which can create problems of its own.

At Microsoft, we often choose to partially restate time-based data back to the start of the current fiscal year, unless historical comparison is deemed particularly important. This enables us to keep current-year reporting consistent with itself, while keeping the cost of restatement under control. We also try not to restate more than once per quarter, to keep the impact to users to a minimum and create a sense of stability in the data.

Finally, it is very important to communicate clearly and assertively about changes to data. Clear communication that spells out the impact to users in ways they can understand makes a big difference to the way such changes are received. For particularly impactful changes, it can be a good idea to identify the most important users and reach out personally, not just to send the message about the change, but also to verify explicitly that it has been received. This avoids arguments after the change from these users that they "never saw" the e-mail (or e-mails) notifying them of the change.

TECHNOLOGY

It's not within the scope of this chapter to go into a lot of detail about technology choices for building out big data systems. What we'll cover here is how to think about the portfolio of technology that you provide users with to enable them to access the data they need in a way that is most appropriate to them.

All Users Are Not Alike

In the early stages of building out a data function, a particular group of similar users may drive many of the requirements. It might be a group of deep analysts who need to drill right into the data, or a group of executives who need a scorecard, or some engineers who need quick-twitch metrics on feature performance. It makes sense, of course, in the context of reputation building, to tailor the systems you deliver to this "founding" group of users. But it is well worth considering how the data might be used by a much broader group that will have much more diverse needs so as to build some flexibility to serve that broader group when the time comes.

Figure 10.2 shows a simple segmentation model (with slightly frivolous names) for users of data systems.

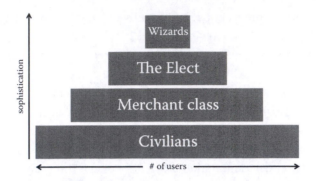

FIGURE 10.2
A simple segmentation model for data system users.

The profiles of these different groups are as follows:

- *Civilians*—Generalist users with no specialized data skills. Primarily looking for static (or very lightly "pivotable" numbers in easy-to-consume formats (e.g., prepopulated templates or reports). May use the data on a regular (e.g., weekly) basis, but needs stay fairly constant.
- *Merchant Class*—More sophisticated users for whom data/analysis is not a core competency or part of their primary role, but who are called upon to pull data for a wider range of reporting/lightweight-analysis scenarios. May be familiar with end-user tools such as Excel Pivot Tables or Tableau.
- *The Elect*—Fairly specialized users who have some significant aspect of reporting or analysis as part of their role. Will make extensive use of standard querying tools (e.g., building their own reports in Excel); will have capabilities to perform moderately technical data manipulation (for example, may be able to join data together from two sources and publish the results).
- *Wizards*—Highly specialized users for whom analysis is their entire role. Possess high-end data retrieval, modeling, and/or data manipulation skills. Frequently require data that is not to be found in managed publish points.

As the pyramid shape of the figure suggests, in most organizations the preponderance of users is at the less sophisticated end of the spectrum, with the Wizards making up a very small proportion of the overall population. But between organizations, and even within the same organization

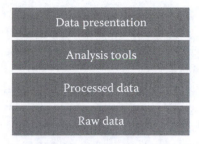

FIGURE 10.3
A simplified big data stack.

in different groups or divisions, there can be significant variation in the specific shape of the pyramid.

Understanding the shape of this pyramid for your organization will help you to plan and prioritize the data systems that you invest in. Many architectures for big data systems look like Figure 10.3.

The characteristics of these layers are as follows:

- *Raw Data*—The relatively unprocessed data (often very large in size) that represents the lowest level of granularity. Typically stored in a massively parallel storage system like Hadoop.
- *Processed Data*—A version of the raw data that has been processed, perhaps to create aggregations (e.g., daily sets of numbers, or visitor profiles) and perform other augmentations. Much less unwieldy than the raw data, but still requires specialist skills to extract for analysis.
- *Analysis Tools*—Tools such as data cubes or ad hoc query builders such as Tableau that provide managed access to the processed data for analysis.
- *Data Presentation*—Reports, dashboards, and templates that surface the processed data to users in preconfigured formats and layouts for easy understanding of performance.

At a crude level of approximation, the four user profiles we looked at previously map fairly well to the four layers of this stack, though in the opposite direction to one another; i.e., the bottom-most user profile (the Civilians) is best served by the top-most layer of the stack (the Data Presentation layer).

Once you have assessed the breakdown of your audience (i.e., the shape of the pyramid), this simple model will provide some useful insights into where you should be focusing your technology resources. For example, if you have a preponderance of sophisticated Elect but relatively fewer

Civilian users, it makes sense not to expend resources delivering a great dashboard/reporting environment, but instead to find ways to make it easy for the Elect to gain access to the processed data so they can construct their analysis queries easily.

The major exception to this principle is that the foundations of the stack to need to be secure before you build lots of stuff on top of them. Many data organizations do indeed get started by putting together dashboards and reports for executives. It is quite common in this case to discover that, beneath the neat exterior of a dashboard, data has been hacked together in a very unscalable and unreliable way. Once the dashboards start to become popular, further requests to enhance the data being passed through to them become harder and harder to execute as the spaghetti under the surface starts to get really tangled. Eventually, the whole thing has to be thrown away and rebuilt from the bottom up, which ends up being a very expensive task. So it's wise to ensure the underlying data is being provisioned and processed in a manageable way, even if most of your users will experience it only through dashboards.

SUMMARY

Persuading users to put data at the heart of their day-to-day decision making takes more than just a megaphone about the virtues of data, or an order from senior management to use more data. For users ready to embrace data in their roles, they need to be able to find it, understand it, and most of all, trust it.

To achieve this triad of user acceptance, it helps to focus on the people, processes, and technology that you have in place to deliver data to your organization. By balancing investments across these three areas, rather than, for example, putting all resources into technology, organizations can build the reliability and trustworthiness in their data services that will draw users in and enable them to rely on the data to do their jobs.

11

Extracting Useful Information from Multivariate Temporal Data

Artur Dubrawski

CONTENTS

INTRODUCTION

Many of the important big data sets encountered in practice assume the form of a record of transactions. Each entry in such data typically includes date and time of an event (such as a nonprescription drug purchase transaction or a record of a repair of a vehicle) and a potentially large number of descriptors characterizing the event (e.g., the type, dose, and quantity of the medicine sold or the model year, make, configuration, and description of failure of the vehicle). Time-stamped transactional data can be used to answer various questions of practical importance. Typical applications leverage the temporal aspect of data and include detection of emergence of previously unknown patterns (such as outbreaks of infectious diseases inferred from unusually elevated volume of sale of certain kinds of drugs in a region or new shopping behaviors developing among specific demographic niches of a customer base), prediction of future occurrences of particular types of events (such as imminent failures of equipment or qualitative changes of monitored business processes), and explanation of patterns or events of specific interest (What is special about the particular cluster of customer data? Can we assess and scope geographically and demographically the potential impact of a newly detected escalating crisis?).

In this chapter, we show a few practical application examples of an intuitively structured approach to tackling these types of questions. The approach consists of two fundamental steps, which conceptually combine data mining and machine learning paradigms:

1. Extraction from data of a possibly very large set of features that, hypothetically or based on application domain expertise, may be informative for the task at hand
2. Use of the extracted features to learn probabilistic models capable of answering posed business questions, while automatically identifying subsets of features that enable the optimal performance at the task at hand

With the exception of some applications where the informative features are known in advance and are readily available in source data, it is often desirable to allow the first step to be highly comprehensive, even exhaustive if possible, to avoid missing potentially useful features. The second step aims to mitigate the resulting complexity and to identify manageable subsets of features that yield practically realizable and effective models.

Large scales of comprehensive searches across potentially highly multidimensional data impose special requirements on the computational feasibility of the proposed process to make it practical. It is often possible to addresses this challenge by using cached sufficient statistics approach. The sufficient statistics data structures store a limited and controllable amount of information about data that is needed to very quickly compute all estimates necessary for analyses or statistical inference. There is usually a one-time computational setup cost involved in creating the sufficient statistics cache, and a memory storage requirement; but as soon as that is done, data-intensive analytic algorithms can retrieve the needed precomputed information from rapidly accessible intermediate storage instead of reaching out to the source databases. We sometimes observe orders-of-magnitude speedups of information retrieval operations when using such caches to support advanced analytics of large data [10]. It is worth noting that the use of cached statistics does not preclude leveraging infrastructural efficiencies of distributed computing systems and algorithms. In fact they can be used jointly for additional improvements of scalability.

The next sections of this chapter showcase a few examples of practical applications of the proposed approach. They involve multidimensional transactional data with a temporal component and illustrate a subset of possible types of business questions that can be asked against such types of data. They also show examples of how the input data can be featurized to allow learning of effective predictive models. The first of these examples involves monitoring the status of public health. It relies on a massive-scale screening through multivariate projections of records of outpatient hospital visits to detect statistically significant spatiotemporal increases in the number of patients reporting with similar symptoms and disease signs. The enabling idea is to use cached sufficient statistics to support exhaustive searches across millions of hypotheses and sort them according to their statistical significance. Looking at the most significant detections, public health officials can focus their attention and investigative resources on the most unusual escalations that may be indicative of emerging outbreaks of disease.

The second example looks at mining high-frequency data collected at the bedside of intensive care patients to predict imminent episodes of acute deterioration of their health. The multivariate baseline data is decomposed spectrally and compressed to form a compact but still highly multidimensional model of typical variability of vital signs characteristics obtained from patients who are not in crisis. The new observations are processed in the same way, and their principal component projections are monitored using a control-chart approach for any statistically significant departures from the expectation. These departures are considered as potentially informative of the near-future deteriorations of health. They serve as inputs to a machine-learning algorithm that uses a representative set of annotated examples of health crises to learn how to predict their future onsets.

The third example employs a similar control-charting approach to event detection; however, it uses a bivariate temporal scan, instead of the univariate cumulative sum chart, to extract potentially informative events from large amounts of bank transaction data. Some of these events are then automatically selected by a classification model trained to anticipate upcoming spending sprees by the bank customers.

The fourth and final application example looks at a few challenges of predictive informatics when it is used to support management of fleets of expensive, complicated equipment. The featuring of high-frequency data from vibration monitoring subsystems is achieved by computing a set of temporal derivatives of increasing orders. It can yield remarkably accurate predictors of onset of uncertain vibration exceedence events. It helps detect the opportunities for preventive maintenance of aircraft before faulty conditions actually set in. Another look at the same application context, but using a multistream analysis, demonstrates the ability of a big data approach to dismiss a number of probable false alerts. Some apparent mechanical faults recorded by the in-flight aircraft health-monitoring systems can be therefore classified as benign artifacts, highly explainable by the particular conditions of flight.

EXAMPLE APPLICATION: PUBLIC HEALTH

One of the societally important applications of modern analytics is to support surveillance of public health. Multiple efforts have been staged over the past decade, primarily in developed countries, to leverage statistical data mining to monitor relevant and digitally available information. It includes records of patients reporting to emergency rooms with particular sets of symptoms, volumes of daily sales of certain types of nonprescription medications, lab test requests, ambulance requests, and so forth [3,4,6,11,17]. Any excessive activity manifesting in a subset of such multivariate spatiotemporal data may indicate an emerging disease outbreak. The key benefit that can be provided by big data analytics is the ability to automatically and comprehensively screen the incoming data for escalations that cannot be confidently explained as random fluctuations consistent with historical trends. They likely represent an emerging threat. Computational scalability of modern event-detection algorithms allows for large-scale screenings with a small number of constraints, giving public health officials a timely and complete view of possible challenges. Being situationally aware, they can validate the most significant detections and mitigate emerging crises before they escalate and impact a substantial number of people.

Modern biosurveillance systems will soon benefit from electronic health records and related developments to enable highly specific, granular analyses of data. Comprehensive reporting of individual disease cases with multiple descriptive details (reported symptoms and signs, treatment, patient demographics, relevant medical history, outcomes, etc.), especially from regions where such detailed information was never recorded, will allow multiple beneficial uses of the resulting data. The potential scope includes but is not limited to highly specific syndromic surveillance of infectious diseases, monitoring of populationwide trends of chronic diseases, detection of emerging new health threats, forecasting demand on healthcare resources, tracking long-term trends in disease evolution and effectiveness of treatment, enabling scientific discovery, and other similar objectives.

However, many currently existing public health information systems are subject to various limitations, including spotty coverage, large latencies in data reporting, low resolution and uncertain quality of data when it is available, limited analytic capacity at local and country levels, and so forth. These limitations are further exacerbated by underdevelopment, lacking infrastructure, and limitations of available resources (human and financial), often found in developing countries. And often the developing countries are where the health challenges with a potential worldwide impact emerge first. Their discovery, mitigation, and containment at or near geographic origins are certainly desirable objectives. Luckily, the emergence of universally accessible communication technology has been recently shown to mitigate some of the challenges. It allows deploying practical and affordable biosurveillance systems even in rural areas of developing countries without substantial information technology infrastructure.

One example of such system, the Real-Time Biosurveillance Program (RTBP), involves an application of the event detection technology to multivariate public health data in the country of Sri Lanka [16]. The system relies on simple and affordable cell phones to convey the contents of comprehensive and accurate hand-written records of outpatient visits. This information goes to a central data repository for monitoring, detection of emerging outbreaks of diseases, as well as visualization, drill-downs, and reporting. RTBP has been found practical and effective at rapid and reliable detection of emerging spatiotemporal clusters of disease and at monitoring dynamics of chronic diseases. Its setup required minimal investments in infrastructure, relying on standard cell phone technology to digitize and relay patient visit data (symptoms, signs, demographics, preliminary diagnoses, and treatments) collected at rural (infrastructure-deprived) healthcare facilities from the field to decision makers. The system dramatically reduced data-reporting latencies (from weeks to within 24 hours), allowed collection of high-resolution information (down to the individual case level, and with multiple dimensions) with much more detail than preexisting solutions and at a fraction of their cost. The included comprehensive statistical analysis toolkit has been designed for rapid processing and highly interactive visualizations of the results of statistical analyses, drill-downs, rollups, and various types of reporting, making the RTBP a complete business intelligence solution that enhanced situational awareness of public health analysts and managers. Big data analytics has been the key enabler of effective and comprehensive handling of daily aggregates of 25 data attributes of various arities, yielding almost 100,000 unique conjunctive combinations of attribute-value pairs represented in data, with a theoretical size of the full contingency table in excess of 10^{12} cells.

The analytic component of RTBP relies on the capability of large-scale screening for subsets of data that show statistically significantly increased numbers of current patients. The method of choice is a bivariate temporal scan [12]. It considers, for instance, the number of children with bloody stools arriving this week from the southern outskirts of the city as the target query, and compares that number against a baseline activity such as the current week's count of patients from the southern suburbs less the number of those in the target group, as well as against counts of target and baseline groups observed in the past. The resulting four numbers fill a two-by-two contingency table, and a statistical test of its uniformity is performed (typically, either Fisher's exact or χ^2 test is used). Upon appearance of an unusually high number of patients who belong to the target group, when compared with the size of the corresponding baseline population and with the target and baseline counts observed during historical reference periods, the resulting p-value of the test will be low. The RTBP massive screening algorithm tries a very large number of target queries and produces the list of findings sorted by their p-values from the most to the least anomalous. The cached sufficient statistics framework allows such large-scale searches to complete fast enough for practical, often interactive use [13].

RTBP has been extensively validated on historical epidemiological data. Within seconds of loading the data, the analysts could find emergence of leptospirosis in Sri Lanka (Figure 11.1). Its interactive spatiotemporal analysis tracks probabilities of an outbreak of any named disease or any cluster of cases sharing similar symptoms (thick black line in time series display). When tried on historical data, it detected emergence of clusters of leptospirosis in 2008 and 2009 weeks before they were originally recognized by the officials (who did not have a capable surveillance tool at their

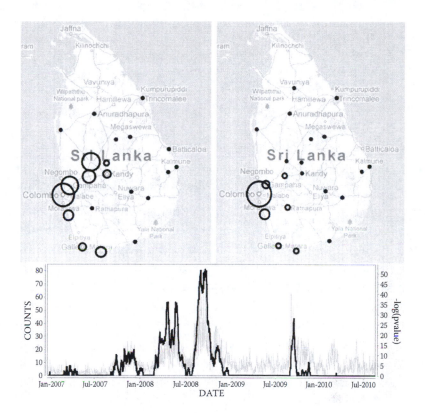

FIGURE 11.1
Retrospective tracking of leptospirosis in Sri Lanka.

disposal at the time). Light gray dashed lines in the time series plot depict the temporal distribution of daily volumes of patients diagnosed with the disease. The alert signal (black) highlights a few periods of unusually high activity of the disease that are automatically flagged by the statistical scanning algorithm. The corresponding geospatial snapshots of the observed diagnosed case distributions for two periods of the highest escalation are shown in the maps. Circles with the radii proportional to the number of cases depict spatial distribution of the disease. The events of 2008 impacted primarily central-eastern provinces of the country. The outbreak of 2009 has primarily affected the capital region and the city of Colombo [6].

Dengue fever outbreaks in Sri Lanka in 2009 and 2010 are thought to be the worst in history. The one in 2009 amounted to 35,007 recorded cases and 346 deaths. An instance of RTBP would have issued warnings in early 2009 about that year's event, when dengue cases just began to escalate, and it would have continued to issue alerts throughout the period of escalated

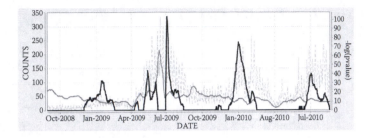

FIGURE 11.2

Dengue fever outbreaks in Sri Lanka in 2009 and 2010 are thought to be the worst in history.

activity of disease. RTBP early warnings would have given health officials valuable time to stage responses and to reduce the impact of the crises.

In Figure 11.2, temporal distribution of daily nationwide counts of dengue cases is plotted with light gray dashed lines. Moving average (aggregated monthly) of cases of all reportable diseases excluding dengue is shown with thin solid gray line, and the RTBP alert signal for dengue is plotted as solid black. RTBP event detection algorithm is sensitive to unusual escalations of dengue activity that could not be explained by simple means such as the overall increase of the number of reported sick patients. Using non-dengue disease counts as a baseline helps mitigate the impact of irrelevant data such as occasional fluctuations in the healthcare system throughput or reporting flaws, allowing for a reduction in the false alert rate. It is interesting to see a side effect of using such a baseline which manifested in the summer of 2009. During one of the periods of peak dengue activity, its alert signal briefly went down because the baseline counts escalate as well. That was due to an independent but simultaneous outbreak of another disease. Newer methods (such as Disjunctive Anomaly Detection algorithms introduced in [14]) can identify coinciding events that affect overlapping subpopulations.

Besides the originally intended goal to detect emergence of notifiable diseases, the system has also shown utility in tracking progression of chronic ailments. For instance, it enabled discovery of a gender division pattern among hypertension patients. The condition is apparently two to three times more prevalent in Sri Lankan female patients than in males. The extent of the difference has not been known to the health officials in the country prior to their use of this technology.

Extensive field validation of RTBP in Kurunegala region of Sri Lanka revealed several dimensions of its remarkable utility. It offers a qualitatively better timeliness of reporting and analysis than any of the preexisting systems because the input data is collected almost instantaneously (worst case, daily) as opposite to four- to eight-week latencies experienced before. It provides a much higher resolution and much more detail in data, leveraging case-level information as opposite to weekly-by-disease aggregates. It also offers unparalleled maintainability and cost-effectiveness. The total costs of operation are lower than with the previously used paper-based notifiable disease reporting systems (attainable 30 percent cost avoidance). Last but not least, it comes with capable analytic software that empowers epidemiologists and public health officials with up-to-date information about the current status and trends in health of populations in their areas of responsibility, enabling rapid responses to emerging crises before they escalate—a capability that had not been available to them before.

EXAMPLE APPLICATION: CLINICAL INFORMATICS

Clinical information systems collect and process various types of data to fulfill multiple objectives that include supporting diagnostic and treatment decisions, scientific research and discovery, clinical trials, surveillance of trends in response to therapies, detection of adverse events in clinical practice, as well as many business functions such as auditing of insurance claim reconciliation practices and fraud detection, to name a few. Many of such data sets assume the familiar form of logs of transactions, or they can be transformed to take such form. Richness, variety of types and form factors, and abundance of the clinical data, combined with multiplicity of potentially beneficial uses of the information it may contain, create tremendous opportunities for application of big data analytics.

One of the many important goals of clinical informatics is to equip physicians and nurses with surveillance tools that will issue probabilistic alerts of upcoming patient status escalations in sufficient advance to allow taking preventive actions before the undesirable conditions actually set in. A recent study [8] conducted a successful preliminary validation of an approach using high-frequency vital signs data (such as electrocardiogram signals, blood pressure, oxygen content, and similar waveform data measured at O(125Hz) frequencies) typically collected at the bedside of intensive care patients. To generate potentially informative events from vital signs, each measurement channel was first segmented into sequences of k consecutive observations. Then, Fourier transformation was performed to obtain spectral profiles of each segment of the raw signal. Multiple spectral profiles, extracted from periods of observation that were considered medically benign (no crises), were then assembled to form a k-dimensional flat table. Principal component analysis was then applied to this table, and the top p components were considered further. Those p components formed a null space spectral model of the expected normal dynamics of the given vital sign. One null space model was built for each measurement channel separately. Each newly observed set of k consecutive measurements could then be processed through Fourier transformation and projected onto the p principal components of the corresponding null space model. Over time of patient observation, those projections produced p time series per measurement channel. Then, a control chart can be applied (in particular, [8] used the cumulative sum (CuSum) chart [1]) to each of these time series and mark the time stamps at which CuSum alerts were raised. These alerts mark moments when the observed spectral decomposition of a vital sign does not match what is expected on the basis of the distribution of medically uneventful data. Each of potentially hundreds of such events may be informative of near-future deteriorations of health. Predictive utility of each type of the automatically extracted events was quantified using training data, which contained the actual health alerts in addition to the vital signs.

To accomplish the task, an exhaustive search across all pairs of CuSum event types (inputs) and alert types (outputs) was performed, where the big data analytics technology (in particular, the T-Cube cached sufficient statistics data structure [5]) provided the enabling efficiency. In this manner, input–output pairs with high values of the lift statistic were identified. Lift estimates the ratio of conditional probability of, in this case, observing a specific type of a health crisis given the recently observed CuSum event of a particular type, to the prior probability of observing the same type of health crisis at any time (irrespective of the presence or absence of any prospective indicators). Under null hypothesis of no relationship between the health crises and detected leading CuSum events, lift should equal 1.0. Input–output pairs with lifts significantly greater than 1.0 can be expected to enable prediction of health status alerts.

In a preliminary study [8], the authors found a few promising indicators of tachycardia episodes with lifts significantly greater than 1.0 and prediction lead times ranging from tens of minutes to a couple of hours. Then, they used a subset of these indicators as inputs for a machine-learning classifier that revealed cross-validation based recall of 85 percent

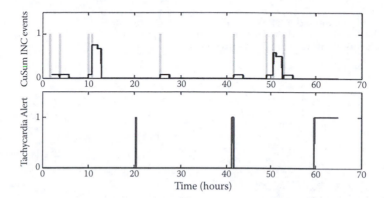

FIGURE 11.3

Frequency (dark gray in the top diagram) of candidate indicators (light gray) typically increases ahead of the onset of tachycardia events (bottom diagram).

at 4.85 percent false-positive rate, and the area under the ROC curve (AUC) score of 0.857. Figure 11.3 depicts an example result obtained in one patient with the presented method. The positive exceedance CuSum events (depicted with light gray spikes, their moving average frequency shown in dark gray in the top diagram) were obtained from one of the principal components of the blood pressure signal. The spikes in the bottom diagram indicate critical tachycardia episodes to be predicted. As can be seen, the frequency of indicator events visibly escalates a few hours prior to the onset of tachycardia occurring shortly past the 20-hour mark of this intensive care unit stay. The same early warning signal is raised again prior to a period of persistent tachycardia starting at about 60-hour mark. The accuracy and specificity of these candidate early warnings has been validated as potentially valuable by practicing cardiologists.

EXAMPLE APPLICATION: FINANCE

The examples above used either multivariate aggregation of the raw data or oddities among spectrally decomposed dense waveforms to identify relationships that may carry predictive power. In a separate case study, we looked at predicting changes in behavior of retail bank customers. We used a scalable implementation of temporal scan algorithm [12] to screen highly multidimensional bank transactions to detect recent changes in spending behaviors of customers. We stratified this data according to

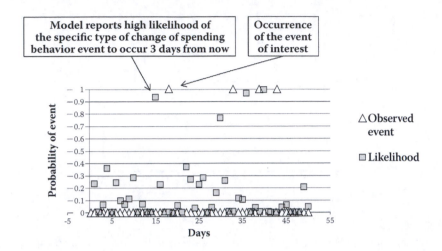

FIGURE 11.4

A big data analytics model can accurately predict one-day spending sprees three days ahead of their occurrence.

a variety of criteria such as age bracket, gender, education, affluence of home neighborhood, and so forth. The algorithm first detects temporal change points in the individual customer's activity by comparing it with their historical records as well as with the current and historical activity of relevant peer groups. The algorithm considered more than 230 different types of such points resulting from multiple stratification criteria mentioned above and from multiple time scales of sought behavioral shifts. Detected changes that could not be explained by random fluctuations of data are then considered as possible predictors of future events such as, for example, one-day credit card spending sprees. Machine learning can be used to automatically select the empirically most useful set of such candidate indicators. Figure 11.4 presents a temporal distribution of events of interest (to be predicted ahead of time, outlined triangles) and likelihood scores produced by the trained model (tone squares). The result has been obtained for one of the bank customers whose data was not used for training the model. This model was specifically tailored to forecast spending sprees supposed to occur three days ahead, and in the shown example it is indeed remarkably accurate at returning elevated likelihoods at this exact interval before the actual occurrences of these events. Cumulative performance at predicting this particular type of spending behavior, measured across several thousand test customers, provides the bank with the attainable positive yield on the order of hundreds of thousands of dollars per annum, net of the costs of processing false detections that occur at the rates that allow desirably precise identification of the events of interest.

EXAMPLE APPLICATION: MANAGEMENT OF EQUIPMENT

Typically, more than 5 percent of the budget of a developed country is spent on the maintenance and repair of equipment and structures [9], and yet too often less than a satisfactory proportion of the inventory is fully available for its intended use. For instance, 2010 mission capability rates of fighter fleets in the U.S. Air Force varied between 52 percent and 67 percent [15]. Managers of expensive equipment must carefully monitor processes that impact their supply chains to ensure the required availability and to control the costs of fleet sustenance. If logistics assumptions are violated, perhaps due to an inadvertent introduction of a batch of faulty spare parts or a change of equipment operating conditions, an unexpected surge of demand on maintenance and supply may develop, reducing availability and escalating costs of operations. In practice, complexities of the underlying processes often make it difficult for managers to recognize emerging patterns of failures before they make a substantial impact. Only when equipment readiness statistics are significantly affected will the notice be taken. Additional costs are often incurred due to expediting root cause investigations and implementing temporary solutions to mitigate the shortages. The ability to discover early indicators of such crises is the key to their effective and prompt mitigation.

The Collective Mind Trending Tool [7] aims to provide such capability. It is designed to notify fleet managers about emergence of one or more of a huge variety of possible problems substantially earlier than was possible before, and to enable pragmatic prioritization of investigative efforts according to the statistical significance of the detections. Recently, it has been validated in one of the U.S. Air Force jet aircraft fleets. Comprehensive statistical searches for fleetwide patterns of escalated maintenance activity yielded 10–20 percent improvement in accuracy of monthly watch lists of potentially problematic components while mitigating the "we do not know what we do not know" challenge. Similar automated statistical analyses help identify unexpected failure patterns in individual "bad actor" components and in individual aircraft. Early detection of systematic failures revealed avoidable replacements of parts. The resulting value of these avoided exchanges across this particular fleet of aircraft is estimated at \$18 million per annum.

The structure of a typical maintenance log of equipment fleet has a striking resemblance to the log of outpatient visits at hospital emergency rooms. Both types of data consist of records of time-stamped transactions with multiple categorical descriptors characterizing each entry. Patient demographics is analogous to the aircraft configuration data, clinical information to the history of use, signs and symptoms to the noticed malfunction modes and their circumstances, preliminary diagnoses and applied treatments to the records self-diagnostic information and repair attempts undertaken, and so forth. The complexities of maintenance data can, however, exceed the levels known in public health domains. Typical equipment maintenance logs we have analyzed would consist of 14–54 data attributes of various arities (besides time), 0.5–6.5 million unique conjunctive combinations of properties, and the theoretical capacity of the corresponding contingency tables ranging between 10^{25} and 10^{93} cells. Comprehensive analyses of such data would not be possible without scalability provided by big data analytics.

Maintenance logs are just one type of data collected about fleets of expensive equipment. Modern aircraft, for instance, produce extensive amounts of self-diagnostic information through the built-in structural, electrical, software, and electronic integrity monitoring systems. These additional streams of data create new opportunities for big data analytics. For example, correlating fault messages logged by the built-in test system with recent maintenance history can be used to quantify effectiveness of repairs and to identify possible unexpected side effects of configuration changes or upgrades.

One of common diagnostic modalities onboard modern aircraft are vibration sensors. Excessive vibrations are responsible for premature fatigue of structures and could shorten useful life of mechanical and electrical subsystems and components, as well as cause faults in electronics. We have recently evaluated the potential utility of big data analytics in processing vibration amplitude data collected with a particular type of sensor onboard more than 300 reasonably homogeneous aircraft over a prolonged period of exploitation, and in a wide range of flight regimes. The data has been featurized by computing dynamic characteristics (such as temporal derivatives of increasing orders) from the time series of specific vibration frequency channels. The resulting set of multiple numeric features was then fed to a machine-learning classifier (in particular, a Random Forest model was used [2]) with the binary output labels formed by the presence or absence of the actual vibration exceedence alerts during a period of 10 to 40 flying hours into the future. We hypothesized that many types of mechanical changes in aerospace structures begin relatively slowly and could be manifested in early stages by relatively miniscule changes in the observed patterns of vibrations, before they escalate to a level that requires alerting flight crews as well as ground mechanics of a possible problem. If we were successful at reliably predicting imminent vibration alerts a few good flight hours ahead of the onset of the actual crises, it would enable preemptive maintenance of the aircraft before flight safety was compromised and before significant repairs were required. It would allow improved reliability and safety of flight, while reducing the costs of maintenance.

Figure 11.5 shows the results of cross-validation of alternative approaches to predicting vibration exceedences recorded by one particular type of onboard sensor. The horizontal axis reflects the recall rates of the vibration alerts that actually took place, while the vertical axis shows the correct prediction rates. The hash line depicts performance of a random predictor, the dashed line uses time since the last exceedence as the only input

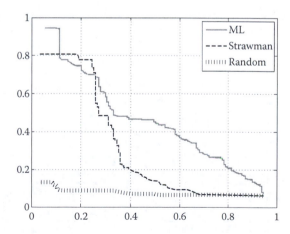

FIGURE 11.5

Precision (vertical axis)–recall (horizontal axis) characteristic of the model trained to predict vibration exceedences using dynamical features of the observed vibrations (solid line) substantially outperforms a simpler technique that uses time since previous exceedence (dashed line).

feature, and the solid line is our method of choice that learns to predict future alerts from multiple dynamical characteristics of the observed vibrations. At the 50 percent recall rate, which is when half of all actual exceedences recorded after 10 and before 40 flight hours from now are correctly predicted by the algorithm, almost 50 percent of the early warnings are correct (truly positive). This accuracy is about 2.5 times higher than that of an alternative that simply leverages the sequential character of occurrences of the vibration exceedences. The utility of the proposed machine-learning approach is even more evident at higher recall rates. If the user requires that 70 percent of all events are announced 10–40 flight hours ahead of their actual onset, the performance of the strawman method cannot be distinguished from random, but about one-third of the alerts (four times the baseline) issued by the machine-learning model are correct.

How does this performance translate to operational benefits? Figure 11.6 provides a characteristic with respect to one variety of pragmatic criteria. The horizontal axis denotes the number of preventive inspections triggered by machine-learning generated early warnings, and the vertical axis corresponds to the number of flights that originally were plagued with the particular vibration exceedences that the preventive maintenance would have helped avoid. This analysis assumes that the current operating procedure requires the ground crew to perform an inspection

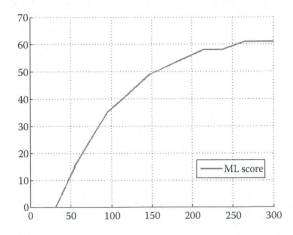

FIGURE 11.6
Operating characteristic of the preventive maintenance model. Vertical axis: Number of flights during which vibration alerts would be avoided. Horizontal axis: Number of additional maintenance actions.

and associated maintenance after each flight with at least one instance of such vibration alert. The use of early warnings allows performing it before these flights. We assume that such action would eliminate vibration exceedences that would have happened during the next flight, as well as any other exceedences if they form a sequential cluster (for the sake of this exercise, the cluster is assumed terminated when the gap between the last exceedence in the current cluster and the next event is greater or equal 20 flying hours). Hence, the benefits of early warnings are measured with the number of flights for which vibration alerts could have been avoided when using the machine-learning-based prognoses. These benefits increase, and the associated flight safety risk decreases, along the vertical axis of the graph in Figure 11.6. The cost of this operating procedure is measured with the number of preventive maintenance episodes that will need to be conducted in response to the early warning alerts. It is depicted along the horizontal axis of the graph. Subsequent points along the characteristic result from varying the sensitivity threshold of the machine-learning predictor at which the preemptive alerts are triggered. The higher the sensitivity the more alerts, leading to higher rates of recall of the actual imminent problems and potentially to a greater number of false positives. The optimal set point can be determined dynamically, for example, based on the current availability of technical personnel. In this case, the personnel capacity will translate to a hard limit of the number of preventive inspections that could be conducted in the specific amount of time, and the characteristic will translate that to the corresponding expected reduction of the number of flights with vibration alerts. Note that the preventive maintenance, if effective, would eliminate the need of postflight maintenance normally triggered by the in-flight alerts. Alternatively, a desirable operating set point could be obtained by establishing a specific cost/benefit tradeoff. For instance, responding to the 150 strongest machine-learning alerts would have eliminated 50 flights that would involve vibration exceedence alerts. This proposal may be feasible as long as the value of the avoided flight safety risk plus the improvement of equipment availability compensates the increased effort of the maintainers plus the cost of the expended consumable resources.

Similar experimental setups can be used to support human understanding of processes and patterns manifested in complex temporal data. Let us take as an example the familiar aircraft vibration alerts. As indicated before, high standards of flight safety enforce thorough processing of each

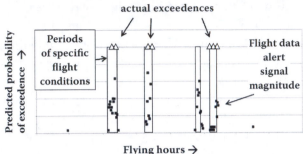

FIGURE 11.7
Machine-learning model identifies vibration exceedances that are explainable by the specific flight conditions and likely do not indicate a technical fault.

alert issued during flight and require ground crew technicians to investigate root causes in order to isolate and fix failures if they are in fact present. However, luckily, in practice many such alerts cannot be linked to any identifiable technical issue. A valid hypothesis states that at least some of them could be triggered by specific flight conditions as opposite to actual failure modes. If we were able to produce a model that could reliably correlate occurrences of certain types of vibration exceedances with specific flight regimes, such alerts could be potentially dismissed as "fake failures," allowing substantial savings of troubleshooting efforts by the ground crew technicians. To test the concept, we have built such models for the fleet of aircraft considered above.

An example result is shown in Figure 11.7. The model trained to predict a certain type of in-flight alerts using a 60-dimensional vector of flight parameters (pressures, angles, engine parameters, status of subsystems, declared phase of flight, etc.) produces a signal (plotted in solid squares) that temporally overlaps three out of four times with the bursts of vibration exceedances (outlined triangles) recorded during this flight. In addition, elevation of the predictive signal coincides with the aircraft being in a specific flight regime, which after expert evaluation was found to be a plausible explanation of these alerts. Plausibly explainable alerts would not require troubleshooting follow-ups by ground crews, saving time and money and keeping the aircraft available for the next flight without delay. This is one of many examples of the ability of big data analytics to find useful explanations of the observed phenomena when the complexities and the amounts of the underlying raw data make it extremely difficult for humans to process and comprehend.

SUMMARY

We have demonstrated a big data analytics approach designed to support discovering and leveraging informative patterns in large-scale multi-dimensional temporal data of transactions. This type of data is abundant in many domains of human activity. Our approach can be adjusted to specific application scenarios by customizing the featurization of the source data and by selecting the appropriate machine-learning algorithms to provide predictive capabilities. We have shown a few instances of societally and commercially beneficial use of the proposed approach. These examples leverage comprehensive screening of large databases for multiple different aspects of change, which in turn may help explain current events and carry information about the future.

ACKNOWLEDGMENTS

This material is based upon work supported by the National Science Foundation under award number 0911032. Many thanks to Michael Baysek, Lujie Chen, Gilles Clermont, Madalina Fiterau, Roman Garnett, Xuewei He, Peter Huggins, Yogi Koasanto, Katsuji Kurihara, Ming Liang, Rajas Lonkar, Saswati Ray, Maheshkumar Sabhnani, Norman Sondheimer, Nuwan Waidyanatha, and Yiwen Xu for contributing information that inspired this text.

REFERENCES

1. Basseville, M., and Nikiforov, I.V. *Detection of Abrupt Changes: Theory and Application.* Prentice-Hall, Englewood Cliffs, N.J. 1993.
2. Breiman, L. Random Forests. *Machine Learning* 45 (1): 5–32, 2001.
3. Burkom, H.S., Murphy, S., Coberly, J., and Hurt-Mullen, K. Public Health Monitoring Tools for Multiple Data Streams. *Morbidity and Mortality Weekly Report (Supplement)* 54: 55–62, 2005.
4. Dubrawski, A. Detection of Events in Multiple Streams of Surveillance Data. In *Infectious Disease Informatics and Biosurveillance,* Eds. D. Zeng, H. Chen, C. Castillo-Chavez, W. Lober, and M. Thurmond. New York: Springer, London: Dordrecht Heidelberg, 2010.
5. Dubrawski, A. The Role of Data Aggregation in Public Health and Food Safety Surveillance. In *Biosurveillance: Methods and Case Studies,* Eds. T. Kass-Hout and X. Zhang. Boca Raton, FL: Taylor & Francis, 2010.

6. Dubrawski, A., Sabhnani, M., Fedorka-Cray, P., Kelley, L., Gerner-Smidt, P., Williams, I., Huckabee, M., and Dunham, A. Discovering Possible Linkages between Food-borne Illness and the Food Supply Using an Interactive Analysis Tool. 8th Annual Conference of the International Society for Disease Surveillance, 2009. Available online at http://thci.org/syndromic/conference2010/09abstracts.aspx

7. Dubrawski, A., and Sondheimer, N. Techniques for Early Warning of Systematic Failures of Aerospace Components, *2011 IEEE Aerospace Conference*, Big Sky, MT, March 2011.

8. Lonkar, R., Dubrawski, A., Fiterau, M., and Garnett, R. Mining Intensive Care Vitals for Leading Indicators of Adverse Health Events. *Emerging Health Threats Journal* 2011, 4: 11073—DOI: 10.3402/ehtj.v4i0.11073

9. McGrattan, E.R., and Schmitz Jr., J.A. Maintenance and Repair: Too Big to Ignore. *Federal Reserve Bank of Minneapolis Quarterly Review* 23 (4): 2–13, Fall 1999.

10. Moore, A., and Lee, M. Cached Sufficient Statistics for Efficient Machine Learning with Large Datasets. *Journal of Artificial Intelligence Research* 8: 67–91, 1998.

11. Rolka, H., Burkom, H., Cooper, G.F., Kulldorff, M., Madigan, D., and Wong, W.K. Issues in Applied Statistics for Public Health Bioterrorism Surveillance Using Multiple Data Streams: Research Needs. *Stat Med.* 26 (8): 1834–1856, 2007.

12. Roure, J., Dubrawski, A., and Schneider, J. A Study into Detection of Bio-Events in Multiple Streams of Surveillance Data. In *BioSurveillance 2007, Lecture Notes in Computer Science 4506*, Eds. D. Zeng et al., pp. 124–133, 2007.

13. Sabhnani, M., Dubrawski, A., and Waidyanatha, N. T-Cube Web Interface for Real-time Biosurveillance in Sri Lanka. 8th Annual Conference of the International Society for Disease Surveillance, 2009. Available online at http://thci.org/syndromic/conference2010/09abstracts.aspx

14. Sabhnani, M., Dubrawski, A., Schneider, J. Searching for Complex Patterns Using Disjunctive Anomaly Detection, *ISDS Annual Conference Proceedings 2012*. Available online at: http://www.syndromic.org/uploads/files/Searching for Complex Patterns Using Disjunctive.pdf

15. Shackelford, M.D., and Carlisle, H.J. Presentation to the House Armed Services Committee Subcommittee on Tactical Air and Land Forces. *U.S. House of Representatives*, March 15, 2011.

16. Waidyanatha, N., Sampath, C., Dubrawski, A., Prashant, S., Ganesan, M., and Gow, G. Affordable System for Rapid Detection and Mitigation of Emerging Diseases. *International Journal on E-Health and Medical Communications* 2011, 2(1), 73–90, January–March 2011.

17. Wong, W.K., Cooper, G.F., Dash, D.H., Levander, J.D., Dowling, J.N., Hogan, W.R., and Wagner, M.M. Bayesian Biosurveillance Using Multiple Data Streams. *Morbidity and Mortality Weekly Report (Supplement)*, 54: 63–69, 2005.

12

Large-Scale Time-Series Forecasting

Murray Stokely, Farzan Rohani, and Eric Tassone[*]

CONTENTS

---

[*] Please note that this chapter was taken from "Large-Scale Parallel Statistical Forecasting Computations," in R. Murray Stokely, Farzan Rohani, and Eric Tassone, *JSM Proceedings*, Section on Physical and Engineering Sciences, American Statistical Association, Alexandria, VA, 2011, with permission.

INTRODUCTION

"It's tough to make predictions, especially about the future."

—**Yogi Berra**

Business executives in the technology sector face uncertainty about the future, ranging from unknown business conditions to unforeseeable changes introduced by new technologies. Any tools to quantify or reduce uncertainty can provide an advantage in decision making, such as in capacity planning or in formulating plans for future expansion. Data analysis generally and forecasting in particular can provide such an advantage.

Large-scale statistical computing has become widespread at Internet companies in recent years, and the rapid growth of available data has increased the importance of scaling the tools for data analysis. Significant progress has been made in designing distributed systems to take advantage of massive clusters of shared machines for long-running batch jobs, but the development of higher-level abstractions and tools for interactive statistical analysis using this infrastructure has lagged. It is particularly vital that analysts are able to iterate quickly when engaged in data exploration, model fitting, and visualization on these very large data sets.

Supporting interactive analysis of data sets that are far larger than available memory and disk space on a single machine requires a high degree of parallelism. That parallelism is frequently implemented using shared clusters of commodity machines (Barroso, 2009). We focus here on the open-source R programming language as opposed to commercial alternatives; the availability of the source code facilitates integration into a wide variety of distributed computing environments. Furthermore, when scaling a statistical computation to thousands of nodes, the licensing costs of the commercial solutions typically becomes prohibitively expensive.

This chapter describes a statistical computing framework built on top of distributed infrastructure and how this infrastructure is used for large-scale ensemble forecasting. Ensemble forecasting can be used to analyze millions of time series of Internet services in different geographic regions to provide actionable business intelligence to drive capacity planning, marketing, and other business strategies.

BACKGROUND

Data Analysis in R

Split-apply-combine (Wickham, 2011) is a common strategy for data analysis in R. The strategy involves splitting up the data into manageable chunks, applying a function or transformation on those chunks, and then combining the results. Such techniques map closely to the MapReduce (Dean, 2008) programming model for large compute clusters.

In the traditional MapReduce programming model, the Map function produces a set of intermediate key/value pairs, which are grouped together by intermediate key and then passed to the Reduce function. The Reduce function is passed an iterator over the intermediate inputs, so it can process more records than will necessarily fit inside memory on a single Reduce instance. The MapReduce implementation then automatically parallelizes the computation by executing the Map and Reduce functions over different inputs on a large cluster of machines, handling machine failures, scheduling, communication, and other system management issues.

The lexical-scoping rules, functional programming support, and vector types of R make the language particularly well suited for the MapReduce paradigm. The language includes built-in functions that are local analogs of the Map and Reduce steps. For example, the built-in list apply family of functions, *lapply*, applies a user-provided function to a list of inputs.

A number of parallel apply packages are available in R (papply [Currie, 2010], snow [Tierney et al., 2008]) that allow a user to execute this step in parallel as long as the results can fit in memory on the calling R instance. MapReduce takes this one step further by adding a parallel reduction step for cases when the output of the Map step is too large for a single machine.

Related Work

A survey of common parallel R implementations is available from Schmidberger (2009). These implementations depend on technologies such as MPI or TCP/IP sockets relying on shared network storage for small clusters of workstations. In addition, they require manual preconfiguration of R and needed libraries on worker nodes. In enterprise environments with bespoke cluster management systems, additional approaches are possible.

We work with much larger clusters that may write to other proprietary parallel storage systems such as GFS (Ghemawat, 2003) or Bigtable (Chang, 2006). The scale of these shared clusters precludes manual prestaging of R, and thus we are not able to use these frameworks. Our approach is most similar to the RHIPE package (Guha, 2010), which implements a more complete MapReduce environment with user-provided Map and Reduce functions written in R that run on multiple nodes with Hadoop. In contrast to RHIPE, though, we instead focus on larger-scale clusters where more automated node setup is essential. Furthermore, in our system all definitions in the calling environment are serialized to disk and distributed to worker tasks, allowing the workers to reference functions, classes, and variables using the lexical scoping rules expected in the R language. This allows users to transparently spawn thousands of worker tasks to execute R functions over a subset of their data and then write out intermediate results to the cluster storage systems or return results directly to the interactive instance.

MAP: PARALLEL APPLY

In this section we describe the high-level design and implementation details for a series of R packages facilitating the use of Google data centers for executing massively parallel R code.

Design Goals

Our design goals were based on observations of how the use of R at Google has evolved over the past several years. In particular, these goals included the following:

- Facilitate parallelism of computations on up to thousands of machines without access to shared NFS file systems.
- Make distribution of code and required resources as seamless as possible for analysts to minimize code modifications required to enable parallelism.

- No setup or preinstallation of R or specific libraries should be required on the machines in the cluster. A virtual machine for the workers should be created dynamically based on the global environment and available libraries of the caller.
- Return results of parallel computations in list form directly back to the calling interactive session, as with *lapply* in R.
- Allow the parallel functions to be used recursively, so that MapReduce workers can in turn spawn additional MapReduces.

Implementation Overview

The figure below shows an overview of the basic implementation of our Parallel Map framework. The three main steps of the process are described below.

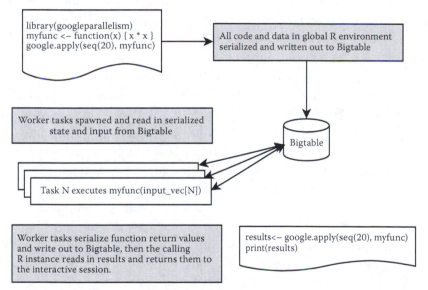

- First, the user's code calls *google.apply()* with a list of inputs and a provided function, *FUN*. An archive is dynamically created on the client including R and all of the needed libraries and then staged to the cluster management system in a data center with available resources. *FUN* and its environment are serialized and written out to a Bigtable in that data center.
- Second, workers tasks are spawned using the dynamically generated virtual machines providing access to all of the R packages that were loaded in the calling instance's R session. These workers read in the serialized environment from the Bigtable, execute the provided

function over a unique element of the input list, and write out the serialized results to a different column of the Bigtable.

- Third, and finally, the calling R instance reads back in the serialized return values from each worker task, performs the necessary error handling, and returns the computed list to the *google.apply()* caller.

The next three subsections provide more detail about each of these three steps.

Lexical Scoping and Serialization in R

To reduce the effort of utilizing Google's parallel infrastructure for statistical computations, we opted to automatically serialize the calling environment and distribute it to the parallel workers. This allows users to reference visible objects from their calling frame in a way that is consistent with the R language, without requiring cumbersome manual *source()* calls of distributed R files on the worker tasks.

The R language's lexical-scoping rules require that free variables in a function be resolved in the environment that was active when the function was defined (Gentleman, 2000). The figure below shows a brief example of a function definition and the bindings of the variables to different calling environments. Serialization of a function thus requires the serialization of the calling environments all the way up to the global environment to ensure that any possible variable references or function calls used in the innermost functions are available when the serialized environment is loaded on another machine. The default R serialization mechanism described by Tierney (2003) handles these details to allow us to stream the complete calling environment from the interactive or batch R instance and the spawned worker tasks.

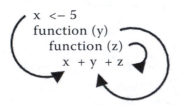

The algorithm below runs on the calling R instance and shows how the input list is split up, and the input function is serialized with the calling environment and distributed to worker tasks. One caveat with this approach is that package name spaces are serialized by name. This means that all loaded packages must be packaged up inside the virtual machine that is dynamically generated and distributed to the spawned worker tasks. Furthermore, any mutable objects, such as user-defined environments, that are hidden within a package namespace are not serialized—a very rare occurrence, in practice, that is the price of not requiring any manual setup of worker nodes.

Algorithm: Task Distribution

```
  # Simple case, we have 1 worker for each list element :
  if (length(x) <= max.workers) {
    assign(".G.INPUT", x, env=.GlobalEnv)
    assign(".G.FUNCTION",
            function(x) { FUN(x, ...) }, env=.GlobalEnv)
  } else {
    warning("length(x) > max.workers, some worker tasks will ",
            "execute over more than 1 input.")
    new.input = InputSplit(x, max.workers)
    assign(".G.INPUT", new.input, env=.GlobalEnv)
    assign(".G.FUNCTION",
            function(x) { lapply(x, FUN, ...) }, env=.GlobalEnv)
  }

  # Step 2. Save the environment of the calling session
  shared.env <- tempfile(".Rdata")
save(list = ls(envir = .GlobalEnv, all.names = TRUE),
       file = shared.env, envir = .GlobalEnv)

  # Add the .Rdata file, R, and packages to stage in our VM.
  packages <- list(VMPKG(files=shared.env))
packages <- c(packages, VMPKG(files=GetRFiles()))

  # Get Bigtable rowkey where results should be written.
key <- GetBigtableKey()

  # Launch the tasks with the created VM.
LaunchRVMs(max.workers, packages, key)
```

Worker Scheduling

In shared-cluster environments with thousands of machines, the runtime of long-term statistical computations will be affected by failures, upgrades, workload changes, task preemptions by higher-priority jobs, and other factors. To deal with these events, individual worker tasks that fail will need to be restarted or migrated to separate machines. In some cases, backup workers may need to be scheduled if some particular workers are taking longer than others due to hardware, network, or contention from other shared workload jobs on that machine. In other cases, we may be able to return when, for example, 95 percent of the workers have completed to provide most of the accuracy of our computation at a fraction of the runtime cost compared to waiting for all workers to complete.

There are two parameters that we expose to the callers for scheduling their R worker tasks: (1) the total number of failures we will tolerate from an individual worker task, and (2) the total number of worker failures across all tasks. The first parameter should scale with the total runtime of the job and is set to a reasonable default since we do not typically know the runtime of a job before first execution. The second parameter should scale with the total number of parallel tasks that were launched. We also provide deadlines and other scheduling parameters to give users greater control over the worker tasks. Dealing with stragglers and scheduling is an active area of research in MapReduce (Ananthanarayanan, 2010).

Error Handling and Return Values

When the worker tasks have completed, the calling R instance reads in the serialized results from the Bigtable, unserializes the result for each worker, and returns R language results. Depending on the scheduling parameters in use, all of the workers may have completed successfully, some may have failed to run completely because of resource constraints on the scheduling system, or some may have run but reached an exception in the R language code executed on the workers. In all cases, we seek to examine the results and promote errors from any of the workers to the attention of the caller. By default, the worker code is wrapped in a try() so the calling instance examines the returned output after unserializing it from the Bigtable and issues a warning() with the task number and exact error message from any try-errors encountered by any of the workers. If all of the workers returned a try-error, then these warnings are promoted to a stop error.

So far, we have described a massively parallel approach to the common split-apply-combine data analysis paradigm, but we have not fully taken advantage of MapReduce because the results from all Mappers return to the calling R instance—essentially a MapReduce with a single reducer. The next section describes the extensions necessary for statistical computations where the aggregate of the outputs from the machines running the Map function is far too large for the memory of a single machine.

REDUCE

The parallel apply functionality described in the previous section allows the speedup of embarassingly data-parallel jobs onto thousands of tasks. The individual tasks may return a result to the calling function or also generate plots and write out other results to distributed data stores.

There is limited support for streaming statistical computations in R, and so we have taken a hybrid approach for MapReduce-like statistical computations. This approach involves using a scalable query processing system directly over the intermediate outputs to implement the types of aggregations typically performed in a Reduce. Since our parallelism implementation allows individual Map workers to in turn generate separate parallel R applications, possibly running in a different data center, we can chain together a series of computations at the R level and then perform the final aggregation step with a distributed query system.

Data Storage and Serialization

R provides two main mechanisms for importing and exporting raw data: the simple binary serialization interface and comma-separated value (CSV) files of tabular data. The serialization interface, described in the section on lexical scoping, can share code and objects between different instances of R but cannot transfer information between R and other systems. The CSV method, in contrast, is widely used to share data between scientific applications but provides no type-safety or efficient binary representation and scales poorly beyond million-record datasets.

To overcome these difficulties we use protocol buffers (https://developers.google.com/protocol-buffers/) extensively for sharing data between parallel R applications and other systems. Protocol buffers are a language-neutral, platform-neutral, extensible mechanism for serializing structured data. Support for the R language is provided by RProtoBuf (available through the Comprehensive R Archive Network, http://cran.r-project.org). By generating a protocol buffer schema for R *data.frames*, we are able to efficiently write out a binary representation of our data that can be parsed in tools written in other languages safely and efficiently.

Distributed Result Aggregation in Dremel

Individual Map functions written in R can export intermediate results in a variety of formats. We focus here on protocol buffer outputs stored in the nested column-striped representation described in the Dremel paper (Melnik, 2010). R data.frames and lists are written directly to this format from the Map functions in R code. When the Map functions complete, the resulting columnar data files are queried directly using an R-language interface to the Dremel scalable ad hoc query system. In contrast to Pig (Olston, 2008), Hive (Hive Development Team, 2011), or Tenzing (Chattopadhyay, 2011), these queries execute immediately against the data in place, without having to launch separate MapReduce jobs over the data.

In these sections, "Map" and "Reduce," we have described the design and implementation of R packages that take advantage of the distributed systems available at Google for high-level statistical computing tasks. In the next two sections we present how this infrastructure can be used for statistical forecasting of a large number of time series.

APPLICATION TO FORECASTING

Forecasting at Google

At Google we use forecasting for numerous purposes, including evaluating performance and anomaly detection. We forecast many quantities (such as queries, revenue, number of users, etc.) for many services (such as web search, YouTube, etc.) and many geographic locations (such as global, continents, countries, etc.), which involves forecasting thousands of time series every day.

These time series exhibit a variety of trends, seasonalities, and holiday effects. For example, the number of Google searches for the query *pizza* grows with a different rate compared with the query *car insurance*.[*] The figure below shows that the two queries also differ in their behavior during the end-of-year holiday season, when pizza queries spike while car insurance queries dip. Consequently, we may need to use different models to forecast pizza and car insurance queries.

Building and updating forecasting models individually for thousands of different time series is expensive, impractical, and requires a considerable

---

[*] All data sets used here are publicly available from Google Trends, http://www.google.com/trends/.

amount of human intervention—highlighting the need for a generic forecasting methodology that is robust and provides an adequately accurate
forecast for each time series. In this section, we focus on how the *google-
parallelism* package in conjunction with Google's infrastructure can be
a useful, practical, and inexpensive method for building, evaluating,
and engineering such a forecasting methodology in the R programming
language. A high-level overview of our forecasting methodology is provided in the next subsection, but further details are beyond the scope of
this chapter.

Brief Overview of Forecasting Methodology

As opposed to fine-tuning a single model, we generate forecasts by averaging ensembles of forecasts from different models (Armstrong, 1989, 2001;
Clemen, 1989).

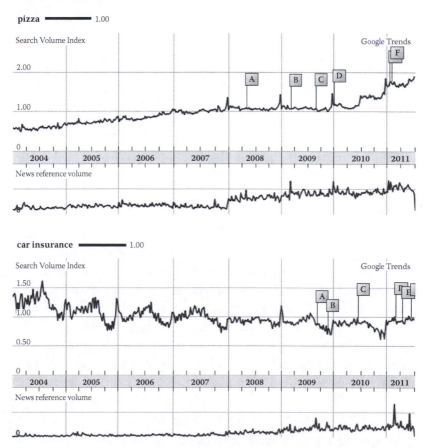

Trend and Seasonality for Pizza and Car Insurance Queries from Google Trends

The idea is to reduce the variance and gain robustness by averaging out the various errors from individual models. The figure below shows the ensemble of forecasts for weekly *pizza* searches. The black solid line in the middle is the trimmed mean* of individual forecasts at each point in time. This forecasting methodology does not provide the best forecast for every single case but works well in large-scale forecasting, where it consistently produces adequate forecasts with minimal human intervention.

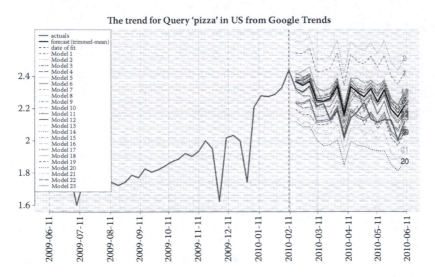

The trend for Query 'pizza' in US from Google Trends

The Ensemble of Forecasts for U.S. Pizza Queries

The robustness of ensemble averaging and the convenience of using R come at a price. Combining multiple models makes it difficult to quantify the uncertainty associated with the forecast process—that is, we cannot build confidence intervals or perform statistical inference. Using simulation-based methods is a typical solution to the problem, but these methods are computationally intensive, particularly on the scale at which we seek to operate. In the next subsection, we describe how the *google-parallelism* package can help us in building forecast confidence intervals using parallel simulations.

---

* The top and bottom 20 percent of individual forecasts are trimmed at each point in time.

Forecast Confidence Intervals

Forecasts inevitably differ from the realized outcomes, or *actuals*. Discrepancies between forecasts and actuals reflect forecast uncertainty or true differences. Because our ensemble methodology does not provide a measure of statistical uncertainty, we generate simulation-based confidence intervals, which necessitates a large number of computationally intensive realizations. We use the general framework described in the previous sections to generate these confidence intervals over many more time series than was previously possible.

We apply a computationally intensive simulation method called the *bootstrap* (Efron, 1987, 1994) to the forecast residuals each week to project a sample of trajectory paths for an arbitrary number of periods into the future. We extract the distribution of simulated traffic at each time to compute the uncertainty associated with different attributes of the time series, such as year-over-year growth values and daily, weekly, and quarterly totals.

The figure below depicts the algorithm used for simulating the realizations of time-series paths. For one realization of values in the next n weeks, we repeat the following three steps n times:

1. At the training end date, we forecast the next week's value.
2. We adjust the forecast value in Step 1, multiplying by an adjusting factor (a randomly generated number based on the distribution of historical one-week-out forecasting errors).
3. We add the adjusted value in Step 2 to the history as a new actual and move the training end date to the next week.

•——•	History
●	Train end data
•——▶	**Forecast next week**
- - - - -	Random adjustment *
•·········•	Simulation path

* Based on historical 1-week-out errors

Iterative Forecasts

The figure below depicts 1,000 realizations for the normalized number of weekly *pizza* searches for 13 weeks starting at our training end date,

February 16, 2010. At each time t, we take the $\alpha/2$ and $1-\alpha/2$ quantiles of the realizations as the lower and upper bounds of the $(1-\alpha)100$ percent forecast confidence interval. These intervals are pointwise, and for 95 percent confidence regions we expect 5 percent of the actuals to fall out of the bands.

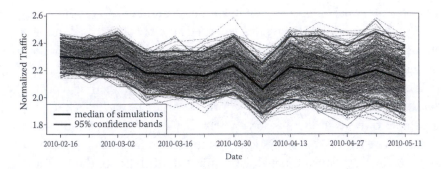

One Thousand Realizations of Pizza Traffic Trajectories

To get 1,000 realizations for the next year (52 weeks), we need to run the forecasting code $1000 \cdot 52 = 52,000$ times. A single run of the forecasting code takes about 5 seconds, so computing a one-year-long confidence region would take $5 \cdot 52,000 = 260,000$ seconds, almost 72 hours, on a single workstation, which is impractical for our purposes.

For forecast simulations, we can parallelize only the between-realization forecasts, while within-realization forecasts must be run on the same machine due to the iterative nature of the method—each forecast for the same realization uses the output of the previous forecast in the chain as an input. Overall, the R package reduced the running time in the above example to 15 minutes (about 300 times faster). Experimental measurements of the task setup costs and runtime distribution of the tasks is presented in the section "Experimental Results."

Forecast Evaluation and R MapReduce

To ensure that proposed changes to our forecast parameters and models improve accuracy in general, and not only for a particular time series, we need a comprehensive performance evaluation suite over the large set of time series that we forecast. We use the R parallelism functionality described in the previous sections to build a scalable forecast evaluation system. After trying out a change in our forecasting code, the output of this system is used to decide whether or not the proposed change should be implemented. Our evaluation system consists of four major parts, which are depicted in the figure below:

- A Google *datastore* (Bigtable) that stores a set of time series to forecast.
- A *forecast mapper* that parallelizes the current and the updated forecast on a Google data center for the time series in the data store (Part 1) at different prespecified training end dates. The output of each forecast is an R data.frame with columns specifying the time series, the forecasting model, the training end date, the forecast/actual date, the length of forecast horizon, and the forecasting error, (forecast – actuals)/actuals.
- The intermediate data.frames are saved on GFS in the nested column-striped format explained in the section "Reduce."
- A *forecast reducer* that uses the Dremel query system to aggregate the results of the forecast mapper and provides information regarding the forecast performance, such as mean absolute percentage error (MAPE) metrics.

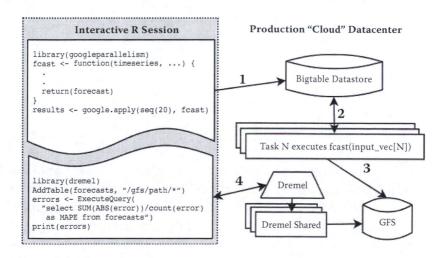

On a single computer, it would take weeks to generate historical forecasts at the scale of Google data. The forecast mapper uses the *googleparallelism*

package to regenerate hundreds of thousands of historical forecasts in a matter of hours: 100,000 forecasts would take less than two hours on 1,000 computers. Also, the output of forecast mapper contains millions of data. frame rows, which makes the aggregation step very slow using standard R data manipulation. For 1,000 time series in the datastore and 100 different training end dates, the output of forecast mapper would have more than 20 million rows. Using the R Dremel package, we can perform basic aggregations over this 20-million row data set in seconds. For example, we can easily compute the MAPE for different forecasting models and for a particular forecast horizon (like one-year-out forecasts) in only a few seconds.

Experimental Results

This section provides empirical results of the runtimes for the iterative forecast simulations. The table below shows the mean and 95th percentile runtimes for the five parallel jobs used to generate the results in the "Application to Forecasting" section. Each task generates one realization of traffic for the next 15 weeks (from the training end date) using iterative forecasts (explained in "Forecast Confidence Intervals" and depicted in the figure there).

Simulation Run	Startup Time (s)		Run Time (s)	
	Mean	95%	Mean	95%
1	48.3	88	249.4	266.1
2	40.8	67	260.7	283.1
3	43.3	74	312.6	343.0
4	37.4	61	283.5	304.0
5	32.3	44	249.5	264.0

These results demonstrate the motivation for some of the scheduling parameters described in "Worker Scheduling." The long tail of straggler jobs is responsible for a disproportionate amount of the total runtime. On a large shared cluster the exact cause of the runtime differences could be due to workload differences, hardware capability differences, network congestion, or hardware failures. The effect is much more pronounced for longer-running jobs and is one of the reasons that setting a deadline or scheduling duplicate tasks for the stragglers can help improve total runtime performance, as is suggested by the figure below.

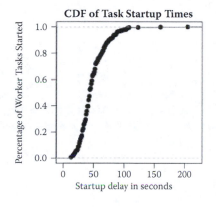
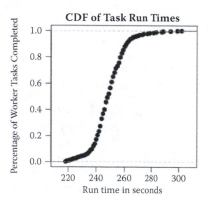

CONCLUSION

In addition to the applications described here, the *googleparallelism* R package has been applied to a variety of problems at Google requiring large-scale statistical analysis. Since the initial development of the package, analyst teams have launched more than 64,000 parallel statistical jobs using an average of 180 machines each.

Importantly, this parallelism is available to analysts without any experience with Google's engineering infrastructure, dramatically expanding the set of people who can take advantage of the system—and allowing analysts to direct their creativity toward their problem domain without worrying about the infrastructure.

ACKNOWLEDGMENTS

Many other statisticians, engineers, and data analysts have made contributions to Google's evolving infrastructure for large-scale statistical computations. We would like to first acknowledge the work of Karl Millar for the bindings he developed between the R language and Google's predominantly C++ infrastructure. John Rothfels first wrote bindings between R and Bigtable, which were a useful prerequisite for scaling up to larger data sets. Josh Wills, Pete Wilson, Raj Shenoy, and Steve Scott also made significant contributions in building the infrastructure for high-level statistical computing in R in Google datacenters.

REFERENCES

Ananthanarayanan, G., Kandula, S., Greenberg, A., Stoica, I., Lu, Y., Saha, B., and Harris, E. (2010), "Reining in the Outliers in Map-Reduce Clusters Using Mantri," in *Proceedings of the 9th USENIX Conference on Operating Systems Design and Implementation*, Berkeley, CA: USENIX Association, OSDI'10, pp. 1–16.

Armstrong, J. S. (1989), "Combining Forecasts: The End of the Beginning or the Beginning of the End?" *International Journal of Forecasting*, 5: 585–588.

Armstrong, J. S. (2001), "Combining Forecasts," in *Principles of Forecasting: A Handbook for Researchers and Practitioners*, New York: Kluwer Academic Publishers, 417–439.

Barroso, L. A. and Hölzle, U. (2009), *The Datacenter as a Computer: An Introduction to the Design of Warehouse-Scale Machines*, Synthesis Lectures on Computer Architecture. San Francisco: Morgan & Claypool Publishers.

Chang, F., Dean, J., Ghemawat, S., Hsieh, W. C., Wallach, D. A., Burrows, M., Chandra, T., Fikes, A., and Gruber, R. E. (2006), "Bigtable: A Distributed Storage System for Structured Data," in *OSDI '06: Proceedings of the 7th Symposium on Operating Systems Design and Implementation*, Seattle, WA: USENIX, pp. 205–218.

Chattopadhyay, B., Lin, L., Liu, W., Mittal, S., Aragonda, P., Lychagina, V., Kwon, Y., and Wong, M. (2011), "Tenzing: A SQL Implementation on the MapReduce Framework." *Proc. VLDB Endow*, VLDB Endowment, pp. 1318–1327.

Clemen, R. (1989), "Combining Forecasts: A Review and Annotated Bibliography." *International Journal of Forecasting*, 5: 559–583.

Currie, D. (2010), *papply: Parallel Apply Function Using MPI*, R Package Version 0.1–3. http://cran.r-project.org/src/contrib/Archive/papply/papply_0.1.tar.gz

Dean, J., and Ghemawat, S. (2008), "MapReduce: Simplified Data Processing on Large Clusters." *Commun. ACM*, 51: 107–113.

Efron, B. (1987), "Better Bootstrap Confidence Intervals." *Journal of the American Statistical Association*, 82: 171–185.

Efron, B. (1994), *An Introduction to the Bootstrap*, New York: Chapman and Hall.

Gentleman, R., and Ihaka, R. (2000), "Lexical Scope and Statistical Computing." *Journal of Computational and Graphical Statistics*, 9: 491–508.

Ghemawat, S., Gobioff, H., and Leung, S.-T. (2003), "The Google File System," in *SOSP '03: Proceedings of the 19th ACM Symposium on Operating Systems Principles*, Lake George, NY: USENIX, pp. 29–43.

Guha, S. (2010), RHIPE: A Distributed Environment for the Analysis of Large and Complex Datasets. http://www.rhipe.org

Hive Development Team (2011), "Hive," https://cwiki.apache.org/confluence/display/Hive/Home.

Melnik, S., Gubarev, A., Long, J. J., Romer, G., Shivakumar, S., Tolton, M., and Vassilakis, T. (2010), "Dremel: Interactive Analysis of Web-Scale Datasets," *Proc. VLDB Endow.*, 3: 330–339.

Olston, C., Reed, B., Srivastava, U., Kumar, R., and Tomkins, A. (2008), "Pig Latin: A Not-So-Foreign Language for Data Processing," in *Proceedings of the 2008 ACM SIGMOD International Conference on Management of Data*, New York: ACM, SIGMOD '08, pp. 1099–1110.

Schmidberger, M., Morgan, M., Eddelbuettel, D., Yu, H., Tierney, L., and Mansmann, U. (2009), "State of the Art in Parallel Computing with R." *Journal of Statistical Software*, 31: 1–27.

Tierney, L. (2003), "A New Serialization Mechanism for R," http://www.cs. uiowa. edu/~luke/R/serialize/serialize.ps.

Tierney, L., Rossini, A. J., Li, N., and Sevcikova, H. (2008), *SNOW: Simple Network of Workstations*, R package version 0.3-3.

Wickham, H. (2011), "The Split-Apply-Combine Strategy for Data Analysis." *Journal of Statistical Software*, University of California, 40: 1–29.

13

Using Big Data and Analytics to Unlock Generosity

Mike Bugembe

CONTENTS

INTRODUCTION

Today millions of people are posting pictures and digital videos online. Mobile phones and social media enable us to track and share many aspects of our lives including what we eat, drink, and do for exercise. Many are open to sharing or talking about their interests, their jobs, brands that they like, recent transactions that they have made, and a lot more. As a result, nearly every decision point, activity, or transaction is generating some form of data; and this explosion of information is what we now call *big data*.

Big data has successfully captured the attention of most organizations today, with C-suite executives optimistic about the substantial business benefits that they expect to gain from big data initiatives. Organizations like IBM, Amazon, and Netflix have managed to harness it, successfully analyze it, and most importantly, use it to realize game-changing benefits. But these benefits should not, by any means, be restricted to profit-seeking organizations; in fact, it has more recently become apparent that big data and analytics will result in one of the most fundamental breakthroughs that the charity sector has seen in the last 30 years.

An entire volume can be dedicated to explaining exactly why and how big data can result in significant benefits for charities. This chapter, however, will provide a summary on how big data and analytics can address one key aspect of the sector, unlocking generosity. Before we embark on that journey, it is crucial that we understand one of the most critical conditions required for any big data or analytics initiative to succeed. This condition applies to all types of organizations, including charities and not-for-profits that are looking for big data and analytics to flourish and produce the benefits that it promises. Big data and analytics need context.

CONTEXT FOR BIG DATA

Many will think that context is the most obvious condition required for big data to succeed and therefore the subject tends to be taken for granted; however, it is surprising how many organizations invest no time in this and then wonder why they struggle to get value out of big data or their analytics initiatives. It is important to stress that it is not the only condition for success, but it is definitely one of the key ones. Tom Davenport in his book *Competing on Analytics* refers to this as a distinctive capability. In his research he found that the organizations that managed to get the most value out of analytics are the ones that have a clear and obvious distinctive capability. It is no coincidence that the organizations he cited are those that are commonly used as examples of successful implementations of big data.

To unlock generosity, big data's distinctive capability must be to understand people—to try and figure out why they are generous and what triggered or drove that decision. This understanding of people must go beyond the commonly sought-after demographics and transactional behavior (in the case of generosity, this could be historical giving transactions) and must look deeper at understanding psychological and biological aspects that form the foundation of human decision making. Surfacing this knowledge will neatly expose the areas where big data can weave its magic and demonstrate its benefits.

Many of the ideas presented in this chapter are not entirely new; they are actually a synthesis of research in biology, psychology, and behavioral economics. Ultimately, for big data and analytics to succeed in unlocking generosity, we need to understand what makes people tick, how they make their decisions to be generous, what triggers and symbols will stimulate them to take action and give to address the needs of all—from those suffering from a rare illness or hunger to the billions in poverty surviving on less than a dollar a day.

It is for this reason that I will require you to be patient as I spend a little time analyzing the biological and psychological aspects that influence our decision to express generosity.

ANALYZING GENEROSITY

It turns out that there are a vast amount of studies on the subject of generosity; the dictionaries define it as "the quality of being kind and generous" (Concise Oxford Dictionary Online) or a "willingness and liberty in giving away one's money, time, etc." (Collins Dictionary Online). We can actually use the iceberg model, frequently used for systems thinking, to extend these definitions.

The iceberg model is based on the notion that 10 percent of the total mass of an iceberg is above the water and 90 percent of it is underwater. It is that 90 percent that the ocean currents act on and what creates the iceberg's behavior at its tip. Generosity can be looked at the same way (Figure 13.1).

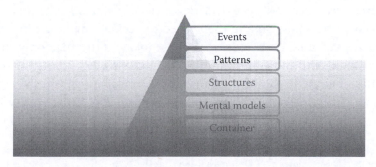

FIGURE 13.1
Systems-thinking iceberg.

We consider the acts of giving purely as the visible signs of generosity; this means that the opposite is true where the decision not give is also an event that could occur. These acts form patterns, which are often guided by underlying social structures and mental models, which are all held in place by values and beliefs also known as the container.

These beliefs and structures are often invisible, and these invisible constructs determine how and when someone will be generous. There are a myriad of articles and research papers on this subject, and for this chapter there are three important points that we need to understand about generosity.

The first is that generosity is natural, both innate and biological. For big data this means that it is a trait that we do not have to induce within people. Secondly, it activates only after the construction of a level of trust on both the psychological and biological planes. Finally, for the events or the acts of giving to materialize, the request has to be considerate of the giver.

Generosity Is Natural

There is a common belief that we are a perfectly designed social animal, one who seeks to cooperate for the benefit of our species and as a result it generally feels good when we are generous; allowing for any philosophical arguments here, it is widely accepted that the act of generosity feels good and when not followed through can leave us feeling unfulfilled. The fulfillment that we get is perhaps nature's way of telling us that it is OK and we should do more of it.

An interesting experiment described in the journal *Nature* (David G. Rand, Joshua D. Greene, and Martin A. Nowak, "Spontaneous Giving and Calculated Greed"*) also demonstrated that we are inherently generous. Here the researchers conducted an experiment in which individuals were provided with some cash and then asked to decide how much to donate to a particular fund. Participants who were told that they had only 10 seconds to make the decision gave more than those who were given more than 10 seconds to make the decision. Since impulsive decisions have their foundations in intuition, the researchers concluded that generosity is an

---

* Rand, D.G., J.D. Greene, and M.A. Nowak. (2012). "Spontaneous giving and calculated greed." *Nature* 489, (20 September), 427–430. doi:10.1038/nature11467.

intuitive human response. It is only when given time to rationalize that we calculate our way to a selfish decision.

This is good news for big data. The challenge of using data and analytics to influence behavioral change is made easier if the desired behavior is a natural human reaction.

Generosity Requires the Construction of Trust

Trust is a feeling defined as "a firm belief in the reliability, truth, or ability of someone or something" (Concise Oxford Dictionary Online). Typically, trust is formed around people with a common set of values and beliefs. It is the foundation on which all relationships are built, and when trust exists between human beings, some amazing things seem to occur.

Paul Zak, a professor in economics at Claremont Graduate University, was able to establish a relationship between the degree of trust and the prosperity of a country. Countries where trust is high are mostly rich or growing very fast, and less-affluent countries were found to be significantly low in trust. He went on to find that trust seemed to enable more transactions between individuals, which in turn stimulated economic activity. These findings begin to expose one of the key aspects of generosity; if economic activity requires trust, then surely a transaction like generosity requires the same foundation. In fact one of the stated barriers to generosity gleaned from a vast array of surveys is the givers' lack of trust toward the charity, particularly in reference to what the charity does with their donations.

Having established that trust is key, we need to know how to stimulate it. Paul Zak, whose work postulations have earned him the nickname "doctor love," believes that this calculation is biological; his studies identified the trust molecule, oxytocin, which is able to be externally inhibited and stimulated. This is fantastic news for big data; essentially this means that there are signals that the brain can receive to create a biological reaction that will enhance trust. While Zak's research is fascinating, con artists have known about this from as early as the fifteenth century and have successfully found out how to stimulate it to manipulate behavior for their benefit. The three-card Monte immediately comes to mind.

The fact that charlatans have used these stimuli for hundreds of years may suggest that these stimuli are not that difficult to identify. We seem to have a natural ability to spot these signals. Simon Sinek uses a fantastic example of the American in the metro in Paris, who upon overhearing another American accent on the metro formed an immediate bond with the stranger as his accent signaled that they had a common bond in this foreign place.

Quite simply, the expressed set of common beliefs and values stimulates trust in people. The number and type of signals required depends on the individual and the situation. We as humans do this assessment naturally, but big data can form these bonds too.

THE REQUEST MUST BE CONSIDERATE

So far we know that giving is a natural, instinctive trait; however, for it to materialize we need the presence of the molecule oxytocin. This molecule as we have discussed can be stimulated as well as inhibited through various signals, which are different for each individual. There is a final piece of the puzzle before we let big data loose on the problem. That is, the mode of the request.

When asking for something, the only way to maintain the instinctive reaction to trust is to be considerate when we make the request. This means that it needs to take into account the giver's circumstances. If I as a giver do not have money on me, I shouldn't be badgered; the requester must be reasonable in understanding that about me. Another consideration may be that I have just given to someone else and I simply cannot give to you too as well. The considerations neatly match many of the observed barriers to generosity that we have found in our research, and these include

1. I really cannot give to everyone.
2. How do I know if your cause is legitimate? I don't trust it.
3. What are you actually doing with the money?
4. I cannot afford it now.
5. Charity communications are inappropriate.
6. In the past, charities have never thanked me.

To illustrate the power of a considerate way to ask, I will refer to an experiment that Simon Sinek, the author of *Start with Why*, conducted on a homeless person.

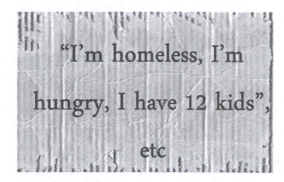

FIGURE 13.2
Typical homeless sign.

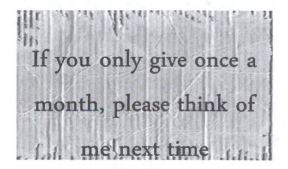

FIGURE 13.3
Updated homeless sign.

Simon Sinek came across a homeless person who was holding up the typical sign that a homeless person holds, resembling Figure 13.2: "I'm homeless, I'm hungry, please give."

With this sign the homeless person was making only about $20 a day. Changing the mode of asking to be considerate had a game-changing impact, with the homeless person earning more in an hour than previously in a day (Figure 13.3): "If you only give once a month, please think of me next time."

The updated request did several things by being considerate; it showed an understanding of the givers' values, beliefs, and possible constraints. The sign created oxytocin by sending the signal to the giver that

1. I know you cannot give all the time.
2. It is your call; don't worry if you don't give today.
3. My cause is legitimate; I will still be here.

Big data can be used to build an understanding of people so that we can be aware of the sorts of signals that will resonate with them, those that are common to their systems of thinking, values, and beliefs. With big data we can also get a hint of their constraints, past experiences, financial and social status, age, and income level. All of these are data points that we need to build trust and to be considerate and therefore unlock generosity.

WHY IS BIG DATA IN A POSITION TO SOLVE THIS?

As mentioned earlier, the social nature of people is changing. With individuals tracking significantly more of their data, we can see and learn a lot more about them. The rise of smartphones and other mobile sensors such as those found in the latest Nike Plus shoes, the inclusion of GPS in our cars, and the increased use of social media and the web for daily transactions are all contributors to this explosion of data. This has led to people, things, and brands being more interconnected than at any time before.

The main reason all of this data has suddenly become available is that it is cheaper to store. When storage was expensive, there was little appetite to keep all of this information. A terabyte of data used to cost in the area of $14 million, and today the price for the same amount is now around $70. This exponential cost reduction has coincided with the increased adoption of mobile phone technology and use of the mobile Internet in places where five years ago there were no hard lines available to get access to the web. Information is not a respecter of boundaries or barren landscapes, and as a result we are increasingly demonstrating our natural desire to share, communicate, and cooperate.

Today tech-savvy people could easily record a full behavioral trail of their lives, and this would be available for capture and storage; this data could be collated, mined, and reviewed. While this is exciting, it is also bordering on creepy. Analysts, data miners, and data scientists therefore have a responsibility to use all of this available information responsibly.

The significance of having all of this information on an individual means that we can analyze and model what makes them tick. Possessing a working model that shows us the process as well as the factors that either dissuade or influence someone to be generous, signifies that we have the means to inspire greater generosity and ultimately meet the challenge of unlocking generosity.

HOW BIG DATA AND ANALYTICS UNLOCK GENEROSITY

Big data and analytics can enable charities to learn so much about individuals. The information available can literally provide personally identifiable signals, behaviors, values, and beliefs. Big data can be used to figure out when someone is ready to start giving, the right time to attempt to retain an existing giver through cross-selling or upselling, which individuals are perfect to acquire, and how to ensure that they have a pleasant experience.

In a world where storage is cheap and the funds set aside for acquisition and growth are limited, big data and analytics are perfectly suited to maximize all of the internal efforts of a charity that is attempting to unlock generosity. This means that big data can reveal actionable insights that are cost-effective and maintain a positive return on investment.

With a thorough understanding of the mechanics of generosity, we now know exactly what to look for in the deep blue oceans of data. This section will outline a five-step approach that can be used to extract valuable nuggets of information from big data, while ensuring that the effort is cost-efficient and beneficial to the short- and long-term success of the charity.

The goal of the five steps is to develop an understanding of who the current supporters are, why they give, and key traits and characteristics that can be used for future acquisition efforts.

STEP ONE: ENRICH THE DATA WITH DEMOGRAPHIC AND SURVEY DATA

A previous donor will have traces of their historical transactions in the charities database. These traces are typically supported by the name and home address of the donor. On its own, this information is enough to build a really basic understanding of the existing donor. While this level of analysis can show interesting regional and financial inferences, it will fall short of providing enough to be able to deduce a common set of values and beliefs.

Inferences at this level are often inefficient and difficult to use. Just to illustrate the problem, my neighbors are in their 80s and have retired yet we have the same postal code, so using a basic regional segmentation and communicating to both my neighbor and me in exactly the same way is likely to alienate one or both of us. More will need to be done to this data for the charity to build a true understanding of who is giving to them and why.

More value can be generated from the data by enhancing it with additional data sets. This process of enhancing the data can turn a single support contact point, such as their postal address, into richer cross-channel access with e-mail and mobile. The typical first step to enhancing the data is to add additional demographic and survey response data. For this process, there are two sources of data that immediately spring to mind—Experian and TGI (although now called Kantar Media).

Experian has invested heavily in the capture of a vast amount of information on society trends, using a wealth of comprehensive demographic data sources and market research. They have variables including age, social class, gender, and income levels of most adults in the United Kingdom. In my experience they have managed 85 percent match rates against millions of donor records.

TGI, a company established in 1969, is also an incredibly valuable tool for charities. They have established themselves as one of the market leaders in market research with the ability to reveal valuable insights in consumer choices. From their work it is possible to make inferences like, if you go to the ballet, you have a higher chance of choosing to buy a BMW.

Appending this data is not a simple case of adding absolutely every variable available. If you have a smart architect and the ability to create a solid database structure, then be my guest. A more efficient approach is to use sample data and build models to identify which variables help form logical clusters and which ones are significant enough to be regarded as part of a predictive or analytical model.

Once the useful data points have been identified, resegmenting your customers will form a richer understanding of who typically gives to you. Suddenly, it will become clear if there is a particular age group or social class that gives to your charity—the volume and value of the transactions can be also be cross-referenced with their income data and their age, which will provide further insights and trends. Valuable segments can be defined with their associated donation behavior monitored over time. This richness of data begins to shed light on key characteristics of individuals and their preferred behavior.

It will be possible to identify groups of supporters that are more likely to volunteer, fundraise, or give monthly. It will show the impact of a supporter's age on their approach to being generous. For example, the use of descriptive statistics may reveal that younger supporters are more likely to volunteer than to give monthly; it may show that event-related fundraising (such as related to a marathon) is actually most popular among the 40–55 year olds from a specific social class as opposed to being popular with the younger, fitter demographic.

If we take a moment to reflect on the goal of unlocking generosity by establishing common beliefs and values as well as being considerate, it should become apparent that by simply adding this data, a charity can identify key characteristics of an individual that resonate with specific opportunities to be generous.

However, much of this is still inferred, and while it is richer than the basic transactional data, certain characteristics such as the organizations they work for, time pressures, family and religious values, opinions, and sentiments would enhance this even further. It is necessary to know more about an individual than simply their age and income. This is the arena for big data.

STEP TWO: ENRICH TRANSACTIONAL DATA WITH RELEVANT BIG DATA

Big data provides the perfect platform for identifying more valuable information about your supporters. It provides a different dimension to the data that we have already talked about. With big data we can find out how an individual thinks and makes decisions. We can see how private an individual is, what interests they have, brands they like, and so much more. Arbitrary data points, such as whether they exercise regularly or not, can prove to be significant. Gone are the days when businesses could wait months for surveys or focus groups. Most of this information is available in vast quantities and various forms as big data.

Social media is one of the most obvious hosts of such data. Interestingly, on the topic of social media, oxytocin rears its head again. Paul Zak, "the love doctor," mentioned in his most recent TED Talk that interactions on social media induced a double-digit release of oxytocin in the brain. This is another piece of fantastic news for big data; the confirmation that social media interactions can biologically induce trust is something that all organizations must pay attention to.

One of these social sources is LinkedIn, which can provide valuable insight on an individual and has personally identifiable data from more than 100 million users. Each of these users has at one point or another uploaded their basic employment details, full curriculum vitae, and a host of additional data including phone number, address, and education history. LinkedIn also tells us how individuals are earning their income and what industries are attracting specific types of people. This sort of information is particularly good for shedding light on the constraints that need to be considered when developing the message for an "ask." For charities that look to foster long-term relationships with companies, this source of information will prove incredibly valuable.

Facebook and Twitter are also fantastic sources of big data. There are over 900 million accounts in Facebook, which probably holds the largest variety of personally identifiable data on individuals. This includes data on conversations, family photos, records of places users have been, places users have eaten in, births, marriages, and deaths. The information on Facebook is so diverse that it could also be used as demographic data verification. The Facebook open graph neatly groups a list of actions such as *liked*, *listened to*, and *watched* to a list of objects such as *a song, a movie*, or *a brand*. This creates a logical structure for the data; for example, your supporter watched (the action) a documentary (this is the object) on starvation and poverty (these would be the attributes of the object). This allows for a very structured analysis of countless numbers of variables to get better insight on individuals.

Both Facebook and Twitter also provide insight on sentiment. This is typically produced through the analysis of the comments that people write. The blogosphere and microblogosphere (e.g., Twitter and its competitors) provide useful information into what groups of supporters and prospects are thinking and saying to one another. There are organizations and agencies that focus entirely on sentiment generated in social media and have proven to develop some really interesting results.

Another valuable category of data that these sources provide is information on who influences their supporters to be generous. Mistakenly, brands sometimes believe that they are best placed to build trust with a customer, but this is not always the case. Trust between friends is in most cases far stronger than trust between a brand and an individual. Influence is therefore likely to be one of the most valuable data points in social media, as it generally means the trust between the supporter and the influencer already exists and therefore the charity should aim to foster relationships with the influencer.

Justgiving is a fantastic demonstration of this phenomenon. Survey results show that more than 25 percent of individuals who decided to fundraise did so simply because they saw someone they knew do it. Interestingly, some of this data also showed that the influencer doesn't even have to be a friend or someone they know; all it requires is an individual who emits the common values and beliefs to inspire and motivate an individual.

All of these data points provide a significantly richer picture on who the supporters are, the sorts of messages that could be drafted to inspire trust, and removing any barriers preventing an individual from being generous.

This data could be used to develop accurate profiles and allow charities to classify and segment their supporters, based on individual demographic data, transactional, behavioral, social, and sentimental insight. Accurate profiles for various supporter types will enable charities to communicate more relevant messages and increase the value of the existing users by cross-selling and upselling.

Getting the messages right is one sure way of building trust, and by using the available data we can get insights into their needs. Strong messaging will encourage the supporters to remain engaged; it will generate the view that the charity is a trusted information provider.

Today supporters are expecting more personalization, so it is important for charities to deliver on these expectations.

Like the demographic and survey-based data, you will have to model it against your objectives to determine which variables are significant, which ones share interactions, and which ones enable strong differentiation when segmenting.

STEP THREE: FUSE THE DATA AND BUILD A SINGLE SUPPORTER VIEW

From the previous step we can see that there is a vast amount of data available, but we have also highlighted that space is cheap these days; so with a good database architect, this is the most opportune time to consider building a single supporter view (SSV). Consolidate all of the key variables from Facebook, LinkedIn, Experian, and TGI as well as some sentiment scores if they have been modeled into an SSV. What this will give you is a full historical analysis of an individual.

You will be able to identify where they have generated maximum value and what mode of generosity seems to suit them. The SSV will enable the charity to see whether an individual enjoys fundraising, volunteering, ad hoc appeal-related giving, or regular monthly donations. This insight begins to shape what a user is doing and more importantly what attributes about them seem to be predictors of their preferences.

For more sophisticated segmentation, a charity can prepare a "giving graph" for each individual, showing what they typically do at certain stages in their life and predicting what they are likely to continue to do once they hit certain milestones such as getting married and then having children. All of this can be inferred just by creating a single supporter view and enhancing the data with the extra variables sourced from big data.

Structuring all of this data will provide quick access to the facts so that predictive and analytical models can be built. It will expose the great diversity among the supporter base but also the commonalities. By focusing attention on commonalities, large populations can be reached in ways that seem more personal, and this is what supporters expect today.

The final step is an additional data source but built internally. To finally unlock generosity, the focus has to move from propensity and likelihood to understanding why.

STEP FOUR: MODEL THE DATA AND BUILD A MODEL OF WHY THEY GAVE?

Modeling the data from the sources described will provide some additional insight on how people decide to be generous. Data points such as the company they work for and the type of role they have in their organization could be significant variables in determining what type of message they should receive. If this data is merged with the books they have read and movies they have seen, one could begin to determine whether an individual's message preference is more analytical or emotional. Would they prefer to know what the charity is doing with the money or would they prefer a compelling emotional story.

There are different reasons or motivations for why people decided to give, and these have been neatly summarized in a book called *Fundraising Analytics* by Joshua M. Birkholz (2008).[*] The summaries of each motivation describe what a typical individual would look like or transact like—it is a summary of what would resonate with each individual. Big data can be used to identify each of these traits, such as, are they religious? Do they have a passion for museums? Do they tend to respond to disaster appeals? Birkholz talks about the following:

1. Loyalty—Typically this type of motivation is earned by the organization as a result of consistently meeting a specific need until the supporter goes there automatically. They would do so because the organization has built a level of trust that almost guarantees that they will always consistently meet their needs. Finding these people is getting more difficult because so many organizations are now operating in the same space. However, someone who has lost a loved one but has received regular support from a charity during that period is likely to be loyal.

2. Global impact—These givers are those whose motivation is the cause: if you look at their giving behavior you can see that they would have given to different charities but each of them support the same cause. For example, one may have given to several child abuse charities and is obviously not loyal to any one of them. This person needs to know the impact and tends to be analytical. We can find these people on aggregate databases; companies like justgiving.com, where over 12,000 charities have transacted, would be fantastic at identifying people who are likely to be motivated by global impact. The sources of big data can help us see if natural clusters form around these sorts of individuals; as an example, all of them might have studied economics and typically work in banks—no loyalty to a charity but focused on the impact. The charities that communicate impact to this sort of individual are tapping into the common values and beliefs and inspiring trust. Interestingly, these individuals also tend to give large amounts.

---

[*] Birkholz, Joshua M. (2008). *Fundraising Analytics: Using Data to Guide Strategy* (The AFP/Wiley Fund Development Series).

3. Personal interest—Similar to the global impact but more focused on local impact in their area; therefore the impact of the causes will tend to be something more visible, such as a local monument, theater, school, park, or playground. Supporters of arts and museums can easily be spotted on social media by identifying their interests.

4. Duty—These are typically faith-based givers; generally they will give to religious organizations but also others. The fact that they have given to religious organizations tends to be the first indicator, and out of duty they will also give to a range of other causes. Again big data and social media will provide the right data to identify these individuals very easily.

5. Empathy—These are givers during the tsunamis and very public disasters. They are more spontaneous and difficult to make loyal. These individuals can be spotted by analyzing their job roles and income—they are typically focused on their income and so would donate small amounts more frequently, unlike the decision maker that is more asset focused.

STEP FIVE: TEST, LEARN, AND MODEL RESPONSE

Sometimes companies forget that a large amount of the analysis is based on propensities. The suggested models of understanding people are all based on what they are likely to do, but few of them are based on how people responded to an "ask."

Therefore, after all of the models have been built, tests can be designed using various channels and modes of communication with a range of biases on the amount of creative content. This completes the 360-degree view of an individual. You will have an indication of propensities and what they are likely to do, and with this you will have metric-based evidence on how they are likely to respond to a specific "ask."

CONCLUSION

We have shown that big data holds a valuable amount of information, and fusing it with your transactional data can tell you who is supporting your cause and why. Using these two points alone, and armed with a thorough understanding of how generosity works, big data and analytics can provide insight into areas where common beliefs and values can be expressed to gain trust. It gives charities an understanding of people's circumstances to enable them to tailor their messaging. Using big data to get the additional information and then executing the messaging correctly will unlock generosity.

Charities should not feel squeamish about leveraging big data to inspire generosity. Instead they need to focus on establishing a privacy policy that is transparent about how data is collected and used. Recent studies have shown that generally the younger, more tech-savvy generation is fairly relaxed about sharing data. The social nature of people is significantly changing, and people are happy to share information to receive a more personal experience.

Most importantly, solving this riddle will lead to millions of people being fed, better quality of life for those with terminal illnesses, cures to diseases, and improved lives of those suffering from poverty. All in all, generosity will contribute to a better life for all of us.

14

The Use of Big Data in Healthcare

Katherine Marconi, Matt Dobra, and Charles Thompson

CONTENTS

INTRODUCTION

Big data is defined elsewhere in this book, but it has many attributes that apply to the large electronic sources of health data being created, managed, and analyzed by healthcare providers, health organizations, and patients and their families. Data from genetic mapping, pharmaceutical tracking, public health reporting, digital x-rays, CAT scans and laboratory results, payer and provider data, insurance claims data, and consumer online behavior adds up to petabytes of information. What makes this data so exciting is that big data has the potential to improve individual and population health, make the business of healthcare more cost-effective, and lead to new treatments of chronic and infectious diseases. In healthcare, the success of enterprisewide electronic information will be measured by its contributions to improvements in individual and population health.

We are in a new era of availability of health data that enables us to transform the data to usable health information and devise better ways to manage individual and population health outcomes. But the ability to combine data into large and useful information remains a significant challenge and will take unexpected twists and turns before its full potential is realized. Current practices and today's IT investment and strategic decisions can either promote or limit tomorrow's successes. In this chapter we discuss the types of big health data and its impact on patient, provider, and organizational health decision making. The chapter ends by discussing possible future trends and threats to using big data to improve the delivery of health services.

Some view data (as does the McKinsey Global Institute, 2011) as being "big" because it is just ahead of the culture and time period's methods of data storage and analysis. Big data combines information from different sources and is analyzed to change our practices; it should improve patient outcomes and improve the nation's healthcare delivery system. This concept of rethinking health information is not a new one. In 1854, John Snow (UCLA, nd), a founder of epidemiology, modernized methods of how we investigate and treat epidemics, specifically the transmission of cholera. He collected data in a new way, combined it with nonhealth information, and thought differently about it. Although his information covered slightly less than 200 sick individuals, by mapping their location along with the locations of noninfected individuals and the London water supply, he produced "big data" for that time period. He identified the source of a cholera epidemic, how it could be stopped, and introduced us to population-based health. John Snow pictured commonly available information differently and stopped an epidemic from spreading (Figure 14.1).

Sources of today's big health data can be grouped onto four categories based on American Informatics Management Association (AIMA) informatics domains:

- data associated with the delivery of clinical care
- public health survey and surveillance information
- genetic and medical research–related information
- healthcare-consumer-driven information

Big data is not simply drawn from each of these sources; it relates information among them in new ways. It also links to other available social and economic information. For example, it may involve linking traditional health information with nonhealth information, such as sales volume, to track patient behaviors or health conditions. Health managers, as they

FIGURE 14.1
Spot map of deaths from cholera in Golden Square area, London, 1854 (redrawn from original). Source: Snow, J. *Snow on cholera*. London: Humphrey Milford: Oxford University Press; 1936. Copied from CDC website: http://www.cdc.gov/osels/scientific_edu/SS1978/Lesson1/Section2.html.

plan enterprisewide IT systems, need to consider these external and internal sources of information that are available for their decision making.

Another modern example can be found in the genetic mapping of the 20,000 to 25,000 human genes and the underlying billions of DNA pairs. The National Institutes of Health 1,000 Genomes Project has made the data freely available on the web for research, the equivalent of "30,000 standard DVDs" (NIST, 2012). Because of the Human Genome Project, we now have screening tests available for a variety of inherited diseases and many potential avenues for advancing treatment. It is a model for shared medical research information that is available to others for further analyses.

Thus, the core principle of big data in health is the ability to combine large amounts of information using different analytic methods to improve clinical and related service delivery decision making. But we should also be aware that because big data influences how we make decisions, it may lead to changes in our organizations' structures and cultures. Big data necessitates working in clinically led teams, rather than the traditional physician-driven care model. It involves sharing of primary medical information among researchers, public health agencies, patients (consumers), and health services. Big data already is changing the way we share health information and deliver healthcare.

TYPES OF BIG HEALTH DATA

Combining clinical, public health, research, and consumer health data into meaningful information is challenging. Medical decision making is very complex, and recording it involves textual information, not just coding. While common data definitions for clinical conditions are in place, such as the *International Classification of Diseases*, Ninth Revision, Clinical Modification (ICD-9-CM) for diagnosis coding, there are gray areas that require further clarification and consensus such as definitions of individual characteristics in research studies and different versions of HL7 messaging standards. The many available software systems to choose from also add to this complexity.

There are policy issues of confidentiality and privacy, where individual information needs to be pooled for analysis without identifying the person. At the same time, there is the need to protect business-sensitive information in a very competitive and regulated medical environment. While these issues exist in other industries, they are magnified in healthcare and have become barriers to realizing the potential of big data. Clinical services, public health, medical research, and consumer-driven information share these common barriers to contributing to care improvement.

CLINICAL SERVICES DATA

For healthcare providers to realize the potential for clinical data to improve their practice and patient outcomes, their organizations must have the technology and capacity to relate information from a number of data sources, including unstructured data and visual information. Not only is this data large, but organizations must be able to acquire it, store it, and analyze it in real time to produce meaningful information for clinical decision making. In this context, meaningful information means results that are easily understood by clinicians, support staff, and administrators (depending on the system).

Clinical Decision Support Systems (CDS) layer on the analytic software to translate clinical data into real-time information for clinical decision making. They apply rules to patient care information to indicate contradictions in care or other outliers. The rules may be a combination of medical expertise and analysis of past illness, diagnoses, and treatment patterns. For CDS to improve care, the system must be acceptable to clinical providers and easily fit into the complex patient–provider workflow of organizations. In one example where the fit was not completely thought through by system implementers and users, information from a CDS bypassed the nursing information and had the potential to lead to medication errors. As an Agency for Healthcare Research and Quality (AHRQ) whitepaper indicates, the timing and ownership of CDS systems are essential to their success (Berner, 2009).

Clinical big data, however, is not only useful for individual patient care; it also makes the individual part of a population. For relatively rare conditions, where previously a specialist might ask one or two colleagues for a second opinion, large clinical data sets give the provider (or clinician) the ability to review treatments for additional patients with similar diagnoses, giving them additional data for clinical decision making. It also provides a base of information for monitoring disease trends, service usage, and quality of care. The National Notifiable Disease Surveillance System operated by the Centers for Disease Control and Prevention (CDC) is a good example. Symptoms are documented in an electronic health record (EHR) at the clinical encounter level, and a diagnosis is coded and entered into a database. The ability to view, aggregate, and analyze this data enables public health practitioners to monitor the occurrence and spread of diseases. As in the John Snow example, clinical data leads to population health management.

To improve quality of care and to change care patterns, big clinical data is impossible without building comprehensive electronic health records (EHRs), longitudinal health records of an individual's health. Comprehensive EHRs include diagnoses, problem lists, current and past medications, results of tests, and treatments from different units and facilities that are accessed by individuals. They form the basis of CDS and other analytic systems. While the percentage of physicians adopting some form of EHR doubled between 2008 and 2011, this percentage still is only 55 percent (National Center for Health Statistics, 2012). Reports from State Health Information Exchanges also show limited progress in information sharing among hospitals and physician practices, but the information frequently is limited to demographics and pharmaceutical information.

This limited data collection and sharing is apparent in the Beacon Community Program grantees (Office of the National Coordinator for Health Information Technology, 2012b). The federal government funded them to provide prototypes of electronic medical record systems. They are important pilot projects for comprehensive EHRs, but most focus on linking information for specific diseases, such as diabetes, heart disease, or asthma or partial health facility functions, rather than the comprehensive data needed to cover patient care that encompasses many different conditions at different health facilities. Figure 14.2 summarizes the current clinical uses of electronic clinical information as described by physicians. The figure indicates the variety of functions that EHRs contribute to as they become more common and comprehensive.

If one looks at all of the certified health IT systems approved through the federal EHR technology program, it is a time of experimentation and

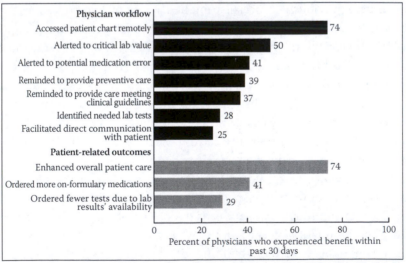

NOTES: Physicians with electronic health record (EHR) systems whose systems or scope of work did not include a specified capability responded not applicable. These responses are included in the denominator for percentages. Data represent office-based physicians who reported having adopted EHR systems (55% of sample). The sample includes nonfederal, office-based physicians and excludes radiologists, anesthesiologists, and pathologists. SOURCE: CDC/NCHS, Physician Workflow study, 2011.

FIGURE 14.2

Percentage of physicians whose electronic health records provided selected benefits: United States, 2011. http://www.cdc.gov/nchs/data/databriefs/db98.htm.

flowering of platforms to create large clinical health data systems. The Office of the National Coordinator for Health Information Technology's (2012) certified Health IT Product List provides a myriad of systems meeting meaningful use requirements. The systems are needed to promote data standardization that will allow data exchange (interoperability) among organizational entities and their many IT systems. A software company executive states that with any type of acquisitions companies can have "from 50 to 70 business systems alone" (Tucker, 2012). Multiple EHRs need to be integrated into a manageable number of systems that are interoperable, thus easily transferring information from one system to another.

Healthcare managers today have many options in planning their enterprisewide EHR solutions. Managers may choose to opt for commonly used systems, such as Wextler Medical Center's use of the EPIC system in its four hospitals to link facility functions including its inpatient system, emergency room system, revenue cycle system, patient scheduling, and operating room system (Guerra, 2012). Others have opted to build interoperability among existing systems and on integrating clinical decision support systems within them. A good example of interoperability can be found in the work of Health Information Exchanges that are creating interfaces among different physician and hospital electronic systems, allowing exchange of patient data to facilitate efficient healthcare delivery.

Of importance in choosing EHRs with big data in mind, providers and administrators of clinical services need to decide how to store the large amounts of data available to them in forms that facilitate their real-time analyses for quality improvement. Some of the key management decisions to enable these systems to produce big data include the availability of standardizing for different order sets; security, multiple clinical services, and clinician teams within facilities; enterprise management; imaging software development; and linking to analysis and knowledge management applications. The National Institute of Standards and Technology's (NIST, 2010; 2012) user-centered design provides one process to guide organizations through these decision-making processes.

The federal government has provided both support and constraints for the growth of electronic medical records and big data. Meaningful Use requirements, which are tied to federal Medicare and Medicaid Incentive Payments, are facilitating this development through the definition and required reporting of health measures and usability standards, such as pharmaceutical interaction checks (Centers for Medicare and Medicaid Services, CMS). Meaningful Use has three phases that are being phased in through 2015: Stage 1 is data capture and sharing basic clinical information; Stage 2 focuses on capturing and sharing advanced clinical processes; and Stage 3 captures improvements in quality, safety, and efficiency. Because it is being implemented in different phases, it can be used as a guide for the development of comprehensive EHRs.

Because Meaningful Use focuses on the development of a limited set of common measures that must be reported to the federal government, it may focus providers on meeting federal standards rather than on developing a comprehensive EHR that meets their own needs. Additionally, the construction of usability standards for healthcare data is lagging behind other federal health EHR standards and requires further development, and federal rules for patient consent and information sharing need to be reconsidered, given this emerging era of big data.

The federally driven Accountable Care Organizations (ACOs) have potential to link patient care among organizations through EHRs. They can provide new opportunities for amassing the wealth of health information available into large data sets for clinical decision making. Funding for ACOs is tied to patient care across different services, necessitating EHRs that can be used to analyze populations of patients, rather than just individuals. No matter which direction the organization of clinical health services takes, EHRs are the wave of the future. In *What's Ahead for EHRs: Experts Weigh In,* The California Health Foundation (2012) discusses the next generation of EHRs: innovative systems that facilitate the use of large pools of information. Their report and a review of current health big data efforts show that we are only in the initial stages of using big data to improve health outcomes.

PUBLIC HEALTH SURVEY AND SURVEILLANCE INFORMATION

Public health information systems range from those that store individual health information for public health surveillance such as immunization or infectious disease reporting, to real-time alert systems for drug interactions, disseminating research findings, and reporting unlikely clusters of unknown or rare conditions. The focus of this information is on protecting the public's health, rather than individual health. Information from health surveillance systems, such as CDC's Notifiable Diseases reporting, and surveys, such as the National Interview Health Survey, has existed for decades. But as pointed out by experts in this area, their information often is not linked or interoperable among reporting organizations, including the cities and states involved in the surveillance systems. The growth of public health information has outpaced our capacity for storage, interpretation, and use. Similar to clinical care, it is an area where coordinated efforts are needed among health facilities and with city, state, and federal health agencies.

An early twenty-first century World Health Organization (WHO) surveillance system is a potential model for future worldwide surveillance. During the severe acute respiratory syndrome (SARS) epidemic, the WHO created a virtual laboratory model using the phone, video, and Internet to monitor and respond to the outbreak. With today's advanced technology, efforts can go beyond this and allow for even quicker reporting, analyses of information, and responding to unusual health events.

One recent example of analyses of a large set of information for improving population health was published in the September 21, 2012, *Morbidity and Mortality Weekly Report*. By combining time-trend rat inspection information with census data that covered a population of 770,000 individuals and approximately 35,000 residences in 12 Bronx, New York, neighborhoods, New York City was able to estimate the prevalence of rats, a known health risk (CDC, 2012). To realize the full potential of this information as big data, the city might consider linking this data with neighborhood clinics and other surveillance information.

The U.S. government is taking some steps to grapple with its diverse health incident disease reporting systems. BioSense 2.0 is an effort by the CDC to reduce the costs and increase the feasibility of state and local data systems that will communicate with each other. The Food and Drug Administration (2012) is undertaking a similar effort to monitor product safety—the Sentinel Initiative to pool existing resources so that large amounts of data can be processed to quickly produce needed information. It also is supporting a Virtual Laboratory Environment to produce innovative analytics for using the information currently available throughout the United States.

Both policy and resource issues need to be addressed to make large sets of public health data available for linkage and analysis to improve population health. First is the flow of information between and among cities, states, and the U.S. government. Data sharing and linkage with each other and with other surveillance information is limited because of a lack of data standardization, structured ways to get clinical information into EHRs, nonuse of standard health information exchange protocols, and the privacy and security required for records that identify individuals. Additionally, updating historical surveillance and survey systems requires resources frequently not available to state and local health agencies. These are not insignificant barriers and need to be considered when prioritizing future forays by public health into big data.

MEDICAL RESEARCH DATA

Within the medical research community a huge amount of information exists, but it is tied to specific grants and institutions. Tension exists between the pull to share information for quicker development of new treatments and the need to patent information to protect profits. At the national level, The National Institutes of Health (NIH) has a number of disease-based initiatives to share information for use in further research. Besides its Genomes Project, for example, the National Heart, Lung, and Blood Institute (2013), NIH has developed the Cardiovascular Research Grid and the Integrating Data for Analysis, Anonymization, and Sharing initiatives to enable researchers to easily store and share information. It not only uses technology to store information but also emphasizes communication and education about the system. The success of the Cardiovascular Research Grid and other efforts will be measured in their ability to advance prevention, diagnosis, and treatment beyond the individual research results and meta-analyses that we see today.

Medical research also is advancing in its use of big data through mathematical modeling. Pharmaceutical companies are using predictive modeling to design new drug formularies and to modify existing ones. From creating mathematical models for neurology clinical trials, to characterizing the genetic determinants of heroin abuse, and to geomapping infectious diseases spread, disease modeling is an important medical research tool.

Once again, common definitions, data standardization, and advanced analytical software will facilitate sharing of huge data sets among researchers. The PhenX project led by RTI International and funded by the National Human Genome Research Institute (NHGRI) (Hamilton et al., 2011) is one example of how to plan and produce big data for genetic research and ultimately impact public health (Hamilton, Strader and Pratt, 2011). Genetics and epidemiological research are being integrated to provide research-ers with high quality and low burden measures that can be included in genome-wide association studies (GWAS) and other types of studies. With large population studies producing large amounts of information about exposure to potential carcinogens, weak causal relationships, such as the association of environmental factors with genetic characteristics, now can be studied. But barriers to pooling data and the meta-analysis of existing studies include lack of common exposure measures and associated analyt-ics. The PhenX project is producing a toolkit to solve these barriers; it is stretching the science of medical research analytics.

A 2010 Position Statement on Data Management and Sharing signed by 17 organizations from five countries highlights the policy and political bar-riers that need to be overcome for big data in medical research to reach its full potential. The agreement points to the current complexity of country policies and procedures for sharing research information and it defines the principles by which such data sets can be used by others to improve the public's health. Signatories include NIH, Agency for Healthcare Research and Quality, and the Bill and Melinda Gates Foundation. *A Call for Action on Health Data from Eight Global Agencies,* including the WHO, states similar principles for the timely sharing across countries of "health financ-ing, health workforce, service access and quality, intervention coverage, risk factors, and health status" information. Its principles center on "devel-oping a common data architecture, strengthening performance monitor-ing and evaluation, and increasing data access and use" (Chan et al., 2010).

These agreements show that the major public and foundation funders of medical research agree on the principles of data sharing. However, the mechanics of storing and accessing data sets still are being worked out. In a 2011 conference, participants stressed that the technological systems for research repositories exist; it is the impact of data sharing on research careers, intellectual property, and profits that must be agreed to. This is especially true in the pharmaceutical industry, where big health data is a reality.

CONSUMER-CENTERED INFORMATION

Patient-driven care is a commonly used concept in health services. The IOM (Institute of Medicine) defines patient-centered care as: "Health care that establishes a partnership among practitioners, patients, and their families (when appropriate) to ensure that decisions respect patients' wants, needs, and preferences and that patients have the education and support they need to make decisions and participate in their own care" (IOM, 2001, pp. 5–6). Its meaning can vary but its underlying concept is that individuals manage their health status by actively seeking information about their health and that they and providers communicate with each other. These efforts, along with capturing and analyzing consumer-driven health information, are caught up in the lack of comprehensive EHRs and connected surveillance systems. Because most health services IT efforts focus on EHRs and other electronic records attached to organizations, rather than tied to consumers, the development of comprehensive longitudinal health records remains a challenge. While consumer-accessible medical records and information is recognized as important, the business models for organization and analyses still need development.

In a 2011 survey, CDC reports that less than 50 percent of people use the Internet to learn about health information. Less than 10 percent communicate with providers by e-mail (CDC, 2012). Security and privacy concerns are a major factor in limiting this interaction. But there is a huge potential for big data analyses of consumer-driven information. This potential includes not just Internet information patterns but usage of remote patient monitoring for conditions such as diabetes or asthma and other electronic devices.

One model for the analysis of consumer Internet behavior can be found in a 2003 National Cancer Institute funded study. Researchers Bader and Theophanis (2003) partnered with Ask Jeeves to analyze the feasibility of measuring cancer hits on Ask.com. Their analysis showed the types of cancers queried and the types of content queried, such as symptoms or treatment. Their methodology forms a framework for today's much larger Internet-driven health data analyses. Not addressed in their article is how this information then could be used to improve consumer searches—the purpose of big health data. A more recent article by Socha et.al. (2012) maps information about users of a library-based phone health literacy service with Census information. The authors found that combining information can identify geographic areas and populations that the phone service is not reaching.

Another source of big data is remote patient monitoring. Remote patient monitoring, which produces real-time information not just for individual behavior but for patterns of behavior and associated treatments, is expected to more than double by 2016—from a $8.9 billion to a $20.9 billion market (Lewis, 2012). The data produced requires systems that can handle large amounts of information, especially if visual imaging is remotely transmitted, but not only is detection of illness made easier for consumers, it also presents opportunities for analyzing areas of business growth.

For healthcare executives, now is the time to lay out strategies for the roles that consumers will play in their organization's service delivery electronic interactions. At one end of the spectrum consumers can be made part of a clinical "shared decision-making" process. A paper by Swan (2009) shows how consumer involvement might be achieved. They are educated about their options and listened to regarding their wishes for clinical procedures. In the middle, there will at least be opportunities for communication and questioning of medical personnel using mobile phone texting and other electronic devices. At the opposite end of the spectrum, consumers can be viewed more passively as readers of web information on health, with companies then analyzing and shaping where their information comes from. Health organizations need to define how they will interact with their public before they consider their IT systems.

At the least, they should have plans for the analyses of their market's Internet behaviors that can be used to build new consumer services, attract new patients, and retain existing ones. The websites of large health organizations, such as Kaiser Permanente and the Cleveland Clinic, contain a wealth of medical information waiting to be mined for consumer use patterns. These organizations also allow patients to use the Internet to access their medical information and to interact with physicians, providing opportunities for analyses and improvements in their business processes.

CREATING ANALYTICAL TOOLS THAT DELIVER INFORMATION FOR CLINICAL AND BUSINESS DECISION MAKING

Big data in health must draw from multiple IT platforms and multiple types of information, ranging from text to disease coding and billing information. Health organizations first need to resolve these types of IT issues so that analytics can be created to produce real-time and useful information. A number of software tools are available for large data sets. Some are specific to one area of health, such as CDC software for analyzing specific surveillance and survey data sets; others are not specific.

Choosing one or more analytical tools starts with common definitions. One of the more complex areas in healthcare that must be made manageable before EMRs and big data sets can be built is getting clinical data into the EHR, such as through the use of clinical order sets. In a case study on Clinical Decision Support Systems, Clinovations (2013) started with approximately 1,300 computerized provider order entry sets that physicians used in six hospitals. Through a consensus process with the clinicians (that also could have been augmented with statistical modeling of order set data) all clinicians were given a chance to develop standard order sets. The result was 354 electronic order sets for use in an EMR and clinical decision support system.

Big data also requires a skilled analytic workforce that combines research and statistical skills frequently found at universities, large public health agencies, and consulting organizations in addition to clinical staff involved in the delivery of health services. Thus, an unlikely combination of health data management and software skills, statistical analyses, experienced medical care, and data literacy is needed. In essence, while discussions of the big data workforce frequently concentrate on data scientists or analysts, in healthcare a team approach is required. The combination of medical knowledge, engineering, computer science, and communication is too rare a skill set for an organization to depend on in one person. For the healthcare executive to free teams for this work, it means considering the time, staffing, and resources that must be devoted not just to information storage but to end uses including analytical and decision-making processes. It requires ensuring that clinical and other patient staff have time built into their schedules for adapting clinical decision-making systems to their institution's needs.

There are broad trends in data analysis software that are likely to provide lasting value to health analytics. For example, Software for the Statistical Analysis of Correlated Data (SUDAAN®) is widely used for survey data, MATLAB® is a powerful tool used for structural modeling, EViews is popular among people interested in analyzing time-series data, MapReduce/Hadoop are a Java-based combination frequently used for data-mining applications, and Statistica and JMP are increasingly used. Other specific applications' main purpose is the displaying of data, such as geographic information systems (GIS) software. In smaller practices and specific health clinics, Microsoft Office tools Excel and Access are frequently used for data analysis. While Access is capable of limited data mining and Excel is capable of basic statistical analysis, neither is a robust replacement for a dedicated software package or for storing big data sets.

For clinical and health business data sets, Statistical Analysis System (SAS) and Statistical Product and Service Solutions (IBM/SPSS) often are the analytical software of choice, whereas among researchers the usage of SPSS lags far behind that of Stata and SAS. For example, in a study analyzing the use of statistical packages across three health journals in 2007–2009, Dembe, Partridge, and Geist (2011) find that of the articles that mention the statistical programs used, 46 percent used Stata and 42.6 percent used SAS, while only 5.8 percent used SPSS. Robert Muenchen's research (2012) indicates that among academics, a wide variety of biomedically targeted statistical programs, most notably Stata and R, are quickly increasing in market penetration.

SAS, SPSS, Stata, and R are examples of how each analytical package has different costs and advantages. The pricing agreements they have vary with the different software publishers. R, as open-source software, is free. Pricing for Stata 12 varies by the version; for example, one of the cheapest versions that can be purchased allows datasets with up to 2,047 variables and models with up to 798 independent variables, with a more expensive version allowing for datasets with up to 32,797 variables and models with up to 10,998 independent variables. The licenses for SPSS and SAS, on the other hand, are annual licenses. The pricing of SPSS is generally such that many of the statistical tools that are included in the full versions of SAS and Stata require the purchase of additional modules that can quickly inflate the purchase cost of SPSS.

In addition to the cost advantage, R and Stata benefit from their easy and relatively rapid extensibility. While the capabilities of each of these software packages has increased over time, the user bases of both R and Stata contribute extensively to the computational power of these software packages through the authorship of user-written add-ons. As a result, Stata and R users generally do not have to wait for the new, cutting-edge techniques to be incorporated into the base version of the software—many have already been written by users, and those with an understanding of the programming languages can script their own.

While Stata and R have an advantage in cost and extensibility, the relative strengths of SAS and SPSS are in the analysis of big data. Using Stata and R is far more memory intensive than SPSS or SAS. This advantage, however, is quickly disappearing with developments in computing, particularly the move from 32 bit Windows to 64 bit Windows. Recent extensions to R further reduce this limitation, allowing data sets to be analyzed from the cloud. Related to this, SAS and SPSS also have an advantage in the actual modeling of big data, particularly in the realm of data mining. SPSS Modeler (formerly Clementine) and SAS Enterprise Miner offer a full suite of data-mining techniques that are currently being developed by R users and are mostly absent from Stata.

Some of these modules are essential to many health scientists, including modules for dealing with survey data, bootstrapping, exact tests, nonlinear regression, and so on. R is always no more expensive than SPSS and SAS; and in the long run, Stata is usually cheaper than SPSS and SAS. These very different costing structures show the time and expertise needed in choosing analytical software.

User-friendliness is certainly one of the many concerns when considering statistical programs. There are likely to be large differences across purposes of what defines user-friendly, in particular between academic and health business settings. As a result, the criteria for user-friendliness is likely to differ across purposes; while decision makers in a corporate setting are likely to view the quality of the graphical user interface as the most important element of a software's user-friendliness, academics will typically view the ease of coding as contributing the most to ease of use.

SUCCEEDING IN A BIG DATA CULTURE

As discussed in the beginning of this chapter, the success of big data in healthcare will be judged by its ability to integrate health and nonhealth information and produce real-time analyses that improve patient outcomes, overall population health, and related business processes. Big data takes the paper-based quality improvement mantra of Plan, Do, Study, Act (PDSA) and brings it into the electronic age (IHI, 2011). This will mean continual changes in the way medicine is practiced and services and research projects are managed, and in every aspect of healthcare delivery. Big data has the potential to change the relationship of consumers and the industry.

The McKinsey Institute Big Data Study points out that the U.S. healthcare system is at a crossroads. It must develop comprehensive EHRs, standardize the way information is collected, and turn it into useful information. If information is able to be standardized and shared, it then can influence patient care and health outcomes. One story that shows how pervasive change must be in our health culture is the transforming effect of patient satisfaction data on health services. We often think of the outcomes of healthcare in terms of patient health and illness severity. But another dimension is patient satisfaction with a facility's services—its cleanliness, the friendliness of staff, and the food that is served. When one hospital set up an ongoing system for measuring and monitoring these dimensions, it was able to make practice changes that raised abysmal patient satisfaction rates. The system led to efforts to instill a culture of service throughout the organization, affecting staff from cleaning crews to surgeons. The facility may not have been able to compete on specialty services with other area faculties, but because it can use data for continuous quality improvement, it can now compete using positive patient experiences as a competitive marketing tool.

As further development occurs in this facility and it is able to link patient satisfaction experiences with patient and care characteristics, it will realize the potential of big data. Similarly, when surveillance data is routinely linked with census and environmental information, the potential for using this information to pinpoint and act upon population health issues greatly increases. Health today is a business, with government public health agencies also adopting common business practices. Big data in healthcare, when it is available electronically, has the potential to make healthcare more efficient and effective.

REFERENCES

Bader, J.L., & Theofanos, M.F. (2003). Searching for cancer information on the Internet: Analyzing natural language search queries. *J Med Internet Res.* Oct–Dec; 5(4): e31. http://dx.doi.org/10.2196/jmir.5.4.e31. Retrieved from http://www.ncbi.nlm.nih.gov/pmc/articles/PMC1550578/.

Berner, E.S. (2009). Clinical Decision Support Systems State of the Art. Agency for Healthcare Research and Quality. Retrieved from http://healthit.ahrq.gov/images/jun09cdsreview/09_0069_ef.html.

California Health Foundation. (2012, February). What's ahead for EMRs: Experts weigh in. Retrieved from http://www.chcf.org/search?query=what's%20ahead%20for%20ehrs&sdate=all&se=1.

CDC. (2012, August 17). QuickStats: Use of health information technology among adults aged ≥18 years—National Health Interview Survey (NHIS), United States, 2009 and 2011. *MMWR Weekly*. Retrieved from http://www.nist.gov/itl/ssd/is/big-data.cfm.

CDC. (2012, September 21). Evaluation of a neighborhood rat-management program—New York City, December 2007–August 2009. *MMWR Weekly*. 61(37): 733–736.

CDC. National health interview survey. Retrieved from http://www.cdc.gov/nchs/nhis.htm.

Chan, M., Kazatchkine, M., Lob-Levyt, J., et al. (2010). Meeting the demand for results and accountability: A call for action on health data from eight global health agencies. *PLoS Med* 7(1): e1000223. http://dx.doi.org/10.1371/journal.pmed.1000223. Retrieved from http://www.plosmedicine.org/article/info%3Adoi%2F10.1371%2Fjournal.pmed.1000223.

Clinovations. (2013). Case study: electronic health records + clinical decision support. Retrieved from http://www.clinovations.com/healthcare-systems-providers.

CMS. An introduction to the Medicare EHR incentive program for eligible professionals. Retrieved from https://www.cms.gov/Regulations-and-guidance/Legislation/EHRIncentivePrograms/downloads/Beginners_Guide.pdf.

Dembe, A.E., Partridge, J.E., & and Geist, L.C. (2011). Statistical software applications used in health services research: Analysis of published studies in the U.S. *BMC Health Services Research*, 11: 252. http://dx.doi.org/10.118/61472-6963-11-252. Retrieved from http://www.biomedcentral.com/1472-6963/11/252/abstract.

Food and Drug Administration. (2012). FDA's Sentinel Initiative. Retrieved from http://www.fda.gov/Safety/FDAsSentinelInitiative/ucm2007250.htm.

Guerra, A. (2012, July 6). Phyllis Teater, Associate V.P./CIO Wextler Medical Center at The Ohio State University. Retrieved from http://healthsystemcio.com/2012/07/06.

Hamilton, C.E., Strader, L.C., Pratt, J.G., et al. (2011). The PhenX Toolkit: Get the most from your measures. *American Journal of Epidemiology*. http://dx.doi.org/10.1093/aje/kwr193. Retrieved from http://aje.oxfordjournals.org/content/early/2011/07/11/aje.kwr193.full.

Institute for Healthcare Improvement (IHI). (2011, April). Science of improvement: How to improve. Retrieved from http://www.ihi.org/knowledge/Pages/HowtoImprove/ScienceofImprovementHowtoImprove.aspx.

Institute of Medicine (IOM). (2001). Crossing the quality chasm: A new health system for the 21st century. Washington, DC: National Academies Press. Available at http://nap.edu/catalog/10027.html

Lewis, N. (2012, July 25). Remote patient monitoring market to double by 2016. *InformationWeek HealthCare*. Retrieved from http://www.informationweek.com/healthcare/mobile-wireless/remote-patient-monitoring-market-to-doub/240004291.

McKinsey Global Institute. (2011). Big data: The next frontier for innovation, competition, and productivity. Retrieved from http://www.mckinsey.com/insights/mgi/research/technology_and_innovation/big_data_the_next_frontier_for_innovation.

Muenchen, R.A. (2012). The popularity of data analysis software. PMCID: PMC3411259. Retrieved from http://r4stats.com/articles/popularity/

National Center for Health Statistics, CDC, HHS. (2012, July). Physician adoption of electronic health record systems: United States, 2011. NCHS Data Brief. Retrieved from http://www.cdc.gov/nchs/data/databriefs/db98.htm.

National Heart, Lung, and Blood Institute. (2013). The CardioVascular research grid. Retrieved from http://www.cvrgrid.org/.

NIST. (2010). NIST guide to the process approach for improving the usability of electronic medical records. U.S. Department of Commerce. NISTIR 7741. Retrieved from http://www.nist.gov/itl/hit/upload/Guide_Final_Publication_Version.pdf.

NIST. (2012, March 29). 1000 genes project data available on Amazon cloud. *NIH News*. Retrieved from http://www.nih.gov/news/health/mar2012/nhgri-29.htm.

Office of the National Coordinator for Health Information Technology. (2012a). Certified health IT product list. Retrieved from http://oncchpl.force.com/ehrcert/EHR ProductSearch?setting=Inpatient.

Office of the National Coordinator for Health Information Technology. (2012b). Beacon community program. Retrieved from http://www.healthit.gov/policy-researchers-implementers/beacon-community-program.

Socha, Y.M., Oelschegel, S., Vaughn, C.J., & Earl, M. (2012). Improving an outreach service by analyzing the relationship of health information disparities to socio-economic indicators using geographic information systems. *J Medical Library Association*, July; 100(3): 222–225. http://dx.doi.org/10.3163/1536-5050.100.3.014. Retrieved from http://www.ncbi.nlm.nih.gov/pmc/articles/PMC3411259/.

Swan, B. (2009). Emerging patient-driven health care models: An examination of health social networks, consumer personalized medicine and quantified self-tracking. *International Journal of Environmental Research and Public Health*, 6(2): 492–525; http://dx.doi.org/10.3390/ijerph6020492. Retrieved from http://www.mdpi.com/1660-4601/6/2/492/htm.

Tucker, T., in Chasan, E. (2012, July 24). The financial-data dilemma. *The Wall Street Journal*, p. B4.

University of California–Los Angeles (UCLA) (n.d.) John Snow. http://www.ph.ucla.edu/epi/snow.html.

Welcome Trust, The. (2010). Position Statement on data management and sharing. Retrieved from http://www.wellcome.ac.uk/About-us/Policy/Policy-and-position-statements/WTX035043.htm.

15

Big Data: Structured and Unstructured

Arun K. Majumdar and John F. Sowa

CONTENTS

INTRODUCTION

Big data comes in two forms: the *structured* data intended for computer processing and the *unstructured* language that people read, write, and speak. Unfortunately, no computer system today can reliably translate unstructured language to the structured formats of databases, spreadsheets, and the semantic web. But they can do a lot of useful processing, and they're becoming more versatile. While we are still some distance away from the talking computer, HAL, in Stanley Kubrick's film *2001: A Space Odyssey*, this chapter surveys the state of the art, the cutting edge, and the future directions for *natural language processing* (NLP) that paves the way in getting us one step closer to the reality presented in that movie.

Lightweight and Heavyweight Semantics

When people read a book, they use their background knowledge to interpret each line of text. They understand the words by relating them to the current context and to their previous experience. That process of understanding is

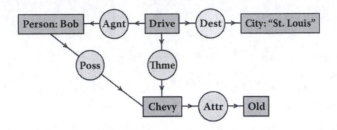

FIGURE 15.1

A conceptual graph for *Bob drives his Chevy to St. Louis.*

heavyweight semantics. But when Google reads a book, it just indexes the words without any attempt to understand what they mean. When someone types a search with similar words, Google lists the book as one of the "hits." That is lightweight semantics. The search engines use a great deal of statistics for finding matches and ranking the hits. But they don't do a deep semantic analysis of the documents they index or the search requests they match to the documents. The difference between lightweight and heavyweight semantics is in the use of background knowledge and models about the world and what things mean. The human brain connects all thoughts, feelings, and memories in a rich network with trillions of connections.

The semantic web is an attempt to gather and store human knowledge in a network that might someday become as rich and flexible. But that goal requires a method for representing knowledge: Figure 15.1 is a *conceptual graph* (CG) that is part of the ISO 24707 Common Logic standard[*] and represents the sentence *Bob drives his Chevy to St. Louis.*

The boxes in Figure 15.1 are called *concepts*, and the circles are called *relations*. Each relation and the concepts attached to it can be read as an English sentence: *The agent (Agnt) of driving is the person Bob. The theme (Thme) of driving is a Chevy. The destination (Dest) of driving is the city St. Louis. Bob possesses (Poss) the Chevy. The Chevy has attribute (Attr) old.* For the semantic web, each of those sentences can be translated to a *triple* in the *Resource Description Format* (RDF). CGs and RDF are highly structured *knowledge representation languages.* They can be stored in a database or used as input for business analytics.

By itself, a conceptual graph such as Figure 15.1 or the RDF triples derived from it represent a small amount of knowledge. The power of a knowledge representation comes from the interconnections of all the graphs and the supporting resources and processes:

---

[*] http://www.iso.org/iso/iso_catalogue/catalogue_tc/catalogue_detail.htm?csnumber=39175

1. *Ontology* is the study of existence. An ontology is the definition of the concepts and relations used to describe the things that exist in an application.
2. A *knowledge base* includes an ontology, the databases or graphs that use the definitions in it, and the rules or axioms that specify reasoning with the knowledge.
3. *Inference engines* process the rules and axioms to reason with and about the knowledge.
4. *Heuristics* use statistics and informal methods to process the knowledge in a variety of ways.

Conceptual graphs and RDF are two notations for representing semantic information. There are many other notations, but they are all based on some version of formal logic combined with an ontology for the subject matter. Information represented in one notation can usually be translated to the others, but some information may be lost in a translation from a more expressive notation to a less expressive form.

A system with truly heavyweight semantics would use large amounts of all four resources. One of the heaviest is the Cyc project, which invested over a thousand person-years of work in developing an ontology with 600,000 concept types and a knowledge base with five million rules and axioms. Cyc supplements that knowledge base by accessing facts from relational databases and the semantic web. Another heavyweight system is IBM's Watson,* which beat the world champion in the game of *Jeopardy!* IBM spent millions of dollars in developing Watson and runs it on a supercomputer with over 2,000 CPUs.

The search engines that process billions of requests per day can't use the heavyweight semantics of Cyc or Watson. But they are gradually increasing the amount of semantics for tagging web pages and interpreting queries. To promote common ontologies and formats, Google, Microsoft, and Yahoo! co-founded schema.org as a nonproprietary source of concept specifications. As an example, schema.org includes a concept called JobPosting, which has the following related concepts:

```
baseSalary, benefits, datePosted, educationRequirements,
employmentType, experienceRequirements, hiringOrganization,
incentives, industry, jobLocation, occupationalCategory,
qualifications, responsibilities, salaryCurrency, skills,
specialCommitments, title, workHours
```

---

* http://www-03.ibm.com/innovation/us/watson/

Any company that lists a job opening on a website can use these concept names to tag the information in the announcement. Search engines can then use those tags to match job searches to job announcements.

With less than a thousand concept types, schema.org has about 0.1 percent of Cyc's coverage of the concepts needed to understand natural language. It has an even smaller percentage of Cyc's axioms for doing automated reasoning. Instead, schema.org depends on the web masters to choose the concept types to tag the information on their web pages. This raises a chicken-and-egg problem. The search engines can't use the tags to improve their results until a significant percentage of web pages are tagged. But web masters aren't going to tag their pages until the search engines begin to use those tags to direct traffic to their sites.

Social networks such as Facebook have more control over the formats of their pages. They provide the tools that their clients use to enter information, and those tools can insert all the tags needed for search. By controlling the tools for data entry and the tools for search, Facebook has become highly successful in attracting users. Unfortunately, it has not yet found a business model for increasing revenue. Their clients devote more time and energy communicating with their friends than with advertisers.

Methods for tagging web pages support a kind of semistructured or middleweight semantics. They don't provide the deep reasoning of Cyc or Watson, but they can be successful when the critical web pages are tagged with semantic information. The health industry is the most promising area for improving productivity and reducing cost by automation. But the huge bulk of information is still in unstructured natural language with few, if any semantic tags. One of the greatest challenges for heavyweight semantics is to develop NLP methods for automatically analyzing documents and inserting semantic tags. Those techniques are still at the research stage, but some of them are beginning to appear in cutting-edge applications.

COMMERCIALLY AVAILABLE NLP SYSTEMS

While we watched in amazement as the IBM Watson supercomputer played *Jeopardy!* in a live TV broadcast, we realized that the field of natural language processing had passed a major milestone. The multiple supercomputing modules of Watson had access to vast troves of data: Big data, processed and used in real time for humanlike natural language understanding had finally taken a step away from science fiction into science fact. Table 15.1 in the Appendix shows that there are companies pursuing this very goal by using the cloud, which promise to provide the equivalent power of Watson's enormous supercomputing resources.

Science fiction had popularized NLP long before Watson: For example, the movie *2001: A Space Odyssey* featured a talking computer called HAL; on the popular 1960s television series *Star Trek,* the *Starship Enterprise* ship's computer would talk to Captain Kirk or his first officer Spock during their analyses. These dreams are getting one step closer to being fulfilled, even though that may still be well over a decade away. For example, the communicator used on *Star Trek,* is now a reality as many of us have mobile audio-visual communicators—the miniaturizing of technology was science fiction then, and science fact now. Siri™, for Apple's iPhone™, is perhaps today's most well advertised natural language understanding system and is swiftly becoming a household word: Behind it is a big data NLP analytics platform that is growing immensely popular in both the consumer and corporate environments. Siri has served to improve the efficacy by which things get done by combining voice and data spoken natural language technology: This improves overall performance for busy people on the go, and ultimately, therefore, contributes to a better bottom line. The miniaturization of computing power is continuing and now reaching into the realms of the emerging discipline of quantum computing, where it may be possible to have all possible worlds of contextual interpretations of language simultaneously available to the computer. However, before we reach out on the skinny branches onto quantum computing, let us consider the shift from typing to speaking and notice that this is essentially a social shift: For example, the shift in driving cars from holding a phone to hands-free talking, to hands-free dialing by speaking out the numbers, or now even asking for directions from the car's computer, we are already approaching the talking computer of the *Enterprise* in *Star Trek.*

For example, one of the business giants is Microsoft. Its business strategy has shifted into building socially consistent user experiences across their product lines such as Xbox Kinect™, Windows™ 8, and especially Windows Phone 8. This strategy will enable developers of "machine thinking" to build their applications into Microsoft products that will already provide the basic conversion of unstructured speech into structured streams of Unicode text for semantic processing. While Microsoft introduced its Speech Application Programming Interface (SAPI) in 1994, the company had not strategically begun to connect social media and semantic analyses with its tools. In 2006 Microsoft acquired Colloquis Inc, a provider of conversational online business solutions that feature natural language-processing technology, and this technology has been improved and augmented for Microsoft products over the past half-dozen years. Not to be left out of the race to build market share by making it easier for humans and machines to communicate with each other, the Internet giant Google™ has pushed forward its agenda for advanced voice-and-data processing with semantic analytics as a part of its Android™ phone, starting with Google-411 service, moving to Google Voice Actions and others.

Nuance™ corporation's SpeakFreely™ and their Clinical Language Understanding (CLU) system, which was used in IBM's Watson, enables a physician to simply talk about and describe the patient visit using a clinical medical terminology in conversational style. The CLU system is revolutionizing the electronic healthcare records industry by directly converting, at the source, the physician, all unstructured data into computable structured data.

In the Department of Defense and law enforcement markets, the Chiliad™ product called Discovery/Alert collects and continuously monitors various kinds of large-scale high-volume data, both structured and unstructured, and enables its users to conduct interactive, real-time queries in a conversational natural language along the lines of the conversation that Deckard, the role played by Harrison Ford, had with his photograph-analyzing computer in the movie *Blade Runner,* by Ridley Scott. Both Chilliad and SpeakFreely, while not consumer-oriented products, are harbingers of things to come: that conversationally advanced user interfaces based on full unrestricted natural language will become the de facto standard in the future. Which set of technologies needed to achieve this is a race yet to be won.

Some companies are addressing specific market sectors. Google Glass™, for example, is focusing on the explosive medical information and health records market: data such as heart rate, calorie intake, and amount of time spent walking (or number of footsteps) can be collected for patients using various mobile apps, pedometers, heart monitors, as well as information contained in their medical records from other physicians. All of this amounts to a lot of data: very big data. And Google™ is betting on using its powerful cloud computing to perform, the same infrastructure that powers its successful web search engine, on the semantic and natural language data analytics domain to improve healthcare. A user-friendly dashboard will be ubiquitously accessed and displayed via Google Glass.

So what are the features that would be common to any big data natural language understanding?

Our viewpoint is that they possess the following characteristics:

1. *Seamless User Interfaces*—The application of advanced speech recognition and natural language processing for converting the unstructured human communications into machine-understandable information.
2. *A Diversity of Technologies*—The use of multiple forms of state-of-the-art information organization and indexing, computing languages and models for AI*, as well as various kinds of retrieval and processing methods.
3. *New Data Storage Technologies*—Software such as Not Only SQL (NoSQL) enables efficient and also interoperable forms of knowledge representations to be stored so that it can be utilized with various kinds of reasoning methods.
4. *Reasoning and Learning Artificial Intelligence*—The integration of artificial intelligence techniques so that the machine can learn from its own mistakes and build that learned knowledge into its knowledge stores for future applications of its own reasoning processes.
5. *Model Driven Architectures (MDA)*—The use of advanced frameworks depends on a diversified and large base of models, which themselves depend on the production of interoperable ontologies. These make it possible to engineer a complex system of heterogeneous components for open-domain, real-time, real-world interaction with humans, in a way that is comfortable and fits within colloquial human language use.

The common theme in all of this: *The key to big data is small data.* Small data depends crucially on the development of very high quality and general models for interpreting natural language of various kinds: For example, the ability to handle short questions and answers is the key to handling big numbers of questions and answers, and this capability depends on good models. Unlike statistical systems that need big data to answer small data questions, the paradigm has become somewhat inverted.

A recent study[†] shows that over 50 percent of all medical applications will use some form of advanced analytics, most of which will rely on

---

[*] AI: Artificial Intelligence, the broad branch under which natural language understanding resides.
[†] http://www.frost.com/c/10046/sublib/display-report.do?id=NA03-01-00-00-00 (U.S. Hospital Health Data Analytics Market).

extraction of information from textual sources, compared with the paltry less than 10 percent today, and that most of the needed approaches to do this successfully will depend on a variety of models and ontologies for the various medical subfields. For example, the *2012 Understanding Healthcare Challenge* by Nuance™* corporation lists the following areas of growth: emergency medical responder (EMR)/point-of-care documentation, access to resources, professional communications, pharm, clinical trials, disease management, patient communication, education programs, administrative, financial, public health, ambulance/emergency medical services (EMS).

Traditionally, tools for business intelligence have been batch-oriented extract-transform-load (ETL) data integration, relational data warehousing, and statistical analytics processes. These pipelined, rigid, time-consuming, and expensive processes are ill-suited to a conversational NLP interface, since they cannot adapt to new patterns without the aid of a programmer. Therefore, they are unsuited for the big data era. The world and its information are now resident within huge collections of online documents, and efforts at manual translation of knowledge, even crowdsourcing, are impractical since the humans would need to be perfectly rational, consistent, coherent, and systematic in their outputs. Today, search for key terms is still a domination approach to get results, but in reality, we want results as well-formed answers from knowledge bases that in turn have been built on text bases: The critical path in developing a successful natural language solution rests in the fundamental design decision matching between various available component technologies (either open source or from vendors), the application domain requirements, and the available models.

Next question: What drives big data NLP? There are five key points:

1. *Entity Identification*—This is needed to extract facts, which can then populate databases. Fact bases are critical to having the basic information needed for almost any kind of decision making. However, what kind of processing is needed and used to extract the salient, relevant facts (or in expert parlance, the *named entities* from free-form text)? What are the impediments to language variability and scalability, and what techniques work and which ones hold promise?
2. *Language Understanding*—The grammar and meaning of the words in a language are needed to extract information as well as knowledge

---

from texts, which is not the same as extraction of facts. For example, business rules (while they also depend on the extraction of facts) tell you how a certain business process are to be operationalized, and the extraction of business rules can be used to automate or analyze a business. In the case of the law (as another domain), the capture of legal jurisprudence, for example, can be used to analyze for forensics in cases. However, how does one disentangle the real requirements for a text-information extraction engine? What are the costs, techniques, and methods that are the best in class in performance and scale?

3. *Causal and Explanatory Reasoning*—In almost any kind of analytics process—medical, financial, national security, banking, and customer service, there are processes that forms dependent chains where one thing must happen before another. The ability of the computer to perform reasoning about what is going in a text depends on its ability to formulate scenarios of activities and to create explanations based on its understanding. This requires being able to reason, to make hypotheses (especially with ambiguous sentences as we shall show later on) and to formulate plans. All of these are components of the traditional research branches of AI.

4. *Voice and Data*—This is a huge industry that has grown from button-pushing interactions into conversational interactions. The kinds of systems used are pervasive in most customer support activities, from booking trains to planes and getting support for your computer. What makes the handling of voice and data, interactive speech, and media interfaces different for textual NLP and NLU? The key differentiator is that spoken language is most often broken up into islands of meanings with interjections, noise, and ambiguities in sound and content.

5. *Knowledge Representation and Models*—Models depend on ontologies, and in order to build an ontology, a method to represent knowledge must be chosen. Models apply to all the areas in (1) through (4) but add an entirely new dimension to big data: the ability to perform what-if reasoning to produce explanations and predications by handling language in terms of knowledge content, which includes facts, information, rules, heuristics, feedback from the user, exploratory question answering (in which there are no "right" answers), and hypotheses. In speech systems, for example, knowledge-oriented natural language processing can look at the interactions across all of the islands of information and facts as they are spoke to derive the final meaning.

Given that we have presented some high-level points about natural language processing from a technical requirements perspective, without producing a first-year course on natural language, we can now turn to the key business decision (and cost) factors in implementing a big data NLP/NLU system: namely, the technology approach (or strategy); the big data systems integrations options; and finally, dealing with ambiguity and context, especially as it usually occurs in contextually dependent freely spoken language.

Technology Approach

A technology approach represents the choices made for handling big data NLP in an end-to-end, cradle-to-grave life cycle: knowledge representation, implementation language, and systems integration. A given technology approach will have a total cost of ownership for a specific capability, and this is a choice that is usually made as a consequence of a requirements process (which is often itself developed as a scenario of uses and use cases). For example, the needs of a system for call-center call routing where a user can listen to choices and respond by pressing a button to select the route to a human agent will have a simple template-based natural language generation and understanding component with a voice-and-data interface. However, a system for knowledge extraction may need to handle the complexities of natural language such as discourse representation, intratextual references, resolving analogies, metaphors and similes, or allegories into thematic, semantic knowledge structures and storing these for use in an interactive question answering module.

Each technology will depend on whether the data is unstructured, structured, or semistructured: For example, template-based methods work best when the data is regularly structured, such as text in the form of an invoice or the format of an address. For other types of text inputs, for example, when there is little background ontology available and the data is completely unstructured, statistical methods are favored. When good background resources and an ontology exist, the linguistic approach delivers superior results to the statistical approaches. The best is usually a hybrid combination of several approaches since data typically is partially a mix of unstructured, semistructured, and fully structured components. There are a number of basic technology approaches, but the field is so diverse that a full compendium of the plethora of approaches would itself require many books to complete. However, from a bird's-eye viewpoint, the diaspora of technical approaches broadly falls into a few groups, which we have outlined as follows:

1. *Statistical (Mathematical) Methods*—These methods all use a number of mathematical equations and statistical properties of words and collections of texts. Algorithms that you may find out more about on the web that are representative of the mathematical approach have such names as Latent Semantic Analysis (LSA), Vector Space Methods (VSM), or Hidden Markov Models (HMM). While these terms refer to highly technical and detailed recipes for counting and ranking words and phrases in a text for analysis or indexing, they essentially do not require any background knowledge to work and so are fast to implement and very scalable.

2. *Template Methods*—These methods have been around with us since the 1960s. Templates are basically sentences with missing parts to be filled in. For example, take the simple sentence "The price is $10.00." This sentence can be made into a template by using variables denoted by the underline, "___ price is ___," so that whenever the sentence matches the exact same words, in the same order, then the price can be collected. This template can collect information such as "Book price is $9.00" and "Beans price is $1.75." A fancier form of templates is to use so-called regular expressions that compile templates into very efficient computer programs (formally called finite state automata) that can process massive volumes of text that is semi-structured with regular repeating patterns (like invoices, order processing, and addresses) at extremely high speed.

3. *Linguistic Methods*—These are the most sophisticated of approaches and generally need a background base of knowledge, ontology, a knowledge representation, and a variety of recipes by which text is assigned to concepts that identify the meanings. For example, models such as Discourse Representation Theory (DRT) model the meaning of not only sentences but also how they relate to each other in paragraphs and the whole text. Other models, such as Rhetorical Structure Theory, express how the topics and focus of the text is related to the intent of the author to the reader. Linguistics methods also cover such things as what it means to interpret and answer a question, using a model of user questioning so that domains such as customer product servicing can be handled effectively by cataloging and storing all the questions that humans have answered and

modeling these into the knowledge base of an automated system so that call-center costs can be saved. While it takes time to build linguistic models for NLP, they are the most powerful and the deepest of techniques with the highest potential payoffs and returns on investment.

Of course, these techniques are available to use in through a number of vendors, the newest of which are entering into the cloud-based model of Software as a Service (SaaS). The vast majority of tools are provided by many of the familiar names in big business, such as IBM, SAS and others; however, there are many fast and high-growth opportunities in emerging niche markets, and these are served often by smaller high-tech startups. Table 15.1 in the Appendix provides a landscape of types of companies that use NLP/NLU extensively and provides a quick-start guide for you to get out on the web to see what they're up to, what they provide, and what you can use if you are considering using this technology in an application.

Implementation and Systems Integration

Implementation choices boil down to either rolling out your own NLP system, which will usually has a very high cost, to choosing ready-made or open-source components and libraries of software and integrating their functionalities into a desired capability. The systems integration approach is the most cost-effective because, as an integrator, no research and development of the core components is needed; however, the burden falls on architecture and design as well as thoroughly understanding the pros and cons of software language choices (Java, C, C++, C#, Scala, Erlang, Prolog, Haskell, etc.) and integration approaches (CORBA, Java-RMI, TCP-sockets, etc.) for a target device set (iPhone, Android, laptop, desktop, web-services based, thick or thin client, etc.). In addition, there are several areas in which systems integration and testing will be highly domain dependent. For example, applications in medical informatics will need rich background data in the form of dictionaries, thesauri, ontologies, and databases that need to be coded and associated to the natural language processing strategy and technology approach. In the case of applications that serve a wider audience, for example, in customer relationship management and support, the requirements for powerful and seamless NLP are very high: I am sure I am not alone in stating that every once in a while

I will encounter a so-called "help" system online or on the telephone that is still a far cry from the quality of help a real human provides.

As everyone knows, computers use 1s and 0s, so a programmer could string together the appropriate sequence of 1s and 0s to write any program: in reality, this would be rather impractical if not impossible to achieve as the program grows in size, complexity, and diversity of concepts and algorithms. Enter the evolution of programming languages and paradigms of integration—all with the purpose of being able to write software at a higher level of complexity and hiding the fine-grained 1s and 0s that are, in the end, always produced to run on a given computer and operating system. Languages are constantly evolving from lower levels, being closer to the 1s and 0s, such as "Assembly" code to higher levels, with the newest languages, such as Scala™, that encapsulate cloud and large-scale concurrent programming concepts seamlessly. Some very high level but older logical languages, such as Prolog, are seeing resurgence as new techniques and methods, as well as advancements in compiler design, have overcome the limitations of the past. Today, the most popular programming language is JAVA, followed by C/C++; and then others such as Python, Prolog, Lisp, Haskell, and Scala form their own niches. The main problem with mainstream languages like Java and C are that they are not designed for reasoning tasks: every reasoning algorithm has to be painstakingly written at a very low level, and therefore the costs are high. In contrast, and especially with more recent language designs for Prolog for NLP agent technologies and Scala as a backbone for cloud technologies, higher-level programming may soon be coming to the mainstream for NLP.

In the world of big data, and for the distribution of NLP tasks, the choice of language, such as Prolog or Scala or Java, and many other options can all benefit from the approach originally taken by Google and now available open source as Hadoop* as well as the precursor Grid Computing principles to build a cloud with NLP service components. For example, Epstein, regarding Watson, states†:

> Early implementations of Watson ran on a single processor where it took 2 hours to answer a single question. The DeepQA computation is embarrassing parallel, however. UIMA-AS, part of Apache UIMA, enables the scaleout of UIMA applications using asynchronous messaging. We used

* http://hadoop.apache.org/
† http://www.aaai.org/Magazine/Watson/watson.php

UIMA-AS to scale Watson out over 2500 compute cores. UIMA-AS handles all of the communication, messaging, and queue management necessary using the open JMS standard. The UIMA-AS deployment of Watson enabled competitive run-time latencies in the 3–5 second range.

To preprocess the corpus and create fast run-time indices we used Hadoop. UIMA annotators were easily deployed as mappers in the Hadoop map-reduce framework. Hadoop distributes the content over the cluster to afford high CPU utilization and provides convenient tools for deploying, managing, and monitoring the corpus analysis process.

VivoMind™ Research, for example, believes in the IBM approach and is developing its own next-generation language and reasoning technologies by developing a state-of-the-art object-oriented Prolog language agent compiler (called Pi-Log™) to be released in 2014: after all, Prolog formed the critical NLP core of IBM's Watson.*

Ambiguity and Context

Natural languages are the most complex and sophisticated forms of communication and knowledge encapsulation, but today, it is not yet possible to program a computer in plain natural language. However, strides are being made that would enable one to program a computer in a controlled natural language.

The major problems facing the NLP and NLU systems integrator are that language is highly variable and flexible in use from one individual to the next. The freedom of language affords humans a wide variety of contexts: Context is all-important and context usually arises out of a situation. If I am at a billiard table, I can use the word *bank* as, "I banked it," in describing a shot; but if I am depositing money at an ATM, that same statement would mean something completely different. In online help systems, context-sensitive is particularly important. To restrict context, one approach is control what words a user can use. A controlled natural language would only understand language in a highly rigid form—but this can be learned by humans: for example, the medical language of radiology reports, or the controlled language of the ATIS (Air Traffic Information System) has been learned by humans and used by machines effectively. The choice in developing, buying, or using an NLP system faces the challenge of how to handle

---

* http://www.cs.nmsu.edu/ALP/2011/03/natural-language-processing-with-prolog-in-the-ibm-watson-system/

vague, ambiguous statements, or at the very least, in advising the user that the inputs were not handled or recognized. This can be tricky. Consider the following set of sentences from a computer's perspective:

1. *Fruit flies like a banana and time flies like an arrow:* is there a kind of insect called "time flies"?
2. *I saw the man on the hill with a telescope:* did the man have the telescope or was it the person watching the man on the hill?
3. *He was a lion in the fight:* how can human be an animal (of course, this is an analogy)?
4. *He banked it:* was it a billiard shot? a trip to the teller at bank? or did he maneuver a plane?
5. *She spilled the beans:* did she vomit or did she tell the truth or did she spill beans literally?
6. *John went through Harry to get to Paul:* physically? Or what?
7. *They were marketing people:* were they in the slave trade or salespeople?
8. *He sat down to eat and drink with a cigar:* did he actually literally both eat and drink a cigar?
9. *The man said that he did not do it:* the man or someone else?
10. *Nobody was found and no one came:* murder or someone called "Nobody"?
11. *This, that, and the other were the choices:* choices of what? Apples? Bananas? Investments?

While these sentences are by no means exhaustive of the possibilities, the roadmap to success will be driven by very careful business use-case and scenario design to ensure that the NLP system can cope with ambiguous inputs and not lead into some sort of automation-surprise (like, for example, draining the users' accounts by some misconception in an online NLP banking system of the future).

Equally important is modality of interaction in language: spoken or written. The advent of the controlled "alphabet" (ASCII) for the computer keyboard is in evolution into a controlled "language" for spoken communications, (such as Siri™), and this means that the concept of NLP and NLU is tied in deeply with speech generation and recognition. For example, a template-based NLP system can trigger processing whenever it encounters the pattern "X costs Y dollars": So X can be apples, oranges or land; and Y can be dollars, pesos, yen, or euros. But the computer has no understanding that this is a quantitative statement. The beauty of a controlled language system is that it has the simplicity of templates but also includes the component of knowledge representation for richer reasoning that basic template systems cannot provide. In contrast to quantitative data input, qualitative natural language data input is a particularly difficult area for computation since most qualitative descriptions are rich with adjectives and nuanced language. Today, the most aggressive efforts to develop systems that can understand qualitative viewpoints are the social mining NLP systems that attempt to understand user sentiment or market opinion.

FUTURE DIRECTIONS

Research projects worldwide are pioneering new NLP methods that promise to make major breakthroughs within the coming decade. Three projects that have already been used in significant applications illustrate the current directions: the Cyc Project, which has developed the world's largest ontology; the IBM Watson Project, which beat the world champion in the *Jeopardy!* game; and the intelligent Prolog language-based agents at VivoMind™ Research, which use Stanford's CSLI Verb Ontology* that was a gift from IBM to Stanford for the public domain. These resources are being successfully used for mining materials science information from science and technology journals for a U.S. Department of Energy (DOE)† program.

Cyc has evolved into an open-source community with some domain-specific closed-source components, and the company is continuing to evolve. The history of Cyc and the lessons learned paved the way for us all.

Today, Watson requires a supercomputer to support its algorithms, but today's laptops are more powerful than the supercomputers of the 1990s. Before long, systems at the level of Watson will run on an ordinary server, then a laptop, and eventually a hand-held wizard. Perhaps these or other systems will lead to ultrasmart clouds of autonomous algorithms that "know" which NLP tasks they are best suited for. Perhaps groups of NLP processes can self-aggregate into useful workflows without programmer effort. New languages and algorithms may emerge. Perhaps the semantic

---

* http://lingo.stanford.edu/vso/
† https://www1.eere.energy.gov/vehiclesandfuels/pdfs/merit_review_2011/adv_power_electronics/ ape032_whaling_2011_o.pdf

web will evolve into the cognitive cloud in the future. Several new startup companies (as shown in Table 15.1 in the Appendix) are already beginning to deliver fully cloud-based NLP solutions that eliminate the need to have a supercomputer at home.

What does the future hold for big data analytics here at VivoMind? We are building on the intelligent agent paradigm, which we believe will lead to ultrasmart clouds of autonomous algorithms that "know" which NLP tasks they are best suited for. In effect, the agents program themselves. We can use ordinary language to tell them what to do, not how to do it.

SCALA, the emerging new language that builds on the JAVA JVM, will also provide momentum into the cloud-based NLP approach: Multilingual NLP clouds and interoperability of intracloud NLP components as well as the emergence of the big data cognitive web are still very much in research phases with lessons learned from current semantic web efforts that many see as the Cyc of yesteryear. We leave it to reader to develop the cognitive cloud of the future as a kind of world-covering software brain where questions, answers, and explanations can be synthesized on demand.

APPENDIX

Cloud-based NLP (Table 15.1a) is a fast-growing area and is a fast track for any company that has a unique solution to offer customers in the big data analytics arena without having a high up-front investment. According to McKinsey,* the market sizes are in the hundreds of billions of dollars for these areas of big data NLP.

There are many solutions vendors with customizable NLP solutions (Table 15.1b), in the form of reconfigurable applications and frameworks, which are at a higher level than just being components or developer tools sets. These applications can be rapidly configured for domain-specific tasks and can be quickly scaled to large volumes by replication of applications onto a server farm. The initial configuration costs are kept fairly low since the frameworks come with helper applications for rapid data ingestion.

At the simpler end of the spectrum, especially for specialty jobs, such as address processing and order processing where the format and layout of the text fits regular patterns, then the template-based methods are very

---

* http://www.mckinsey.com/insights/mgi/research/technology_and_innovation/big_data_the_next_frontier_for_innovation

TABLE 15.1a

Technology Platforms and Vendors

Platforms	Applications	Technology Sources
Cloud NLP Services	You design your application; the cloud API vendor provides all the algorithms. Cut down coding and total cost of ownership. Applications: • Social Network Mining • Open-Source Information Analyses • Blog, Website and News Analyses	**Alchemy**: http://www.alchemyapi.com/ **Nerd**: http://nerd.eurecom.fr/ **Ramp**: http://www.ramp.com/mediacloud **Bayes Informatics**: https://www.bayesinformatics.com/node/3 **Hakia**: http://company.hakia.com/semanticrank.html **Semantria**: http://www.semantria.com/ **Exalead**: http://www.3ds.com/products/exalead/products/exalead-cloudview/overview/ **Zemanta API:** http://www.zemanta.com/
NLP Application Services	Applications: • Market Intelligence • Sentiment Analysis • Social Opinion Mining • Trends Analyses • Continuous News Monitoring • Web-Site Monitoring	Accenture Technology Labs: http://www.accenture.com/Global/Services/Accenture Technology Labs/default.htm Adaptive Semantics Inc.: http://adaptivesem antics.com/ **Linguastat**: http://www.linguastat.com/ **Connotate**: http://www.connotate.com Visible Technologies: http://www.visibletechnologies.com/trupulse.html **RiverGlass**: http://www.riverglassinc.com/Fast: http://www.fastsearch.com/ Mnemonic Technology: http://www.mnemonic.com **Chilliad**: http://www.chiliad.com Crawdad Technologies: http://www.crawdadtech.com/ **Lymbix**: http://www.lymbix.com/ **Northern Light**: http://www.northernlight.com **Nstein**: http://www.nstein.com **Recorded Future**: http://www.recordedfuture.com

hard to beat for speed and scalability. In the case of patterns of semis-tructured texts with a regular language, for example, the Air Traffic Information Systems dialogs, template-based systems are ideal for infor-mation extraction.

When proprietary know-how, trade secrecy, as well as sources and methods form the cornerstone of the business-use case, then it is hard

TABLE 15.1b

Technology Platforms and Vendors

Platforms	Applications	Technology Sources
NLP Solution Vendors	NLU solutions for various industries that use a variety of algorithms and methods in order to achieve performance, scalability and results. Applications: • Social Network Mining • Open-Source Information Analyses • Blog, Website, and News Analyses • Market Intelligence • Sentiment Analysis • Social Opinion Mining • Trends Analyses • Continuous News Monitoring • Website Monitoring • Web Scraping	**Attensity:** http://www.attensity.com **Autonomy:** http://www.autonomy.com/ **BBN:** http://www.bbn.com/technology/knowledge/semantic_web_applications **Bitext:** http://www.bitext.com/ **Brainware:** http://www.brainware.com/ **Chilliad:** http://www.chiliad.com **ClearForest:** http://www.clearforest.com/ **Lextek International:** http://www.lextek.com/ **LXA Lexalytics:** http://www.lexalytics.com/ **NetOwl:** http://www.netowl.com/ **SAS:** http://www.sas.com/text-analytics/text-miner/index.htm **Lingpipe:** http://alias-i.com/lingpipe/ **Topic Mapper:** http://www.ai-one.com/
NLP Template-Based Sytems	Keyword and key phrase extraction templates using word lists or thesauri. Applications: • Web Scraping • Key Term Extraction • Key Phrase Watch List Monitors	**Carrot:** http://project.carrot2.org/ **Kea:** http://www.nzdl.org/Kea/ **Sematext:** http://sematext.com/products/key-phrase-extractor/index.html **Maui:** http://code.google.com/p/maui-indexer/ **Keyphrase Extractor:** http://smile.deri.ie/projects/keyphrase-extraction

to beat a good set of optimized commercial software developer toolkits (SDKs) and/or open-source technologies for customized programming of an application or solution (Table 15.1c). Open-source tools are improving, and IBM's Watson used many open-source components. While we have provided a broad-strokes overview, there are many more companies and specialty component technologies on the market. Some, like the intelligent agent–based approaches like Connotate™, already have an early and strong lead with this very promising approach for scalable and distributed natural language processing.

TABLE 15.1c

Technology Platforms and Vendors

Platforms	Applications	Technology Sources
NLP Toolkits	These vendors provide all the algorithms in the form of specific language application programming toolkits. Applications: • Medical Data Mining • Healthcare Records Analyses • Financial News Analyses • Extraction and Loading of Unstructured Text Into Databases • Customer Help and Support Systems	Cognition: http://www.cognition.com/ Connexor: http://www.connexor.com/ Digital Reasoning: http://www.digitalreasoning.com/solutions/ Expert System: http://www.expertsystem.net/ Extractiv: http://extractiv.com/ IBM: http://www.ibm.com/developerworks/data/downloads/uima/ Ling-Join: http://en.lingjoin.com/product/ljparser.html Lingway: http://www.lingway.com/ Q-go: http://www.q-go.nl/ SAP: http://www.sap.com/solutions/sapbusinessobjects/in dex.epx Teragram: http://www.teragram.com/oem/ Temis: http://www.temis.com Vantage Linguistics: http://www.vantagelinguistics.com/ Xerox: http://www.xrce.xerox.com/Research-Development/Document-Content-Laboratory
NLP Open-Source Tools	This is the classic build-versus-buy scenario. An Internet search resulted in many tool suites, and this is simply a sampling, not representative of the total available. Wikipedia list of open-source NLP tools: http://en.wikipedia.org/wiki/List of natural_language_processing_toolkits	Stanford NLP–Stanford University (an Extensive tool suite, GPL): http://nlp.stanford.edu/software/index.shtml Balie—Baseline Information Extraction (University of Ottawa, GNU GPL): http://balie.sourceforge.net/ FreeLing (Universitat Politecnica de Catalunya, GNU LGPL): http://nlp.lsi.upc.edu/freeling/ Gate—General Architecture For Language Engineering (Java, University of Sheffield, LGPL): http://gate.ac.uk/ MALLET—Machine Learning for Language Toolkit (Java—University of Massachusetts—Common Public License): http://mallet.cs.umass.edu/ NLTK—Natural Language Tool Kit: http://nltk.org/ Ellogon—Visual NLP (C++, LGPL): http://www.ellogon.org/

Index

Page numbers followed by f indicate figure
Page numbers followed by t indicate table